Salman Rushdie and Translation

Also available from Bloomsbury

Salman Rushdie: Contemporary Critical Perspectives edited by Robert Eaglestone and Martin McQuillan
Salman Rushdie's Cities: Reconfigurational Politics and the Contemporary Urban Imagination by Vassilena Parashkevova
Salman Rushdie's Midnight's Children: A Reader's Guide by Norbert Schurer

Salman Rushdie and Translation

Jenni Ramone

Bloomsbury Academic India
An imprint of Bloomsbury Publishing Plc
BLOOMSBURY
NEW DELHI • LONDON • OXFORD • NEW YORK • SYDNEY

First published in India 2018
First published 2013
Paperback edition first published 2015

Bloomsbury Academic India
An imprint of Bloomsbury Publishing Plc
BLOOMSBURY, Bloomsbury Academic India and the Diana
logo are trademarks of Bloomsbury Publishing Plc

This edition published with permission from Bloomsbury Publishing Plc,
50 Bedford Square, London, WC1B3DP, UK

British Library Cataloguing-in-Publication Data
A catalogue record for this book is available from the British Library.

Library of Congress Cataloging-in-Publication Data
A catalog record for this book is available from the Library of Congress.

ISBN 978 93 87863 64 4
10 9 8 7 6 5 4 3 2 1
For sale in the Indian subcontinent only

Bloomsbury Publishing India Pvt. Ltd
Second Floor, Building No. 4
DDA Complex LSC, Pocket C – 6 & 7
Vasant Kunj, New Delhi 110070
www.bloomsbury.com

Typeset by Deanta Global Publishing Services, Chennai, India
Printed and bound in India by Replika Press Pvt. Ltd.

For Seren

Contents

Acknowledgements

I began this project as a doctoral student at Loughborough University, and I am very grateful for the advice and support I received from my supervisory team Professor Roger Ebbatson and Professor John Schad, and from my examiners, Professor Julian Wolfreys and Dr John Brannigan.

Introduction

Colonial and postcolonial translation

Translation and colonialism are fundamentally connected, as Susan Bassnett and Harish Trivedi have argued in *Post-Colonial Translation* (1999). Bassnett and Trivedi insist that translation is not 'transparent' or 'innocent', but is instead a 'highly manipulative activity' between unequal participants from different cultural systems.[1] Bassnett and Trivedi also observe the meaningful historical congruence of colonial expansion and the concept of the 'high-status original' that might be compared with a mediocre translation. This concept was ultimately extended from texts to systems, so that inevitably: 'Europe was regarded as the Great Original, the starting point, and the colonies were therefore copies, or "translations" of Europe, which they were supposed to duplicate'.[2]

Bassnett and Trivedi's research has shown that for centuries, texts were translated into European languages 'for European consumption', and that these texts were selected for their specific suitability for European readers.[3] In addition to the material function of the translated text, the manner in which it is translated is clearly significant. Colonial translation effects a colonization of the text in the same way that the wider colonial project conquers subjects and spaces. Colonial translation involves the reinterpretation of metaphor in two ways: primarily, a colonial translation involves the erasure of 'foreign' metaphor, but in addition, there is an imposition of colonial metaphor on to the translation. This frequently meant heavy editing and mediation of the text, in order to erase culturally specific metaphor, and impose colonial metaphor on to that text. For instance, in addition to his frequent comparisons between 'Oriental' and Western stories and poetry, in the notes accompanying his translation of the Rubaiyat of Omar Khayyam, Edward Fitzgerald openly disregards 'Persian' metaphor in favour of his own European description. Discussing the phrase 'the white hand of Moses' from the fourth stanza, Fitzgerald imagines this 'whiteness to be more suitably represented 'not, according to the Persians, "leprous as Snow," but white, as our May-blossom in Spring perhaps'.[4] Fitzgerald is just as quick to consider erasing stanzas altogether where he considers the imagery to be unpleasant, as in the example of stanza XLIII. He writes:

> According to one beautiful Oriental Legend, Azrael accomplishes his mission by holding to the nostril an Apple from the Tree of Life. This, and the two following Stanzas would have been withdrawn, as somewhat *de trop*, from the Text, but for advice which I least like to disregard.[5]

Similarly, he is eager to 'improve' the versification, describing his decision to alter the rhyme scheme which he describes in the original as 'a strange succession of Grave and Gay'. His translation omits some of the 'Gay' to correct his idea that this 'recurs over-frequently in the Original'.[6]

In colonial India, the first translation was Charles Wilkins' translation from Sanskrit to English of the *Bhagavad Gita*, which was followed by William Jones's *Sacontala*. These were seen as emblems of the achievements of the colonial project which, according to Governor-General Warren Hastings, would far outlast the British presence in India.[7] Translators were among the first of the Orientalists in India whose work enabled British colonial rule; the British approach was to gather, translate and use existing literary and legal documents rather than imposing an entirely new legal system on India. William Jones was one of these translators, along with Abraham-Hyacinthe Antequil-Duperron. Jones's work for the British East India Company provided a stepping stone from scholarly to outright imperialist Orientalism. The first British Viceroy of Egypt, Cromer, applied the knowledge of the Oriental gained through translation and other scholarship, using his 'personal canon of Orientalist wisdom'[8] as a body of so-called knowledge by which to work. It was this that led to the establishment of the Oriental/Occidental binary that Said explored in Orientalism, where the Oriental was perceived to be 'irrational, depraved (fallen), childlike, "different"'.[9]

Postcolonial translation

In response to this highly mediated colonial translation process, postcolonial literature has responded with postcolonial intralingual translations which aim to retell a historical event, the story of a location or a literary text. Maria Tymoczko has described this kind of translation process as one that aims to re-present not just one text, but a culture, comprised of a language, a literature, a legal framework, a history and so forth.[10] Postcolonial literature has often responded to colonial discourse with direct retellings of canonical literature, retold from a postcolonial perspective. This kind of retelling can be categorized as translation, according to Roman Jakobson's model of three translation types. Roman Jakobson's three categories of translation bear witness to the many ways in which translation has been conceived by linguistic, literary and cultural theorists. Roman Jakobson's categories of contemporary translation theory are 'intralingual' translation, a rewording of signs in one language with signs from the same language; 'interlingual' translation, or the interpretation of signs in one language with signs from another language (translation 'proper'); and 'intersemiotic' translation or the transfer ('transmutation') of signs in one language to non-verbal sign systems (from language into art or music).[11] 'Intralingual translation' best describes the way that Rushdie's work performs (or becomes a) translation: this form of translation enables stories to be retold for new audiences or in a new historical moment. Examples of intralingual translations of literature written with a postcolonial perspective include Jean Rhys's *Wide Sargasso Sea* in response to *Jane Eyre*, Maryse Conde's *Windward Heights* which retells *Wuthering Heights*, J M Coetzee's *Foe* which rewrites *Robinson Crusoe*, and Peter Carey's *Jack Maggs*, a postcolonial retelling of *Great Expectations*. There are many retellings of *The Tempest*, a potent symbol of coloniality, especially in the Caribbean; well-known translations include Aime Cesaire's *A Tempest* and George Lamming's theoretical retelling, *The Pleasures of Exile*. Other postcolonial texts perform acts of translation and retelling within new stories.

Rushdie's texts exemplify this postcolonial need to retell, with *Midnight's Children*, a narrative of the independence and Partition of South Asia, most directly performing this retelling of colonial or European versions of that historical period. With their strange magical powers, the midnight's children embody the dubious gift of independence and of the preceding so-called benevolent colonial rule. *The Satanic Verses* is a rewriting of the idea of migration from South Asia to Britain, while *Shalimar the Clown* presents the history of Kashmir anew, by juxtaposing it with the contemporaneous European historical period of the World War II, and thus equalizing those histories.

Approaching Rushdie's work as translation in this way might raise questions about the lengths to which a definition of translation can be put to work. However, the conventionally limited definition of translation that operates in some Western thinking does not represent translation as conceived in some SouthAsian languages and contexts. In Sanskrit, the word for translation, *anuvad*, means 'saying after or again, repeating by way of explanation, explanatory repetition or reiteration with corroboration or illustration, explanatory reference to anything already said'.[12] The sense of translation coming after an original persists in this definition, but the connectedness between original and translation stops there: there is no insistence on faithfulness in grammatical, stylistic or contextual senses.

Rushdie's translation is one of languages and structures as well as stories, and he explicitly produces stories which are inspired by oral narrative forms, while they are written in a new English language in a bid to possess that language rather than allowing those stories to become possessed by the language of the former colonizers. In this way Rushdie has taken up Chinua Achebe's call to use the English language which is inherited by the postcolonial subject, but to make that language a new English that can carry the weight of the formerly colonized subject's experience.[13] Aside from translation theory, the theoretical background for my thesis is largely in postcolonial studies. In particular, I engage with work by Homi Bhabha, Laura Chrisman, Edward Said, Nicholas Harrison, Robert Young, Frantz Fanon and Ashcroft, Griffiths and Tiffin to add to my discussion of some key concerns of postcolonial studies. Susan Bassnett and Harish Trivedi's edited collection of essays, *Post-Colonial Translation*, brings the fields of postcolonial studies and translation theory together, especially in Maria Tymoczko's essay 'Post-colonial writing and literary translation', where it is claimed that 'post-colonial writing might be imagined as a form of translation'.[14] Ashcroft, Griffiths and Tiffin support the idea that translation and postcolonial theories are conjoined:

> In the last few years several critical discussions of post-colonial translation have emerged . . . and a great number of scholars are beginning to address the issue as the theoretical problems of translation in post-colonial countries attracts their attention. The standard problem – "is translation really interpretation" – familiar to all translation theory becomes a crucial issue. Questions of cultural familiarity, the implied construction of the audience, the problems of constructing the "other" have particular relevance in this context.[15]

Linguistic features of Rushdie's work and frequent considerations of desire and of the female body mean that Julia Kristeva's work has been an invaluable source offering methods of interrogating Rushdie's narrative structures and symbolism. The instances of spectacle present in much of Rushdie's writing, and Rushdie's being considered a postmodern writer by many of his contemporary commentators, led to my inclusion of some of the ideas of Baudrillard and Lyotard whose postmodern theories provide further insight into Rushdie's cinematic images and bodily mutations. Reproducing cinematic images in verbal form suggests a further type of translation, one that Jakobson describes as 'intersemiotic'.[16]

In translation

In Rushdie's work, translation always involves temptation and transgression, aspects of translation practice which are implied by the symbolic origin of translation and language difference within the worldviews of the three Abrahamic religions. The construction of the tower of Babel, leading to the subsequent division of human speech, was caused by human transgression: the tower was built in an effort to gain knowledge of God. The division of human speech gave birth to a temptation to translate, hard to resist, just as the tower of Babel was constructed when the temptation to transgress became too strong to resist.

When human language was divided, translation was conceived in order to aid communication. Attempting to heal the linguistic rift, translators transgress linguistic as well as other barriers. As André Lefevere observes: 'translations can be potentially threatening precisely because they confront the receiving culture with another, different way of looking at life and society, a way that can be seen as potentially subversive'.[17] The act of translation is subversive according to the Biblical understanding of translation precisely because the act of translation takes language into human hands and out of God's control in an effort to pre-empt the ideal unilingual future in the advent of glossolalia, after which time there will be no need for translation. The Islamic understanding of human language diversity, important to address in relation to Rushdie whose undergraduate research in Islamic History led to his engagement with the Qur'an in his writing, is slightly different. Umberto Eco writes about a version of language division as told by Ibn Hazm, from his scrutiny of the Qur'an:

> In the beginning there existed a single language given by God, . . . [this] original language was so rich in synonyms that it included every possible language. Thus *confusio* did not depend on the invention of new languages, but on the fragmentation of a unique tongue that existed *ab initio* and in which all others were already contained.[18]

This version of the source of translation is perhaps even more tantalizing, as it suggests that the original state of one common language can somehow be obtained again, because 'in any language men may discover the spirit, the breath, the perfume, and the traces of the original'.[19]

Some translation theorists engage explicitly with ideas of a desire and temptation which compels them to translate – note, for example, Gayatri Chakravorty Spivak's claim that, in order to produce a translation, one 'should adopt a procedure of "love" and "surrender" towards the original'.[20] In many cases, the desire and temptation of the translator is evident through the images and examples used to explain a theoretical approach, suggesting that desire and temptation are inherent properties of the translation process. An example is provided by John McWhorter who, in *The Power of Babel*, claims that his initial awakening into a 'lifelong obsession'[21] with language and translation occurred as a result of his first, childhood feelings of romantic love:

> I fell in love for the first time at four years old. Her name was Shirley and we were both in a piano class. . . . Watching her joyously greet her family, I was shocked to hear that as soon as she started talking to them, I couldn't understand what they were saying! This was the first time in my life that I had ever known that there were languages other than English, and it remains the profoundest shock I have ever encountered . . . I was so frustrated that I cried like the child I was – partly because I felt that this revelation had lost me the girl of my dreams and partly because I was absolutely dazzled by the idea that there were ways of speaking that I could not understand, that there were *other* ways to talk.[22]

The child's desire is defeated by the fact that the object of his affection speaks a different language from him, yet this leaves him 'dazzled', a word that evokes admiration and fascination (or desire) as well as surprise. McWhorter implies that to cross that language barrier in order to fulfil his desire would be a transgression that he could not perform – instead, he 'had lost' the 'girl of [his] dreams'. As if in fear of mistranslation or miscommunication, this event compelled him to learn other languages – he writes, 'I became so obsessed with my language deficit that I left a note on the blackboard for the rabbi . . . asking him how I, too, could learn Hebrew'.[23] Gaining knowledge of Shirley's language, McWhorter implies, the inter-linguistic relationship would not be such a transgression. Entering a foreign language without adequate knowledge is considered to be the transgressive element, in McWhorter's terms.

For Umberto Eco, transgression and temptation combine in the event of translating a passage about a portrait of a young girl wearing an open corset.

Various examples of translations into English and Italian from the original French are examined, but their vagueness frustrates Eco, who wants to know just 'how open was that bodice or corset?'.[24] This detail, Eco suggests, is 'rather relevant since the topic of that scene is the subtle and malicious charm of the aunt at the time of her glorious youth'.[25] Eco suggests that in order to render the image correctly, he must use 13 words instead of the 8, 9 and 10 words in other translations which were closer to the original 'from the rhythmic point of view'.[26] Eco's transgression of rhythm and literalness was performed because of the temptation of the image in the original: 'the relevant element in that visualisation was the exciting and seductive waistline of the young bride, and it was that that I had to make visible, thus abandoning any effort to translate literally'.[27] These examples illustrate the synthesis of translation and temptation at the level of content. Like Spivak, Rosemary Arrojo, in her essay, 'Interpretation as Possessive Love', claims that the process of translation itself involves desire – for Arrojo, the translator is a 'seduced, faithful reader' who is cautious about transgressing, and thus treats the original text with 'extreme fidelity'.[28] As an example, Arrojo suggests that the 'careful "word for word" translation strategy' undertaken by Hélène Cixous 'has a lot in common with a successful love affair' where 'a reader and author' are 'happily brought together'.[29] However, what begins as a loving union soon turns into 'a violent desire to possess' that original text – for Cixous, this takes the form of 'her "transgressive" desire to be in the mother's position' – for the translator who was the 'child' of the author of the original text to become the 'mother'.[30] This possessive desire of the translator is compared by Arrojo to the oppressive nature of 'patriarchy and colonialism'.[31] For Rushdie, though, translation does not necessitate the colonizer's overpowering of the 'native' or the language of the colonizer subsuming that of the colony.

Talking about his work, Rushdie describes translation as primarily a migratory event, occurring when the migrant is 'carried across' a geographical boundary, replicating the etymological meaning of the word 'translation' in the physical movement of the body. In an interview, Rushdie states that

> translation, from the Latin, means "to carry across". Metaphor, from the Greek, means "to carry across". So again this comes back to my preoccupation with the idea of migration. People are also carried across, . . . and I formed the idea that the act of migration was to turn people somehow into things, into people who had been translated.[32]

This idea, equating translation with migration – a key postcolonial concern – has been the focus of much of the work published on Rushdie which alludes to translation in any way. Homi Bhabha's discussion of *The Satanic Verses* in *The Location of Culture*, for instance, sees Saladin Chamcha as a 'borderline figure of a massive historical displacement – postcolonial migration – that is, not only a "transitional" reality, but also a "translational" phenomenon'.[33] However, what emerges from a close reading of Rushdie's fiction is a far more complex relationship between the texts and translation theory. Rushdie's writing explicitly engages with pertinent aspects of translation theory, including the untranslatable, prophetic communication mediated by angels and the madness caused by such communication, as well as the figure of the translator, 'bad' language including bilingualism and dialect, and desire in language, which I will argue replicates the translator's desire to translate. I approach translation in the light of George Steiner's argument, which sees it as 'the arc of communication which every successful speech-act closes within a given language'.[34] One of the ways in which Rushdie's work is inseparable from the act of translation is in its constant preoccupation with translator figures: Saleem Sinai in *Midnight's Children*, Salman the Scribe in *The Satanic Verses*, Aoi Uë in *The Moor's Last Sigh*, the character-narrator retelling the story of *Hamlet* in 'Yorick', and Dashwanth in *The Enchantress of Florence*, for example, can all be understood as translator figures.

Intertextuality

Rushdie's narratives of postcolonial South Asia and South Asian migration can be placed usefully alongside other narratives that aim to tell a postcolonial or anti-colonial version of events. G V Desani's *All About H Hatterr* (1948) has been acknowledged by Rushdie as a key text in the literary presentation of postcolonial India. The novel is, among other things, a dense intertextual web of references to Shakespeare's plays which are imagined by the protagonist's confidant Bannerji to be a manual for life and morality. The novel in many ways renegotiates the place of Shakespeare in India and the after-effects of this symbol of Colonialism. Desani precedes Rushdie in foregrounding language as a fundamental part of identity, and in constructing Indian characters with British literary repertoires.

Indian fiction in English translation has, like Rushdie's work, engaged with language and translation as a fundamental symbol of the post-independence, Partitioned South Asia. Saadat Hasan Manto's renowned short story about the

Partition of India, 'Toba Tek Singh' (1947), describes the complex process of the geographical displacement of asylum inmates following Partition:

> A couple of years after the Partition of the country, it occurred to the respective governments of India and Pakistan that inmates of lunatic asylums, like prisoners, should also be exchanged. . . . Whether this was a reasonable or an unreasonable idea is difficult to say. One thing, however, is clear. It took many conferences of important officials from the two sides to come to this decision.[35]

In the midst of this fairly uncomplicated narrative form is the confused linguistic imagination of the title character, who provides outbursts of bilingual dialogue when asked his opinion about 'the forthcoming exchange of Indian and Pakistani lunatics': 'Uper the gur gur the annexe the bay dhayana the mung the dal of the Government of Pakistan'.[36] The deconstruction of language implies that the exchange of lunatics, the exchange of prisoners and the partition itself may be equally as 'unreasonable' as the exchange of words from one language to another in what could otherwise be a complete sentence.

Significant examples of recent South Asian Diaspora writing in the UK include Monica Ali's *Brick Lane* (2004), a story of migration from Bangladesh to a problematic multicultural London shortlisted for the Man Booker Prize, and Nadeem Aslam's *Maps for Lost Lovers* (2004), longlisted for the Man Booker Prize, winner of the Kiriyama prize in 2005, and described in a number of reviews as reminiscent of Rushdie in its epic quality and political focus. Zadie Smith's *White Teeth* (2000) is also worth mentioning as one of the most widely read narratives of contemporary migration between the UK and South Asia: the separation of twin brothers, one remaining in London and the other sent to Bangladesh for a supposedly more authentic South Asian education engages directly with the notion of the split identity or the hybridity of the second-generation migrant, while it expresses constant uncertainty about place: the London twin engages in juvenile Islamic fundamentalism, while the Bangladesh twin returns a paragon of British Colonial manners and opinions. While Zadie Smith might not deserve the accusation that she is more than a little influenced by Rushdie's writing, there is certainly valuable intertextual commentary between the London Caribbean and South Asian migrants who populate both *White Teeth* and *The Satanic Verses*. Instead of a clash of forces in the guises of theatre and fiction, like the showdown between Saladin Chamcha and Gibreel Farishta on the miniature London stage set, Smith's factions come together to dispute FutureMouse, a scientific experiment in genetic mutation.

First- and second-generation South Asian migrant writers in America include Man Booker prize winning novelist Kiran Desai whose *The Inheritance of Loss* (2006) describes a remote Himalayan border village in the context of globalization, and Bharati Mukherjee, a writer who has been taught on British and American undergraduate modules on South Asian and on American literature for some time. Michael Ondaatje has for decades been a significant literary figure, a Canadian writer with Sri Lankan roots whose works on the search for identity across geographical and spatial borders include *Running in the Family* (1982), an account of a return to Sri Lanka in search of family and community stories sometimes categorized as a memoir, and *The English Patient* (1992), a story of Indians, British and Canadians in the World War II. In this category of very successful migrant South Asian writers Rushdie is a dominant figure, whose most critically acclaimed narrative of postcolonial South Asia, *Midnight's Children*, has won the Booker Prize (1981), the Booker of Bookers (1993) and the Best of the Bookers (2008).

Non-fictional accounts, though far more limited in their potential readership due to the fact that in the main they are generally to be found only in academic libraries, have offered similar counter-colonial representations of South Asian partition and post-independence life and migration. Urvashi Butalia's historical-ethnographic study on Partition, *The Other Side of Silence* (2000), offers first-hand accounts of the physical brutality that occurred at the confused moment of Partition. This is just one example of a text that can be categorized (as Rushdie's novels can) as a revision of postcolonial South Asia. Her work can be read alongside Rushdie's *Shalimar the Clown*, for example, a novel that charts the changes in the formerly peaceful Kashmir and its effects on, in particular, women's bodies.

In others' words

Edward Said writes that 'in the reams of print about Salman Rushdie's *The Satanic Verses*, only a tiny proportion discussed the book *itself*; those who opposed it and recommended its burning and its author's death refused to read it, while those who supported his freedom to write left it self-righteously at that'.[37] Later works on Rushdie, for example, Goonetilleke's study (1998), included detailed explanatory notes revealing the literary, historical, religious and symbolic meaning of Rushdie's references, perhaps in response to this perceived lack of attention to the text itself. Even the most recent criticism, not only of *The Satanic Verses*, but also of Rushdie's work in general, suggests that Rushdie's work can only be read in the context of the fatwa, as the title of Madelena Gonzalez's recent study, *Fiction After the Fatwa*, suggests, explicitly privileging the event as a key concern in reading Rushdie. Though Gonzalez's concern is primarily with the influence of the fatwa on Rushdie's subsequent writing, her approach to transgression is to produce a thought-provoking evaluation of the fatwa's influence – she claims that her 15-year study is 'a case for transgressive aesthetics which seems increasingly viable as a description of [Rushdie's] contribution to literature'.[38] Some of Rushdie's commentators go as far as to suggest that it is impossible to read Rushdie's texts without engaging with the fatwa – Christopher Rollason is an example, who, in an essay on *The Ground Beneath Her Feet*, writes that he 'shall . . . endeavour to read and interpret [the novel] with only secondary or incidental reference to the fatwa'.[39] This approach highlights an ongoing preoccupation with the fatwa which has found a response in Rushdie's memoir, *Joseph Anton* (2012), named after the pseudonym he chose while in hiding, a name constructed from the first names of Rushdie's two favourite authors, Joseph Conrad and Anton Chekhov.

Much work has been done to illuminate the events surrounding the fatwa, and to examine *The Satanic Verses* in the light of the accusations made in the fatwa, including Appignanesi and Maitland's edited collection of articles and essays, *The Rushdie File*, and Malise Ruthven's *A Satanic Affair*, as well as more general works on Rushdie by Catherine Cundy, DCRA Goonetilleke, Daniel Pipes and others.[40] Goonetilleke's and Cundy's works, published by Palgrave and Manchester University Press, respectively, have recently been superseded by updated general works offered by these publishers in 2008, and written by Stephen Morton and Andrew Teverson. These newer studies include work on some of Rushdie's newer fiction, and attest to his continued critical significance while reflecting a slow move away from fatwa-focused responses. As Samir Dayal suggests, there had been 'saturation coverage' of the fatwa.[41] It became clear that the fatwa had become a focus for critical interrogation at the expense of the important things that Rushdie was doing in his texts. Laura Chrisman suggests that, similarly, 'the Rushdie Affair . . . risks obscuring other important dynamics of 1980s Englishness, some of which were recognised by Rushdie himself in a 1984 critical essay, "Outside the Whale"'.[42] Among the most interesting of these neglected areas was the narrative voice and the language used in the narrators' and characters' dialogue, in combination with themes which evoke linguistic questions – for example, the examination of veils and the harem in *Shame* is set against the concept of *takallouf*, a linguistic system of 'tongue-tying formality'. *Takallouf* dictates that only the surface level of polite communication is permissible, it is 'a social restraint so extreme as to make it impossible for the victim to express what he or she really means, a species of compulsory irony which insists, for the sake of good form, on being taken literally'.[43] In other words, *takallouf* is an engagement with the unsayable or the untranslatable, and the veil and the harem can be taken as symbolic of the untranslatable in *Shame* and *The Satanic Verses*, a recurring engagement in Rushdie with the complicated process of translation.

In addition, the fatwa must be viewed from the perspective of the translator. It was actually in translation that the effect of the fatwa was felt the most severely: of course, Rushdie was the major focus of aggression but the various translators of *The Satanic Verses* were seen as easier targets by some, and it is well known that Japanese translator Hitoshi Igarashi was murdered in 1991. Also in 1991 Ettore Capriolo, its Italian translator, was seriously wounded, while in October 1993 the novel's Norwegian publisher, William Nygaard, was shot and seriously wounded. These events followed Rushdie's attempt to prevent the novel from being translated from English into other languages at all. The publishers of the French and Spanish translations were wary, and while the Spanish publisher withheld the translator's name, the French translation was published using a pseudonym to protect the translator. It is still difficult to find the names or professional profiles of some of the translators of the novel. Perhaps the most dramatic incident occurred in 1993 at the Turkish Pir Sultan Abdal Literary Festival; a 2000-strong mob set fire to the hotel where the festival was taking place after the mob was denied its demand that one of the speakers, the Turkish translator of *The Satanic Verses* Aziz Nesin, be handed over for execution according to the fatwa's instructions. Nesin escaped the fire and survived but 37 other festival participants died. Even as recently as 2007 when the first Romanian translation of the novel by Dana Craciun was published, the Romanian Church (whose censorship regulations are part of national law) heavily condemned its publication. If the fatwa is to remain a subject of cultural interest in relation to the public life of Salman Rushdie, then his works cannot be separated from their existence in interlingual translation. Reading Rushdie from a more direct, literary perspective, though, it is in the intertextual relationship between the novels and earlier narratives of colonial and postcolonial India where intralingual translation holds the most promise.

Chapter summary

Questions of the unsaid or unsayable, the untranslatable and the unrepeatable form the basis of the first chapters of this book. Chapter 1 examines moments in *The Satanic Verses*, *Shalimar the Clown* and *Shame* where desire is conveyed by textual ruptures in the form of gaps, pauses, deferrals and silences. In their reflections on translation and in notes and forewords, translators frequently describe translation as a process of desire and seduction. Translation takes place as a result of the translator's desire for the original, and their desire to possess that original and render it anew in translation. In the novels, hunger and gluttony, desire and greed echo the translator's passion for the task of translation, in texts which are ruptured in ways that resemble those 'untranslatable' parts that cause translators the most frenzied energy, that replicate the translators' earliest engagements with translation and linguistic difference.

Chapter 2 considers proposals made by Derrida and others that translation is impossible, to consider the ways in which Rushdie's texts engage with the unsayable and the untranslatable. 'Takallouf' – the idea that all spoken language must be taken literally – is a key aspect of this, which resonates with early translators' loyalty to practices of word-for-word translation. In *Shame*, takallouf is apparently used as a method of restricting women's speech and with it, their physical freedom. Yet, according to Sara Suleri, to render in metaphorical language is to possess. Outside metaphorical language, remaining literal, the women in Rushdie's harems and behind their veils remain un-described, not-possessed by their male relatives. Rushdie's texts transgress the gender boundaries set down by societal codes in order to reveal the women behind the veils and inside the harems. This act of revelation, of saying the unsayable, involves a representation of the harem as the rigorously managed and powerful matriarchal political and economic system, in stark contrast to colonial or Hollywood representations. The harem, then, no longer unsayable, is, by its rendering here, translatable.

Chapter 3 aligns translation with transgression by exploring examples of bad language in *Midnight's Children*, *The Satanic Verses* and *Shame*. Conventionally, the translator's task is perceived as a transgressive one. After all, the translator rebels against the injunction placed upon humanity by God as punishment for building of the tower of Babel, a story that haunts translation theory. Transgressive translation in Rushdie's work is conveyed in key moments where protagonists choose to use transgressive language or to transgress their linguistic boundaries or duties: In *Midnight's Children*, Saleem causes riots when he repeats a rhyme intended to mock the rhythmical patterns of Gujerati. In *The Satanic Verses*, Salman the Scribe tests his prophet Mahound's knowledge and connection to God by altering the prophecies slightly, by selecting synonyms and ultimately raises the question of doubt, which is for Rushdie the opposite of faith. In *Shame*, the active use of obscene language leads directly to violence, so the specific words chosen have physical manifestations. The use of language that is for one reason or another inappropriate – by stepping outside of an allocated linguistic role or identity – leads to physical, bodily impact. Translation, then, is revealed to be not, after all, simply a matter of 'dictionaries and grammars'.

Further chapters deal with methods of translating colonial representation by focusing on literary form, history and theory. Chapter 4 explores the importance of literary form in translation. By examining Rushdie's short stories in *East, West* and the parallel which I suggest exists between them and Goethe's three translation types, this chapter shows that the short story form might be more inherently suitable for translating stories about places, ideas, people and times. The chapter also considers Rushdie's other short stories in these terms.

In Chapter 5, I turn to the need to retell colonial histories, with an exploration of the representation of Kashmir in *Shalimar the Clown* and *Midnight's Children*. When translators translate, they can change the way that a location or a time is perceived by the reader. They can also influence the receiving culture by exposing them to the unfamiliar images and ideas conveyed in the translated texts. *Midnight's Children* and *Shalimar the Clown* both represent Kashmir in a way that undermines the dominant representation of that region. Rather than presenting one straightforward new version of history, though, Rushdie's texts question the legitimacy of historical representation altogether. This is enacted textually by the use of narrative structure which situates Kashmir in the present moment, and evades the sense of an ending that Frank Kermode suggests compels all Western narratives (and their readerships).

Chapter 6 reconsiders the somewhat neglected *Grimus* through Edward Said's travelling theory, the process by which theory might travel, or, translate. *Grimus* was not an especially successful first novel in comparison with his later work. Nor was it particularly well received in Rushdie scholarship. Perhaps one reason for this is the feeling that postcolonial sensibilities were somehow misapplied in the novel to a vague Native American context. Though there are common concerns between postcolonial and Native American contexts, they are not, perhaps, so easily interchangeable. Instead, the novel can be read more fruitfully as an early example of the twenty-first-century meeting between ecocriticism and postcolonial theory. This chapter considers *Grimus* from a postcolonial-ecocritical perspective, and is informed by Said's travelling theory.

In the final chapters of the book, I suggest that Rushdie's engagement with translation practices and theories ultimately points towards a desire to make translation a visible and a free practice, rather than the invisible and faithful endeavour that dominates traditional representations of translation. Chapter 7 considers the ways in which literary texts can make translation and translators visible, in response to the authority of patronage. I explore the patronage of translation and Lawrence Venuti's position on the translator's invisibility, and Rushdie's attempt to make the translator visible again, in *The Moor's Last Sigh* and *The Enchantress of Florence*. The patron is traditionally an important figure in translation, holding a significant level of power over what is translated, for whom and how. The same can be said of art patronage. In this chapter, I explore Rushdie's engagement with visual culture and painting as an intersemiotic translation process, where stories are translated into their visual form and, as in the case of *The Enchantress of Florence*, afterwards translated from art into flesh.

Chapter 8 considers the ways in which Rushdie as a literary figure has been received, and has represented his own public persona. Relevant to this question is Rushdie's appointment as Distinguished Writer in Residence at Emory University. Rushdie's place in the academy (when, previously, he had been very unwilling to define himself or his texts as postcolonial or postmodern, and insisted they were just what they were, just what the reader found) means that it is now more important to consider how the writer engages or has engaged with theories or academic thinking. This chapter also considers ways in which Rushdie has represented the fatwa and its effect on his writing, which is engaged with most directly in two ways: in his writing for children, *Haroun and the Sea of Stories* and *Luka and the Fire of Life*, and in his autobiographical work, *Joseph Anton*, a 2012 memoir of his experience of the fatwa.

The concluding chapter summarizes the importance and the impact of considering Rushdie's work alongside translation theories, and the importance of translation in contemporary scholarship in relation to postcolonial literary studies. An annotated bibliography of texts on translation, on postcolonial and other relevant theories and on Rushdie, is intended to encourage the reader's continued engagement with questions raised in this book.

1

Translation as Temptation: Gaps, Silences, Seductions

In their reflections on translation and in notes and forewords, translators frequently describe translation as a process of desire and seduction. Translation takes place as a result of the translator's desire for the original, and their desire to possess that original and render it anew in translation. In *The Satanic Verses*, this desire is embodied by Gibreel Farishta who is forced to occupy the liminal space of the angel in the role of ventriloquist's dummy, caught between God and prophets, between the postmodern screen and reality and between India and the colonial motherland. The result is madness, conveyed through textual silences and distortions. In *Shame*, the liminal space is occupied by Farah Aziz, whose existence in space outside communication is rendered by broken sentences, and by her haunting of a landscape constructed from fragments: broken shards of mirror and interminable bollards. Her desirability is her undoing, and when hypnotized she is subject to a brutal mistranslation: Omar Khayyam Shakil chooses to believe that she is a willing party to his seduction and impregnation, an act that ultimately removes her from the liminality that had afforded her a kind of power outside linguistic certainty. In *Shalimar the Clown*, textual structures are ruptured with gaps, silences, pauses and deferrals. Hunger and gluttony, desire and greed echo the translator's passion for the task of translation, in text ruptured in ways that resemble those 'untranslatable' parts that cause translators the most frenzied energy, that replicate the translators' earliest engagements with translation and linguistic difference. In all of these texts, translation occurs as a result of temptation, and temptation is rendered through gaps, silences, fractures, distortions and impossibilities.

'*Bugs in the brain*': Translation as Madness in *The Satanic Verses*

Jean Baudrillard describes a culture in which 'communication "occurs" by means of a sole instantaneous circuit, and for it to be "good" communication it must take place fast – there is no time for silence'. He continues,

> Silence is . . . a blip in the circuitry, that minor catastrophe, that slip which, on television for instance, becomes highly meaningful – a break laden now with anxiety, now with jubilation, which confirms the fact that all this communication is basically nothing but a rigid script, an uninterrupted fiction designed to free us not only from the void of the television screen but equally from the void of our own mental screen, whose images we wait on with the same fascination.[1]

Thus, communication must be fast, with no gaps or silence, in order for it to be considered 'good'. The 'anxiety' of silence is evocative of Gibreel's flawed communication with Mahound in *The Satanic Verses* – Gibreel, we read, 'remains silent, empty of answers' (p. 111). And, as a result, Mahound's unanswered questions cause him to provide his own response, which he later believes to be the words of 'the Devil . . . in the guise of the archangel' (p. 123), the 'satanic verses'. The 'rigid script' of Baudrillard's postmodern communication is the film script which Gibreel follows but which fails in his first meeting with Mahound because he doesn't 'know the story', hasn't 'learned any lines' (p. 109). The 'rigid script' also suggests the religious text which cannot be distorted, and which Salman the scribe tried to alter: 'when he sat at the Prophet's feet, writing down rules rules rules, he began, surreptitiously, to change things' (p. 367). Mahound at first 'did not notice the alterations', but later pronounced, in a statement which Rushdie has described as an example of eerie foreknowledge of his fatwa: 'your blasphemy, Salman, can't be forgiven. Did you think I wouldn't work it out? To set your words against the Words of God' (p. 374).[2]

The Satanic Verses poses the question of whether communication with angels is a symptom of madness. In the Bible story, Babel was thrust on to humanity, causing confusion comparable to psychosis. In this confused linguistic space, communication with the Archangel Gabriel and with Gibreel Farishta, takes place. The reliability of human communication with God through the medium of an angel, and of the message produced, is a preoccupation of *The Satanic Verses*. Perhaps angelic communication was made necessary because Babel prevented more direct communication, and angel communication is thus a symptom of the madness caused by Babel. Translation theory is frequently haunted by the idea of Babel and the ideal of a unilingual future, which has its origin in the gift of tongues bestowed on the disciples at Pentecost.[3] Pentecost is thought of as the reverse of Babel, where the phenomenon of glossolalia is equivalent to a 'good' or 'angelic' babble: at Pentecost, the disciples 'were all filled with the Holy Ghost, and began to speak with other tongues, as the Spirit gave them utterance'.[4] St Paul refers to this as speaking in the tongues of angels in 1 Corinthians 13. The passage reads: 'though I speak with the tongues of men and of angels, but have not love, I have become sounding brass or a clanging cymbal'.[5] Without love, communication fails. Similarly, prophecy is subordinate to love, as the passage continues: 'and though I have the gift of prophecy, and understand all mysteries and all knowledge, and though I have all faith, so that I could remove mountains, but have not love, I am nothing'.[6] Language, after Babel, in that unilingual ideal, is seen as more powerful than prophecy:

> 8 Love never fails. But whether there are prophecies, they will fail; whether there are tongues, they will cease; whether there is knowledge, it will vanish away. 9 For we know in part and we prophesy in part. 10 But when that which is perfect has come, then that which is in part will be done away.[7]

This goes some way towards explaining Gibreel's reluctance to perform the role of archangel, and towards excusing his flaws. Gibreel is only temporarily providing a communication channel: one day, such prophecy will 'fail' – it will no longer be required when 'that which is perfect' prevails and communication is unilingual. *The Satanic Verses* addresses the relationship between religious communication, madness and, via the angelic Gibreel Farishta, the postcolonial migrant. Satan is, of course, also a migrant, who like Gibreel, was only temporarily involved in communication between God and humankind, and then became an exiled angel. It is Gibreel's comparable status as a migrant angel which prompts Saladin's devilish appearance and compels him to carry out a cruel revenge on Gibreel in the form of 'little, satanic verses that made him mad' (p. 445) spoken in a multitude of taunting voices in a string of malicious telephone calls.

The Satanic Verses portrays various contagious social conditions, beginning when Gibreel's fame causes feverish but fickle public devotion, manifested in the most religious language when Gibreel is ill in hospital: 'in the mosques and temples of the nation, packed congregations prayed, not only for the life of the dying actor, but for the future, for themselves' (p. 29). Secondly, Saladin Chamcha's diabolical appearance becomes an infectious teenage fashion to imitate as teenagers pretend at devilishness: 'all of a sudden he was everywhere, on the chests of young girls and in the windows protected against bricks by metal grilles . . . the kids in the Street started wearing rubber devil-horns on their heads' (p. 286).

Pretence is the medium of the actor and perhaps equally of the translator: Perrot d'Ablancourt states that in his translation, 'there are many passages I have translated word for word, . . . there are also passages in which I have considered what ought to be said, or what I could say, rather than what he [the writer of the original text being translated] actually said.'[8] In this way, the translator's task is to present their interpretation of inferred meaning more than to provide a faithfully translated alternative text. Much of what the translator infers is based on what is absent from the text, as George Steiner suggests, writing that where 'so little is being said' yet 'so much is being meant', the absence in the text poses 'almost intractable problems for the translator'.[9] Thus, the translator invents, makes up, pretends and bases the translation on something external to the text: a voice in his or her head. It is the presence of something, a second personality or a disembodied extra voice like the one relied upon by the translator, which is often seen as signifying madness, and it is this type of madness that is particularly relevant to the angel experience.

The presence of extra voices or personalities and the idea of possession can be interpreted as prophetic communication with angels, yet instead of being treated as such, these presences account for many diagnoses of madness. As Roy Porter claims, 'these days, the Roman Catholic or Anglican who claims to be filled with the Holy Ghost, or the Devil, is something of an embarrassment, even to his fellow-believers. His priest will try to persuade him that he is speaking metaphorically; and, if he persists, he may be invited to see a doctor'.[10] Perhaps the idea that the insane person contains something additional to other people in the form of voices or possession is one reason for primitive but recent treatments for madness which involve the removal of part of the brain. The lobotomy was the original method of removing problematic extraneous brain matter: 'lobotomies and leucotomies were in vogue for a time as the "heroic" contribution of psycho-surgery'[11] but this was replaced with a far cheaper method of brain reduction, known as a 'modified leucotomy', which was pioneered by the Italian Doctor Fiamberti:

> One cuts the small limited area, in the lower medial quadrant of the frontal lobe, that maintains tension and obsessive thinking, thus relieving the patient without any risk of the "personality deterioration" which often resulted from the old full

> operation. [The doctor] simply pushed a strong needle through the roof of the eye socket and into the lower part of the frontal lobe; then he manipulated the needle in such a way as to cut the appropriate brain tracts. . . . Ordinary psychiatrists could now, if absolutely necessary, undertake a modified leucotomy themselves, without having to summon a neurosurgeon.[12]

Roy Porter suggests that there is a parallel between madness and religion in general, in *The Faber Book of Madness*. He claims that 'religion, one can argue, *all* religion, is delusional *per se*', going on to explain, with reference to Freud, that 'in adopting this stance, which reduced religion to psychopathology, Freud was inheriting the mantle of the more brutal of the Enlightenment *philosophes*, who regarded religion as a morbid thought secretion of sick brains'.[13] Porter suggests that the connection between religion and madness is based on Christian pronouncements, meaning that 'Christianity set faith (or what Freud called 'wish-fulfilment') above reason'.[14] Gibreel's visionary dreams cause him to be pronounced 'a man possessed' (p. 301). Freud treats religious experience as illness or malfunction. Likewise in *The Satanic Verses*, Gibreel's possession is not taken seriously and, instead, is attributed by 'the medical opinion' to 'starvation' (p. 341), or physical problems. Rushdie, it seems, is not entirely in disagreement with the doctors, for Saladin's and Gibreel's experiences of madness can be explained by their mutations after surviving their fall from the aeroplane.

Instead of taking away something from the patient, by using drugs the doctors can 'give' something 'additional', as in Gibreel Farishta's treatment. Here, Gibreel is both an asylum seeker, wandering over geographical boundaries, and an inhabitant of a lunatic asylum. In his case, the borderline between these two senses of the word 'asylum' is blurred. Translation intensifies the confusion between insanity and foreignness, when what cannot be translated becomes imprecise. For Susan Sontag, migration and madness are connected by a metaphorical passport, which provides ease of passage from 'the kingdom of the well' to 'the kingdom of the sick', which is for Sontag the dual kingdom which everyone inhabits.[15] The drugs intended to stabilize Gibreel's wayward mind cause equal but different erratic brain impulses; in his 'bloody jail' of an asylum, 'the drugs made Gibreel clumsy' (p. 434). Sometimes, of course, a drug causes hallucination, instead of curing it – nevertheless, 'some psychiatrists consider the report of hallucinations alone, in the absence of any other evidence of insanity, as warranting the diagnosis "schizophrenia"'.[16]

The hallucination is invariably 'othered', as we see in *The Satanic Verses*, where what is other must be contained: the immigrants are held in a sanatorium;

Saladin Chamcha's metamorphosis is hidden in his rented room; and Gibreel is sent to a rural safe house when his angelic state – or his insanity – is considered so strong that other people should be protected from it. This is reminiscent of early twentieth-century attitudes to insanity and the culture of the asylum, operating within 'a "realised myth": a myth of what an elite group wanted to represent as madness, and madness contained and controlled'.[17] In *The Satanic Verses*, therefore, what is forcibly contained self-destructs or mutates.

The formative years of Gibreel the actor may provide clues about the origin of Gibreel's madness. During adolescence and young adulthood, he first acquires his angelic pseudonym ('Gibreel Farishta' translates as 'Gabriel Angel'[18]). At this point, he identifies with the Prophet, in a response that could be described as a pre-existing condition or suggestibility, which, with the trauma of surviving a fall from a hijacked aeroplane, may be an argument that the prophetic and angelic parts of the novel are simply representative of the playing out of a mental illness, the hallucinations of sickness: 'he caught himself in the act of forming blasphemous thoughts, . . . his somnolent fancy began to compare his own condition with that of the Prophet . . . and after that he began to worry about the impurity in his make-up that could create such terrible visions' (p. 22). Not only does this passage suggest that Gibreel may in fact create the visions which he later experiences as real, but also, that his visions are connected to his lifestyle as an actor: it is his 'make-up' which allows him to create these visions – not his genetic make-up, but the make-up he uses on stage and screen.

Once this stage make-up is removed, Gibreel has no focus. He is left feeling divided by his prophetic dreams; though sleeping in twentieth-century London, he provides prophecies 'from the peak of Mount Cone' in 'Jahilia' to Mahound (p. 126). Though he joins the past with the present, eventually he cannot reconcile his angelic communication with the prophet Mahound with his status as a film star, and commits suicide: '"if I thought the sickness would never leave me, that it would always return, I would not be able to bear up to it." . . . Gibreel put the barrel of the gun into his own mouth; and pulled the trigger; and was free' (p. 546). To be absolutely connected with the past would, of course, be a form of madness – as George Steiner writes: 'to remember everything is a condition of madness'.[19] However, to forget everything (or to be forced to forget everything) may also be a condition of colonialism: as Cundy suggests, 'a lack of consciousness of, or belief in, one's identity can be a specific by-product of colonialism'.[20] Gibreel kills himself because of the conflict between his madness which forces him to remember everything, and colonialism, which compels him to forget.

Catherine Cundy's notion of a lack of belief in one's identity can be seen in Saladin Chamcha's desperation to become what he imagines to be the ideal Englishman, and his inability to tolerate the Indian who he once was, who spoke in Bombay dialect and had a meaningful identity based on his given name. Salahuddin means 'the righteousness of the faith' and Chamchawala means 'spoon-seller'.[21] Because of his shortened name, Zeeny calls him 'my Salad' (p. 54), and Gibreel calls him 'Spoono' and 'Chumch' (pp. 131, 3). A further meaning not made explicit within the novel is provided by Goonetilleke: Saladin means 'sycophant' in Bombay slang.[22] When he anglicizes his name, he not only divides both of those names and therefore divides his self, 'the mutation of Salahuddin Chamchawala into Saladin Chamcha' (p. 37), but he also prevents belief in that original identity because the resulting shortened name is meaningless, or carries frivolous or incorrect meaning. In short, he does not translate – or at least, not without being diminished.

Saladin's false representation is a kind of simulation, connecting Saladin to Gibreel again, for Masqood's hypothesis that angel communication may be falsity equally resonates with Baudrillard's postmodern culture of simulation; Baudrillard questions the idea of sickness:

> Simulation threatens the difference between the "true" and the "false", the "real" and the "imaginary". Is the simulator sick or not, given that he produces "true" symptoms? . . . For, if any symptoms can be "produced", and can no longer be taken as a fact of nature, then every illness can be considered as sustainable and simulated.[23]

Baudrillard goes on to associate simulated sickness with simulation in religion, asking, 'what becomes of divinity when it reveals itself in icons, when it is multiplied in simulacra?'[24] It is the prohibition of simulacra, related to questions of iconoclasts with which Baudrillard engages in *Simulacra and Simulation*. The prohibition of simulacra causes Saleem's family to rebuke his claim of prophetic communication in *Midnight's Children*, encourages Masqood to condemn contemporary communication with angels as lunacy or lies and causes Rushdie's censors to condemn his portrayals of Gibreel and a prophet called Mahound as blasphemous. Baudrillard describes the iconoclasts' fears over the

> Omnipotence of simulacra, the faculty simulacra have of effacing God from the conscience of man, and the destructive, annihilating truth that they allow to appear – that deep down God never existed, that only the simulacrum ever existed, even that God himself was never anything but his own simulacrum.[25]

Gibreel Farishta embodies the simulacrum who wears masks of gods and replicates the image of gods in film, who is unmasked in romantic relationships, and whose images fade when he is no longer believed in, revealing the devotion to him to have been only devotion to a simulacrum.

The angel and ventriloquism

Gibreel Farishta's name translates literally from the Urdu to Gabriel Angel.[26] As a representation of the angel Gabriel, though, at first reading he appears untypical: being 'irresistibly attractive to women', he lives a 'life of scandal and debauch' which consumes his emotional life in an 'avalanche of sex' (p. 25). As well as being eroticized, this is a migrant angel; Gibreel's communication with the Prophet Mahound begins only when he migrates from Bombay to London (Rekha Merchant's accusation renders this migration divinely inspired: 'God knows where you thought you were from').

An angel's role in a process of translation is like the translator's position mediating between an original and a translation. Represented in art, the Angel Gabriel is sometimes portrayed as possessing agency, like a translator who can make independent choices about how to represent an original. Sandro Botticelli's Gabriel depicted in *The Annunciation* (1489–90) appears persuasive and supplicant, delivering God's message in response to Mary's reaction and not in spite of it, employing the translator's art in order to convey a message in the most effective way. Gibreel Farishta, though, is an unwilling and inactive part of the prophetic experience. This is a symptom of the time: Walter Benjamin refers to a weakening of prophecy in the modern period when he suggests that 'theology . . . today . . . is wizened and has to keep out of sight', though, he writes, 'like every generation that preceded us, we have been endowed with a *weak* Messianic power'.[27] Gibreel's function is to communicate a message – which he cannot influence – between God and human. As Gibreel puts it, 'damn me if I know where she's getting her information/inspiration. Not from this quarter, that's for sure' (p. 226), he says of the prophet Ayesha. Gibreel's experience of embodying the angel is consistent with the Islamic idea of a servant angel: the traditional Islamic angel is more susceptible to human will than he is in Judeo-Christian interpretations like Botticelli's rendering of the angel, for example, as, 'according to the prophet Mohammed, [the Angel is] sent by God to earth to search out those places where individuals or groups are engaged in remembering or invoking the Deity'.[28] Because an angel conveys an oral text rather than a written text, the three-way process of repeated words resembles ventriloquism, and the angel becomes a ventriloquist's dummy; this is a difficult role for the accomplished actor Gibreel to perform, and the result of this unwilling mimicry is his confinement in an asylum. According to Gibreel's rejected love-interest Rekha Merchant, the perceived insanity accompanying Gibreel's angelic experience could equally be ascribed to divine will: 'God knows what diseases you brought' (26).

Saladin Chamcha as Gibreel's foil 'wanted nothing to do with [Gibreel's] pathetic personality, that half-reconstructed affair of mimicry and voices' (p. 9). This phenomenon of 'mimicry and voices' is perceived as the opposite of the 'will to live' that rendered Saladin's body hard and inhuman by 'turning his blood to iron, changing his flesh to steel'. The metal entity that Saladin becomes when he and Gibreel fall from the exploded aeroplane is a robotic reconstruction of the human, though, a mimic of the man that was once Saladin. Saladin falls to land not as an aeroplane, but as a robot or even a bomb in his steel and iron construction, and like an unexploded bomb – an unwelcome type of exile – his arrival in England elicits hostility: 'a sealed police van containing three immigration officers and five policemen' became 'all the universe he possessed . . . a universe of fear' (pp. 158–9). Saladin is the mimic; he resembles Naipaul's mimic man and a representation of the 'Pal' discussed by Benedict Anderson in *Imagined Communities* in response to the recollections of Bipin Chandra Pal, who is 'condemned to an "irrational" permanent subordination to the English . . . . It was not simply that, no matter how Anglicized a Pal became, he was always barred from the uppermost peaks of the Raj. He was also barred from movement outside its perimeter'.[29] Saladin expresses 'his determination to become . . . a goodandproper Englishman . . . he would be English, even if his classmates giggled at his voice and excluded him from their secrets, because these exclusions only increased his determination, and that was when he began to act, to find masks that these fellows would recognize, paleface masks, clown-masks, until he fooled them into thinking he was *okay*, he was *people-like-us*' (p. 43). Saladin's mimicry is part of his 'will to live' in England and is enabled by the robotic, masked performance of what he perceives to be adherence to English customs and desires composed of 'tepid, used [bath-]water full of mud and soap'; 'summer pudding, hockey-sticks, thatched houses', 'Yorkshire pudding and hearts of oak', 'ye olde dream-England' (pp. 43, 180). Saladin understands that while developing into a 'goodandproper Englishman', he has become 'an

Indian translated into English-medium' (p. 58). Yet his successful television career is limited to voice-overs or ventriloquism: 'they pay you to imitate them, as long as they don't have to look at you. Your voice becomes famous but they hide your face' (p. 60). The particular translation which he attempts to perform is one which Goethe describes as the type where the 'aim is to make the original identical with the translation' so that the translation is seamless. Goethe warns that 'the translator who attaches himself too closely to his original' which in this case would be Saladin's conception of England and Englishness, 'more or less abandons the originality of his own nation'. In contrast with Gibreel's unwilling ventriloquism as an angel, Saladin's ventriloquism is purposeful: though both characters become translated as a result of their migration, Saladin desires translation while Gibreel resists it, wishing to remain 'an untranslated man' (p. 427).

Ventriloquism and translation coincide in Gibreel's forced prophetic communication. The angel Gabriel is, according to Michel Serres, 'portrayed as the bringer of the good tidings at the origins of both Christianity and Islam'.[30] The term 'good tidings' means gospel,[31] the word of God, and the idea of the angel as intermediary appears in both Judeo-Christian and Islamic portrayals; Malise Ruthven states that the angel Gibreel was the 'revered figure of the archangel who in Islamic tradition brought down the Qur'an from God to Muhammad'.[32] Peter Lamborn Wilson also sees the Islamic version of Gabriel as a physical embodiment of the word of God: 'between his two eyes were written the words: There is no god but God, and Mohammed is the prophet of God'.[33] As Wilson puts it, Gabriel is the 'principle of the Divine Word'.[34] Rushdie's Gabriel, Gibreel Farishta, performs this role with difficulty, wishing to remain 'untranslated'.

Gibreel Farishta contains elements of both the Islamic and the Christian versions of the angel, but he is also a postcolonial migrant and subject to a history of imperialism and geographical movement. It is in resistance to the history of colonial translation, a powerful tool in subjugating the colonized population, that Gibreel is anxious to remain 'untranslated'. This conjunction of religious miracle and recent political history resembles Walter Benjamin's interpretation of the angel of history in response to Paul Klee's 'Angelus Novus', an angel who unwillingly joins the past to the present and future: 'his face is turned towards the past', though the 'storm irresistibly propels him into the future to which his back is turned'.[35] Benjamin's angel of history has 'eyes [that] are staring, his mouth is open, his wings are spread. . . . a storm is blowing from Paradise; it has got caught in his wings with such violence that the angel can no longer close them'.[36] These images are reproduced in *The Satanic Verses*, but instead of representing Gibreel, they are attributed to the Prophet Mahound, whose 'overwhelming intensity' and 'anguish' (pp. 110, 111) act as a beacon to summon the serving angel Gibreel Farishta to the mountain to transmit God's word. In Rushdie, though, it is the prophet rather than the angel who is portrayed with his 'eyes open wide' and a 'rigid' (p. 112) stance. Benjamin's storm becomes Gibreel's: the day begins 'to turn to night, . . . clouds to mass overhead . . . the air to thicken into soup' (p. 112). What does it mean when a prophet is caught in the storm between the past and the future? When a mortal man like Mahound has the power of influence hitherto ascribed to the archangel, the validity of angel communication is rendered questionable, and the power behind the words translated or produced is deferred to the speaker, Mahound. Indeed, the novel expresses doubt about the origin of the prophecies voiced by Mahound: in Gibreel's vision of the revelations, Mahound was the ventriloquist: 'he started weeping for joy and then he did his old trick, forcing my mouth open and making the voice, the Voice, pour out of me once again, made it pour all over him, like sick' (p. 123). Gibreel struggles against his angelic destiny and, in contrast to Benjamin's cold storm, Gibreel creates a heat wave in London, declaring, 'I am going to tropicalize you' (p. 354). Gibreel's insistent tropicalization reverses the colonial desire to impose a familiar lifestyle on the colony, what Bassnett and Trivedi describe as the 'metaphor of the colony as a translation, a copy of an original located elsewhere on a map'.[37] Here the colonized imposes his structure on the former colonizer.

When he fears that he may be propelled unwillingly into an uncertain future by the prophecy that he perceives as mental illness, Gibreel commits suicide. In taking control, he becomes 'free' of responsibility, as Rekha suggests when she tells him, 'nobody ever held you responsible for what you did' (p. 546). The postcolonial angel is able to control his destiny, unlike the angel who serves God without question, as Gibreel first comprehends while walking along an old London street: 'not all migrants are powerless' (p. 458). God becomes the colonial power to which Gibreel responds, in contrast to the imaginary England behind Saladin's mimicry. Rushdie's Gibreel is rebellious and devilish, bloated with power. Because, unlike Saladin, he refuses to serve the colonial power, his angelic status remains incomplete: a migrant angel like Satan, he is denied God's protection, and is kicked out of heaven and into an asylum, where his prophecies become 'bugs in the brain' (p. 434). Confined here, Saladin assumes the position of the devil and the 'puppeteer' (p. 432) of both Gibreel, on whom he wishes to exact revenge, and Allie, Gibreel's lover, through a programme of sophisticated mimicry in the form of malicious 'telephone calls' (p. 443) in various voices: 'little satanic verses' that 'would finish [Gibreel] off for good' (p. 445). Saladin's attempt to embody Englishness is problematized by his relationship with Gibreel, an imprecise opposite, and as Fanon describes in *Black Skin, White Masks*, 'face to face with this man who is "different from himself," he needs to defend himself. In other words, to personify the Other. The Other will become the mainstay of his preoccupations and his desires'.[38] Saladin's white mask is worn in this defensive manner and he constructs Gibreel – the untranslated Indian who threatens to reveal his own Indianness beneath his English mask – as his Other, who, because he blames Gibreel for his detention in the asylum with beastlike migrants, becomes 'the mainstay of his preoccupations and his desires'.

The Prophet Mahound takes on the characteristics which Benjamin attributes to the angel, thereby embodying the word of God. In this way, Gibreel is dissociated from the translation and God's word is translated without interference from the messenger. Gibreel's reluctance to convey prophecy is not limited by time; he feels equally unable to translate God's message to either Mahound or the contemporary prophet, Ayesha. As with Benjamin's angel of history, Rushdie's angel causes a convergence of the past with the present. Frank Kermode suggests that existence out of the historical sequence of time is the definition of the angelic state, and it is interesting to note that Kermode makes this point in relation to psychoanalysis, to make what is a recurrent connection between madness and the angel:

> Angels required their own order of time because they were not pure being, yet were (on most interpretations) immaterial, acting in time yet not of it, any more than they participated in God's eternity. Immutable, not subject to time, they were nevertheless capable of acts of will and intellect, by which change is produced in time.[39]

Historically, angels were not earthly creatures, but because this angel, or the method of translation – the migrant actor Gibreel Farishta – is of human origin and because, as a philandering stage performer he is flawed and weakened by personal vanity and jealousy, the translation of that message fails and the messenger dies. This prevents any future transmission through Gibreel in the form of either religious film or divine instruction. Gibreel is a postcolonial reworking of the angel Gabriel, but unlike the traditional angel, his communication is problematic, suggesting that in turn, postcolonial translation is contaminated by the effects of colonial history (in Gibreel and Saladin these effects are revealed in painful acts of mimicry) and is similarly problematic.

Gibreel survives his fall from an aeroplane and, therefore, cheats history of its sensible ending by staying alive. His future is rendered unstable as it is disconnected from his origin. His visions are depictions of psychological disturbance in response to this lack of historical continuity, caused when Gibreel is forced to reconstruct his life meaningfully according to Kermode's theory in *The Sense of an Ending*:

> To make sense of our lives from where we are, as it were, stranded in the middle, we need fictions of beginning and fictions of ends, fictions which unite beginning and end and endow the interval between with meaning. I called these "concord-fictions", taking them to be like the plots of novels, which often end with an appearance of concord.[40]

The Satanic Verses uses this 'appearance of concord' at its ending, when Saladin, who also cheated death in the falling aeroplane, is able to begin his future free of his past (uniting beginning and end) after the deaths of Gibreel and his father, with whom he has been reconciled: 'if the old refused to die, the new could not be born. . . . he was getting another chance' (p. 547). Taking this stance, Saladin reproduces Gibreel's philosophy, and at the same time expresses the dominant narrative viewpoint, which forms the first line of the novel: 'to be born again, . . . first you have to die' (p. 3). This notion resembling reincarnation, though ancient, is a version of a postmodern preoccupation which Baudrillard discusses in *The Transparency of Evil*, and it is equally in this postmodern sense that the idea should be understood in *The Satanic Verses*, though for Baudrillard, 'to die' does not guarantee that one may be 'born again':

> Nothing (not even God) now disappears by coming to an end, by dying. Instead, things disappear through proliferation or contamination, by becoming saturated or transparent, because of extenuation or extermination, or as a result of the epidemic of simulation, as a result of their transfer into the secondary existence of simulation.[41]

While Saladin is diminished through 'proliferation' when he becomes a teenage fashion icon prior to his mutation back into human form – 'the kids in the Street started wearing rubber devil-horns on their heads' (p. 286) – Gibreel experiences 'contamination', or 'bugs in the brain' (p. 92) which lead to his death. The characters of Gibreel and Saladin resulting from this postmodern rebirth, prone to acts of mutation and miracle, are presented as simulations, and their prophetic dreams and physical transformations are simulations produced by simulations.

Gibreel as angelic communicator also performs the function of storyteller, and when he dies, for his anathema Saladin, 'childhood was over . . . he shook his head; could no longer believe in fairy-tales' (p. 547). Gibreel's suicide weapon was hidden inside 'the wonderful lamp' (p. 546) which had previously embodied all of Saladin's childhood hopes and wishes. When 'Gibreel rubbed his hand along the side of the magic lamp: once, twice, thrice' (p. 546) in a postcolonial reconstruction of the Aladdin story, instead of the riches and harmony desired in the *Arabian Nights* version, the jaded film star produces a gun (the Hollywood response to conflict) instead of 'a fearsome jinnee' from this 'twentieth-century lamp' (p. 546). Saladin's name, shortened in order to anglicize his identity, bears a strong aural resemblance to Aladdin, and perhaps this is one reason for the name change: with a fairy-tale name, the character is able to make ludicrous wishes and to believe that they have come true, and that he has become the 'goodandproper Englishman' (p. 43) that he desires to be. From childhood, 'the promise of the magic lamp infected Master Salahuddin with the notion that one day his troubles would end and his innermost desires would be gratified' (p. 36). By preserving the mythology of *The Arabian Nights*, Saladin represents colonial belief in *The Arabian Nights* myth as a true representation of the subcontinent. This is exposed as fantasy only when Saladin changes his name back to its full Salahuddin and accepts his true identity as not so thoroughly translated, and acknowledging that he was in denial somewhat, as Zeeny tells him when he visits India: 'we cracked your shell' (p. 57). Like the magic lamp which 'infected' the child Salahuddin with desire to change, it is the imagery of sickness that causes his constructed identity to fail: 'after you recover from typhoid, Chamcha reflected, you remain immune to the disease for ten years or so. But nothing is forever; eventually the antibodies vanish from your blood. He had to accept that his blood no longer contained the immunizing agents that would have enabled him to suffer India's reality' (p. 57). Ironically, though, while both he and Zeeny believe that he is being reclaimed by India because of his bout of sickness, his susceptibility to India's diseases means that he more closely resembles the English foreigner that he has chosen to become.

At the end of the novel, Gibreel begins to tell what is the end of his story, and 'also the end of many stories' (p. 543) like the ending of *The Arabian Nights*, when Scheherazade draws all of the strands of her story together in a similar acceptance of her impending death. This ending also represents the end of Gibreel's connection to the past, in a language which has not been used by the character as a rule throughout the story: he begins, 'Kan ma kan/Fi qadim azzaman' (p. 544).[42] The return to this language suggests a refusal to translate, though the written text of *The Satanic Verses* produces the story in translation. This refusal to translate is a reclamation of the voice that was so brutally colonized (by God or insanity). The voice, according to Steven Connor, is 'the voicing of [the] self, as the renewed and persisting action of producing [the] self as a vocal agent, as a producer of signs and sounds, that asserts this continuity and substance'.[43] The difficulty experienced by Gibreel when forced to perform as ventriloquist's dummy is due to this very personal mode of creation, where speech renders the self and communicates the self: 'my voice . . . is me, it is my way of being me in my going out from myself'.[44] Ventriloquism, Connor suggests, causes both 'fascination and menace'. In response to this fearful state, Gibreel takes back his voice.

Gibreel's reluctance to translate carries over into Saladin's character, previously the 'Indian translated into English-medium' (p. 58) who has accepted that he may not have been reliably translated into English after all, if much of the sense which made up his identity was lost. This influence of one character on the other is not surprising – not only because of their initial convergence as 'Gibreelsaladin Farishtachamcha' (p. 5) during their fall to earth from the aeroplane, but also because of the underlying influence on their characters of the construction of the word translation:

> Translation, from the Latin, means "to carry across." Metaphor, from the Greek, means "to carry across." . . . People are also carried across . . . the act of migration was to turn people somehow into things, into people who had been translated.[45]

Carried back across to India, Gibreel tells his story in verse, and this is presented on the page with spacing to denote what would have been its rhythm in its original language. These are alternative satanic verses, spoken by 'the god damned angel of god' (p. 544).

Dreams and distortion

As the angel who delivers the Annunciation, Gabriel or Gibreel performs both translation, and by delivering God's message, Mary's conception, because it is by this message that Mary becomes aware of her pregnancy. The association of translation and conception coincides with that proposed by Benjamin in 'The Task of the Translator' – here he argues that 'translation is so far removed from being the sterile equation of two dead languages that of all literary forms it is the one charged with the special mission of watching over the maturing process of the original language and the birth pangs of its own'.[46] Translation, then, is theorized in terms directly comparable to the function of the character Gibreel: for Benjamin, translation is like a guardian angel charged with the task of watching over the birth of a new religious understanding. By the images he chooses, Benjamin goes on to evoke the other act performed by Gibreel, that of revelation: 'translation keeps putting the hallowed growth of languages to the test: how far removed is their hidden meaning from revelation . . .?'[47] So, Gibreel is a literalization or personification of the angelic trope buried in Benjamin's account of translation; he is the angel of translation.

As ever, the act of translation performed by Gibreel is flawed, and perhaps this is because, in *The Satanic Verses*, the source of what is being translated is depicted as uncertain. Madhu Jain claims that 'the root idea of the novel is that there are no absolutes. . . . It's almost impossible to tell angel and devil apart: Mahound the prophet has a tough time telling the difference between the voice of the angel and the *shaitan* (devil)'.[48] Angels are, themselves, ambiguous – neither masculine nor feminine, human nor divine: 'the angelic . . . condition' is located 'halfway between Allahgod and homosap' (p. 92). It is difficult to communicate with angels or to translate their message if theirs are unreliable voices to start with. Malise Ruthven asks, 'how does the believer in any faith distinguish the voices of God and the Devil?'[49] Disentangling meaning from messages is difficult, and in *The Satanic Verses* this is further complicated by the distortion caused by the level of consciousness at which the angel's message is delivered: through dreams, which Derrida suggests are 'untranslatable'.[50] Angel communication cannot be translated into sense, therefore, as it occurs in the time when Gibreel is dreaming. So how is a reliable narrative to be conveyed? The migrant Gibreel, trying to tell a story which he has difficulty in interpreting, is victim to the psychological barriers suggested by Freud, and in its very terminology, this idea, expounded by Derrida, forces the migrant to think about space as well as time: 'the border between the non-phonetic space of writing (even 'phonetic' writing[51]) and the space of the stage (*scène*) of dreams is uncertain. . . . interpretation has spelled out the elements of dreams. It has revealed the work of condensation and displacement'.[52] A geographical space or structure where human frailty renders messages untranslatable under the gaze of a deity can, of course, only suggest Babel. But it is the Bollywood stage and screen which provides the backdrop to Gibreel Farishta's embodiment of the angel.

In the Bombay of *The Satanic Verses*, Gibreel Farishta is an erotic icon. His private physical description suggests that the extent of his adoration is unwarranted: his co-star Pimple Billimoria claims that his breath smells 'of rotting cockroach dung', an assessment which the narrator confirms was in fact 'a little understated' (p. 13). The public reverence due to his status as a film star is consistently expressed in religious imagery: 'even before he replaced false head with fake tail he had become irresistibly attractive to women. The seductions of his fame had grown so great that several of these young ladies asked him if he would keep the Ganesh-mask on while they made love' (p. 25). Fame renders the individual unusually desirable to their public. This is in part because of the climate of hallucination in which, according to Simon Gottschalk, the postmodern individual lives. In his study of mental illness and postmodernism, Gottschalk argues that people are subject to psychological distortion on a par with madness every day by watching television fantasy:

> From TV screens to computer terminals, from surveillance cameras to cell phones, we increasingly experience everyday life, reality, and others via technologies of spectacle, simulation, and "telepresence". By comparison to individuals living in previous periods, postmodern individuals must now proceed across this hallucinatory landscape, and, perhaps more interestingly, may very well experience it through a consciousness which is inevitably contaminated – encoded – by these new technologies and the logic they promote.[53]

In Rushdie, new technologies contaminate prophecy in the following ways: the 'Mercedes station wagon' with 'air conditioning' and an 'icebox full of cokes' (p. 239) is proposed as a method of transporting pilgrims to Mecca; the telephone that becomes Saladin's means of delivering his 'little satanic verses' (p. 445); and the cinematic angel role that complicates Gibreel's understanding of his prophesying. Madelena Gonzales suggests that when reading Rushdie, 'it would . . . be a mistake to ignore the influence of both Bollywood and Hollywood cinema'.[54] Gonzales draws attention to Rushdie's claim that he writes fiction with the screen in mind – Rushdie says that 'the whole experience of montage technique, split screens, dissolves, and so on, has become a film language which translates quite easily into fiction and gives you an extra vocabulary of literature'.[55] The postmodern consciousness, then, is clearly comparable to Gibreel's psychology and to his encounters with the contemporary prophet Ayesha and her historical counterpart, Mahound. Gottschalk's comments suggest that the influence of 'technologies of spectacle [and] simulation' which Gibreel experiences make him susceptible to hallucination and, therefore, that there is such a thing as the postmodern angel. In fact, Gibreel's celebrated comeback is staged on an extravagant set which is a replica of London in miniature (a perfect setting on which a ventriloquist's dummy may perform). The false landscape of 'counterfeit streets' (p. 422) mimics reality, and therefore represents a sanitized space in which hallucination may be contained. The language used to describe the stage set is appropriately theatrical and interspersed with song, 'musical Podsnappery', to echo 'the madness of the street' (p. 424). If this is a Dickensian London, then the stage set refers to an already fragmented and fluid landscape – as Julian Wolfreys suggests in *Writing London*, 'Dickens comprehends the city in terms of its spaces having texture, and being of a frequently chaotic textual nature, rather than being a series of fixed sites which are unproblematically defined and presented'.[56] Wolfreys also recalls the description of London as the 'modern Babylon' in *David Copperfield*, suggesting that 'Babylon' is 'a virtual cliché in the nineteenth century for speaking of London's unspeakability'. Wolfreys suggests that 'to name London Babylon is to admit to the city being composed of multiple, disparate voices'.[57] In Rushdie, these 'multiple, disparate voices' are migrant voices. In a postmodern context, the migrants' disparate voices are further multiplied and distorted when they are processed through the multimedia equipment adorning the stage set. Even the emotional life of characters becomes subject to the influence of the painted stage, and when Saladin and Gibreel meet here, the scene is one of 'tragedy. – Or, at least the echo of tragedy, the full-blooded original being unavailable to modern men and women, so it's said. – A burlesque for our degraded, imitative times, in which clowns re-enact what was first done by heroes and by kings' (p. 424). The characters become caricatures, and the reader is further distanced when the authorial narrator steps on to the stage and owns his characters: 'my Chamcha may be no Ancient of Venice, my Allie no smothered Desdemona, Farishta no match for the Moor, but they will, at least, be costumed in such explanations as my understanding will allow' (p. 425). In language resembling stage direction, they act out their conflict in the safe space of their pretend London, a city as false as Gibreel's awareness of the bigger one ('Properlondon') outside it: 'Gibreel waves in greeting; Chamcha approaches; the curtain rises on a darkening stage' (p. 425). Gottschalk maintains that although he is not suggesting 'a simple causal link between multimedia and mental disorders', living in the postmodern multimedia society does, however, 'make acceptable psychological dispositions that, although normalized, are fundamentally unhealthy'.[58] Angels may well linger in such unwholesome locations. Gibreel as an actor embodies the effect of unhealthy influences on the postmodern mind, and so suggests a relationship between religious miracle and televisual fantasy.

The idea of simulation and pretence in *The Satanic Verses* begins with the hijacked aeroplane, which corresponds exactly with Baudrillard's theory regarding the way that postmodern events are understood:

> All the holdups, airplane hijackings, etc. are now in some sense simulation holdups in that they are already inscribed in the decoding and orchestration rituals of the media, anticipated in their presentation and their possible consequences. In short, where they function as a group of signs dedicated exclusively to their recurrence as signs, and no longer at all to their "real" end. But this does not make them harmless. . . . it is in this sense that they cannot be controlled by an order that can only exert itself on the real and the rational.[59]

In response to the influence of postmodern events on 'the real and the rational', Gibreel replays his inscribed notions of angelhood gleaned from a society where the angel is eroticized. Gibreel is placed in opposition to 'the real' and performs the angel role according to an erotic, filmic representation which is familiar. His name echoes this performance: Gib*reel* suggests the cinematic reel in contrast to 'the real', off-screen, non-postmodern Gib*real* who would provide an alternative angel figure. The first instance of Gibreel's embodiment of the angel in communication with the prophet Mahound relies heavily on televisual fantasy and on Gibreel's consciousness as determined by his status as an actor. Again, the episode begins with stage directions: 'Gibreel: the dreamer, whose point of view is sometimes that of the camera and at other moments, spectator' (p. 108). Transported to Jahilia, Gibreel is described as 'the camera', 'on a high crane' who looks at 'the actors'. Naming Gibreel effects his mutation: once named, Gibreel briefly becomes the audience rather than the camera, and states, 'who asks the bloody audience of a "theological" to solve the bloody plot?' (p. 108). When Gibreel becomes 'the star' of the piece he is in crisis, has taken on 'too many roles' and stands 'quaking' when Mahound requires revelation, believing he's 'just some idiot actor' (p. 109).

Gibreel is at once the postcolonial angel of history after Benjamin's model, a storyteller, and the actor-angel in a simulated, cinematic landscape. Again, Baudrillard provides an argument to suggest a relationship between these three representations. Gibreel as the storyteller, representative of the fairy tales of childhood, avoids making genuine postcolonial choices in the commercial world by choosing a career in cinema, which is an automatic international passport separating him from a static community, as Baudrillard suggests: 'myth, chased from the real by the violence of history, finds refuge in cinema'.[60] He is briefly exposed to the 'real' world both in Bombay when he loses his faith and in London where he is proved to be a product of hierarchical Bombay society: 'used to servants, he left clothes, crumbs, used tea-bags where they fell . . . unconscious of what he was doing, he went on proving to himself that he, the poor boy from the streets, no longer needed to tidy up after himself' (p. 310). This dysfunction causes Gibreel's forced return to acting, and again he conforms to Baudrillard's model, where 'history exorcised by a slowly or brutally congealing society celebrates its resurrection in force on the screen'.[61] Of course, it is in terms of resurrection that Gibreel describes his life after falling from the exploded aeroplane: 'if you want to get born again . . . you must die' (p. 3).

Resurrected time after time in his acting roles in epic religious cinema, Gibreel Farishta is a desired and revered figure and 'a philanderer of the worst type' (p. 25). His subsequent angel incarnation is eroticized: as he takes on the persona of the archangel, his encounters with the prophets retain the sexual element of the relationships which he had with his fans. Gibreel describes Ayesha as his 'dream-wife' after his one-sided encounter with her:

> The moment her eyes closed he was there beside her, dreaming Gibreel in coat and hat, sweltering in the heat. She looked at him but he couldn't say what she saw, wings maybe, haloes, the works. Then he was lying there and finding he could not get up . . . . When she finished looking at him she nodded, gravely, as if he had spoken, and then she took off her scrap of a sari and stretched out beside him, nude. (p. 226)

His communication with Mahound is homoerotic, and Gibreel is not so passive: 'Gibreel and the Prophet are wrestling, both naked, rolling over and over . . . he's getting in everywhere, his tongue in my ear and his fist around my balls' (p. 122). The eroticized representation of the angel figure is not a new phenomenon. In the Book of Genesis, Jacob wrestles with an angel, and this scene has been depicted in art which, like *The Satanic Verses*, portrays the biblical scene as homoerotic.[62] Peter Lamborn Wilson provides two examples, describing Gauguin's depiction as 'love-play', and also reproducing Delacroix's *Jacob Wrestling the Angel* which shows both figures as semi-naked.[63] I would like to consider the sexualization of the figure of the angel and especially of the Archangel Gabriel or Gibreel, in *The Satanic Verses*, in Islamic and Christian texts, and in art.

The postmodern mind is sated by romantic and dramatic cinema populated by actors like Gibreel who are constructed as figures of desire. This postmodern (and daydreaming) mind may be prone to hallucination, and may be predisposed to interpret this hallucination as, for example, communication with angels.

Shame: Silent paces between

Wolfgang Iser describes the process of translation as a negotiation of the in-between, as

> A mutual mirroring of different cultures. This is due to the fact that the space between does not belong to any of the cultures that refract one another. This makes the space between turn into a condition for self-reflexivity, which can only result in a heightened self-awareness of a culture that sees itself refracted in the mirror of the one encountered.[64]

'Decidedly untraditional',[65] in *Shame*, Farah slips in and out of the border in this space which, like Iser's space of translation, is a 'space between' which really 'does not belong to' either side. Farah's father is a border guard, working in the space between, and like Nietzsche's Zarathustra, she is 'equally comfortable inside' (in her case, in the school room which symbolizes Zarathustra's cave), 'and in the sunlight outside'.[66] She moves easily between spaces; Farah spends most of her time outside, running between the bollards lining the frontier, which is a vast, bleak landscape: 'no wall, no police, no barbed wire or floodlights, no red-and-white striped barriers, nothing but a row of concrete bollards . . . driven into the hard and barren ground' (p. 51). The space between languages is a no-man's land, but it is also an autoerotic space, where Farah seeks what will bring her pleasure. As if trying to contain herself within an imagined boundary, Farah has a compulsive relationship with mirrors, tying broken fragments to the posts with pieces of string so that as she runs past them she can see her image captured and tied to a solid marker: 'as Farah approaches each fragment she sees shards of herself reflected in the glass, and smiles her private smile' (p. 52). Her 'private smile' echoes portrayals of the harem women in Malek Alloula's collection of postcards where women in that secret, private space are captured smiling, apparently in natural yet erotic poses. Like them, Farah has her private space intruded upon by the male gaze. Farah's 'self-reflexivity' is a condition of living in this geographical space which corresponds directly with the space where translation is located, according to Iser. She privately creates the erotic harem in order to make sense of her surroundings. Her contemplation of a geographical space resembles Zarathustra's engagement with 'the meaning of the earth' (as opposed to the meaning of life).[67] Her desire for 'heightened self-awareness' is exploited by Omar, who asks whether she has ever been hypnotized (p. 51). Farah's secret, self-pleasure occurs when she sees herself reflected in a series of mirrors – the multitude of mirrors allows her to gain heightened awareness of her physical form, as she catches glimpses of her body reflected as she moves between those mirrors. In this way, and because this knowledge is gained on the border between territories (resembling Iser's 'space between'), Farah's knowledge of the way that she looks is code for Iser's notion of the 'self-awareness' enabled by translation as a positive, egalitarian and enriching experience. It is no accident that once Farah is forced to give pleasure to the other, to the man, her border-life ends: note that the pregnancy which follows sex with Omar forces her to become contained: their teacher marries her, effacing her name, and she is forced to cross a border and settle in a well-defined geographical space.

Rani Harappa is the other character in *Shame* who develops a relationship with the mirror, but in her case, this is due to her enclosure in a house which, similar to a harem, is full of women whose rivalry and hostility forces her to communicate with her reflected image. Initially, the mirror provides a space for communication where Rani can ignore her seclusion and her husband's rejection, and remember her past with 'inaccurate nostalgia' (p. 94). However, eventually, the 'mutual mirroring' characteristic of this communication means that Rani recognizes the truth of the image reflected in her mirror, and gains that 'heightened self-awareness' through her continued 'self-reflexivity'. Rani's relationship with the mirror, inside the harem, achieves Iser's ideal of a full translation because, by the process of mirroring, she gains greater knowledge. Farah's mirrors cause her to become inaccurately and painfully translated as a result of the brutality of colonization: Omar was driven by the bare expanse of land to perform that recurring postcolonial metaphor for land conquest by raping her, but before he did that, he had to conquer her mind, in a symbolic re-enactment of imperial conquest of the female psyche by recasting the law in apparent support of women's rights.

The inter-space, or no-man's land that the act of translation negotiates, is also akin to Jacques Lacan's conception of the mirror stage. Lacan suggests that the individual becomes transformed on recognizing, and assuming, a self-image:

> This jubilant assumption of his specular image by the child . . . would seem to exhibit in an exemplary situation the symbolic matrix in which the *I* is precipitated

> in a primordial form, before it is objectified in the dialectic of identification with the other, and before language restores to it, in the universal, its function as subject.[68]

This identification occurs before 'identification with the other' and before 'language restores to it . . . its function as subject'. The mirror, then, causes 'self-reflexivity' before the advent of the postcolonial Other, and before the *I* has a linguistic function; therefore, 'self-reflexivity' occurs in a state prior to the imposition of Babel and before the need for translation. Lacan suggests that the raw form would be called the 'Ideal-I';[69] Farah and Rani both see this Ideal-I in their mirrors. Rani is unable to speak once she has identified with the image in her mirror, so operates outside language and weaves her stories. Farah's Ideal-I is destroyed by Omar, to whom she is both the female Other and the postcolonial Other.

Farah's identity is fragmentary, constructed from the 'shards of herself' (p. 52) visible in each fragment of mirror suspended from boundary markers in the barren ground. Her location is similarly split: on term-time weekdays Farah lodges in Q., a town with a fractured, abbreviated name, at a house owned by another half-drawn character: 'an unimportant Jamshed who does not even merit a description'. The fragmentary language used in the passage concerned with Farah supports this construction: speech is spliced with narration ('"Have you ever," he asks Farah Zoroaster, "been hypnotized?"'), constructed from short and contradictory questions which make answers difficult ('Why? Why not? Because I'm fat?'), or omitted altogether: 'there is no need to repeat his speech, or Farah's coarse reply' (p. 51). Farah's speech is sometimes presented in formal, standard English, reflecting her intelligence and education; at other times it is bilingual or coloured by dialect: '"Fun, na?" she yells, "Teep-taap!"', and there is explicit 'silence between them until late afternoon'. Such fragmentary language and the fragmentary self are suggestive of Julia Kristeva's semiotic *chora*, which is defined as 'rupture and articulations (rhythm)'.[70] Kristeva's formulation holds fragmentary language responsible for the ruptured self: the *chora* is 'a mobile, unspeakable, presymbolic source of the divided subject'.[71] Kristeva suggests that 'the mother's body is the ordering principle of the *chora*', yet Farah's mother is absent, so her emergence 'into language from a background of conflict between attraction and repulsion with an image of the archaic mother' is distorted. When Farah looks into fragments of mirror or recognizes the image produced by Omar's admiring gaze (the fragmentary subject sees itself 'in an actual mirror or in the "mirroring" gaze of another person'[72]), the 'idealized image' of herself which is produced may combine the maternal body with her own body. Instead of forcing the separation of child from mother, Farah becomes a 'split subject' by containing her mother's body within her own, and in this way too 'the maternal image is at once a source of fascination and rejection'.[73] Omar's abuse of what was reflected in Farah's mirror transformed her body into the maternal body.

Speech flourishes in an in-between space, because this is exactly the kind of space that provokes translation.

Shalimar the Clown: Translation and disorientation

In place of a sense of an ending, the novels express a sense of waiting in the present moment; both Kashmira and Saleem embody the location of their history. Boonyi's daughter Kashmira's name is changed to India, as if to detach her from her history and geography, or to further anonymize her by giving her a name that includes the vast associations of the subcontinent instead of the more specific connotations of Kashmir. The novel begins with a chapter named 'India' (after the character) whose 'agitated periods of sleep-speech' evoke the memory of an absent mother who 'had been Kashmiri, and was lost . . . like Paradise, like Kashmir' (4). At the end of the novel, in a chapter called 'Kashmira', the character rejects India as her name when she learns that her absent mother, Boonyi (who also had an absent mother), had at birth given her the name Kashmira. Accompanying India/Kashmira's hesitant focalization is an authorial narrator who holds the character-focalizer at a distance. This authorial narrator is the type that Julia Kristeva describes as a 'nonperson . . . an anonymity, an absence, a blank space'.[74] Kristeva suggests that our experience of narrative is reliant on a focalizing character who prevents us from becoming overwhelmed by the disorientation caused by reading the text. When faced with the writer instead of that focalizing character, the reader notices the 'zero where the author is situated'.[75] This sense of emptiness is only overcome when the literary character becomes familiar to us, when 'the *he/she* of the character is born'.[76]

The reader's disorientation is heightened even further if the text contains the characteristics of translation, and the reader is therefore required to work harder to overcome the absence left not only by an author but also by a translator. The same is true of Rushdie's text which, though it is not a translation of an existing story, reinterprets stories, including the story of migration and displacement during World War Two which, in dominant histories, privileges Jewish displacement, but in *Shalimar the Clown*, is concerned with the forced movement of Kashmir's Hindus, and *Romeo and Juliet* which is retold as the story of Kashmiri teenagers Boonyi and Shalimar. Boonyi and Shalimar's relationship is initially scandalous because, similarly to Romeo and Juliet's feuding families (whose story provides an 'original' for which Boonyi and Shalimar's relationship is a 'translation'), the couple come from different religious communities. Once the village accept their relationship as progressive and positive, though, the tragic aspects of *Romeo and Juliet* are rewritten into Boonyi and Shalimar's story. Both lovers are brutally killed as a result of their desire for revenge rather than through love for each other. Because the *Romeo and Juliet* story is distorted in this way, this results in untranslatable desires which can only be fulfilled by the revenge motive. These stories become 'translated' because they are presented in a new cultural and historical context. Thus, the writer of the original story remains in the reader's consciousness as a haunting presence in the text.

The reader again experiences Kristeva's sense of disorientation and anonymity when characters change their names and become more difficult to recognize or hold on to. If a familiar character is disengaged from their narrative, then the reader is thrust even further into that uncomfortable empty space. Such moments of emptiness occur frequently in *Shalimar the Clown*; focalizing characters become detached from the narrative, and the reader becomes aware of the voice of an authorial narrator. Alternatively, this higher voice could indicate the presence of a kind of translator. The good translator has traditionally been expected to remain 'invisible'.[77] Lawrence Venuti disputes this perceived necessity, equating invisibility in the text with a lack of recognition for the translator by readers and publishers,[78] as the translation is then thought of as 'derivative, fake', as being of 'second-order status'.[79] Instead, Venuti argues for making 'the translator more visible so as to resist and change the conditions under which translation is theorized and practiced today', so that 'translations can be read as translations, as texts in their own right'.[80] The translator would presumably need to become more visible in the text as well as in publishers' contracts. That additional presence is what the reader experiences in *Shalimar the Clown*, when the authorial narrator (who becomes a translator by retelling old stories within the narrative) states his presence and motivation. One example of this occurs when India/Kashmira subverts the father/daughter relationship by shouting to her silk-suited, flower-holding father: 'People will think you're my lover' (7). She then watches her father standing on the pavement beneath her open window, but although he is fixed in space in the narrative moment, he is unfixed in her perception: he 'recede[s] into the past', 'each successive moment of him passing before her eyes' (7) and while she is thus entranced, the authorial narrator appropriates her disturbed vision with a reference to the loss India/Kashmira will later feel, conveyed in grand and universal terms: 'This is what loss was, what death was: an escape into the luminous wave-forms, into the ineffable speed of the light years and parasecs, the eternally receding distances of the cosmos' (7). The authorial narrator translates India/Kashmira's emotional response to her father by insisting on the ineffable, the unsayable, that exists between narration and what is narrated. The translator's longing to be included and visible in the text at these moments of disrupted focalization creates a resounding sense of longing in the narration. This hunger and longing is symbolized by both banquets and famine, and is expressed in gaps, absences and a sense of lack of the object of desire. The narrative form of *Shalimar the Clown* is constantly disrupted by broken-down sentence structure and moments of wildly distorted perception, where the focalizing character is suddenly detached from their concrete surroundings and the reader experiences a hallucinatory vision of that location. For instance, when India Ophuls focalizes, this takes the form of repetition of words in very short sentences and clauses, indicating her uncertain and hesitant relationship with the place and person that she focalizes as if she is trying to bring those things into focus by each taste of the word on her tongue:

> Abruptly she would wake . . . convinced, in her disoriented state, that there was an intruder in her bedroom. There was no intruder. The intruder was an absence, a negative space in the darkness. She had no mother. Her mother had died giving her birth . . . . Her mother had been Kashmiri, and was lost to her, like paradise, like Kashmir, in a time before memory. . . . the terms Kashmir and paradise were synonymous . . . . After her father died – her brilliant, cosmopolitan father, Franco-American, "like Liberty", he said, her beloved, resented, wayward, promiscuous, often absent, irresistible father – she began to sleep soundly, as if she had been shriven. Forgiven her sins, or perhaps, his. The burden of sin had been passed on. She did not believe in sin. (2)

The objects or subjects of the short clauses are not connected logically by India, nor is that connection disclosed to the reader. Instead, they are connected by India's unconscious thoughts: the idea of an intruder evokes the concept of a mother, which means Kashmir or paradise, and which in turn suggests her father and then sin. The only certainty of knowledge in this passage is the rush of information about her father, presented in parenthesis amidst the other, unconscious, connections. The difference between the formal presentation of this parenthetical information and the remainder of the passage demonstrates

India's substantial knowledge about her father compared with the other things that preoccupy her mind. The narrative sense behind the list of connections is not made explicit, so the gaps between these ideas open perceptibly.

Though she only later discovers that her name at birth was Kashmira, India has always disliked her name and felt disconnected from it: 'it felt exoticist, colonial, suggesting the appropriation of a reality that was not hers to own' (5). Without her proper name, India embodies the emptiness or 'silences' to which Kristeva draws attention. India structures her narrative through her desire for the unknown Kashmir-Paradise like a perverse kind of homesickness. Susan Stewart notes that homesickness was one of the earliest recorded definitions of the word 'longing', and evaluates narrative structure on this basis, suggesting that 'the location of desire, or, more particularly, the direction of force in the desiring narrative, is always a future-past, a deferment of experience in the direction of origin and thus eschaton [or ending], the point where narrative begins/ends'. [81]

Emphasizing the prophetic aspect of Stewart's idea of an eschaton in her definition, India's search for her origin or history, and Shalimar's search for an ending in what he hopes will also be India's death or ending, is predetermined. This predetermination is caused by the very nature of the characters' longings, which instigate the crossing of geographical boundaries by both characters in order to achieve their satisfactions.

No Kashmira, only Kashmir

Boonyi sacrifices her maternal role in order to return to Kashmir, essentially to return to her childhood, imagining herself able to: 'put it all back the way it had been' while sat at the dinner table with her parents and parents-in-law (220). Boonyi's journey is made possible by the mantra that she repeats: 'there is no Kashmira. There was only Kashmir' (218). The power of this mantra is tangible: it requires all of Boonyi's strength to overcome the distortion of physics which threatens to crush her: 'the weight of the absent girl had grown so heavy that the plane could not carry it over the peaks' until Boonyi 'summoned all her remaining will and let the phantom baby go . . . felt the weight in her lap lessen, felt the aircraft rise' (218). This is a rare example of magic realism in the novel, and corresponds with the similar unlikely journey at the end of the text – Shalimar's escape from prison. Magic realism combines with fairy-tale magic, echoing the combination of colonial and postcolonial representations. The postcolonial is symbolized by magic realism, as Graeme Harper suggests, as this narrative form has become a medium 'for challenging or confirming identity, of recognizing or attempting to negate cultural hegemony, of appropriating imposed forms of social or artistic engagement'.[82] The colonial is suggested by the fairy tale magic, which is the way that magic generally features in Western fictions. The combination in Boonyi's case indicates that the paradisiacal return to innocence and childhood happiness that she requires is unattainable in a postcolonial context; Boonyi must use the more fanciful type of magic found in fairy tales to enhance her wishes. Even this fails, as Boonyi's imaginary happy ending collapses: instead of achieving a return to childhood with a happy family reunion, not only is Boonyi rejected by her community, but her period of gluttony, begun in an attempt to recreate the 36- and 60-course feasts of her childhood, is mirrored: as if in response to her overeating, the village suffers a period of fasting so severe that 'a statewide famine was a real possibility' (300).

Stories and food are equally valuable in *Shalimar the Clown*, because the only available alternatives are 'unpalatable facts' (187). Stories are retold throughout the novel, making a cyclical narrative structure that resembles oral narrative, and signifying the novel's self-conscious concern with narrative form. Those 'unpalatable facts' are what is left when the 'magic spell . . . break[s]' and the 'beautiful fiction' of fairy-tale romance – in one example described as the after-Cinderella story by ambassador Max Ophuls's rejected wife – fails. The linear narrative form of stories which constantly glance towards a happy ending is disrupted in *Shalimar the Clown* because the food-related plot – the stage or page upon which those stories are told – is distorted by gluttony, starvation or intoxication, symptoms or effects of insatiable desire.

2

'*Takallouf*': The Unsayable, the Untranslatable

Derrida has proposed that translation might be impossible. This chapter considers the ways in which Rushdie's texts engage with the unsayable, and the untranslatable. 'Takallouf' – the idea that all language spoken must be taken literally – is a key aspect of this, which resonates with early translators' loyalty to practices of word-for-word translation. In *Shame*, takallouf is apparently used as a method of restricting women's speech and with it, their physical freedom. Yet, according to Sara Suleri in *The Rhetoric of English India*, to render in metaphorical language is to possess. Outside metaphorical language, remaining literal, the women in Rushdie's harems and behind their veils remain un-described, not-possessed by their male relatives. Rushdie's texts transgress the gender boundaries set down by societal codes in order to reveal the women behind the veils and inside the harems. This act of revelation, of saying the unsayable, involves a representation of the harem as the rigorously managed and powerful matriarchal political and economic system, in stark contrast to colonial or Hollywood representations. The harem, then, no longer unsayable, is, by its rendering here, translatable.

Takallouf is 'a form of tongue-tying formality' which renders a speaker unable to challenge spoken words or to 'express what he or she really means', instead insisting that, 'for the sake of good form', words are 'taken literally' (p. 104). *Takallouf* is introduced in *Shame* to explain the meaning of Raza Hyder's apparent caution for his wife's delicate health when he insists that she stay at home instead of accompanying him on an 'arduous trip' to the Commander-in-Chief's reception party in Karachi. The only explicitly 'untranslatable' word in *Shame*, this term refuses 'to travel across linguistic frontiers' (p. 104), not even for the sake of Raza and Bilquis Hyder's marriage, and 'when *takallouf* gets between a husband and a wife, look out' (p. 104).

The novel's focus upon the unspeakable and the untranslatable at the core of a marriage between the future prime minister and a girl famous for the green *dupatta* (or scarf[1]) that covered her sudden nakedness after an explosion which blasts away her clothes invites a reading of the unspeakable and the untranslatable which has at its centre two factors: the covering and uncovering of the female body and the public/private dichotomy. The notion of a public/private dichotomy does not apply in a society where the home is both the domestic space and the location of the political centre, as Leslie Peirce argues:

> Feminist scholarship has challenged . . . Western notions of a public/private dichotomy, in which the family is seen as occupying private, non-political space. . . . the most superficial acquaintance with Islamic law and evidence of its application in the early modern Ottoman period demonstrates that the family was viewed as intrinsically political.[2]

N. M. Penzer supports Peirce's claim, suggesting that the women who lived and worked in the imperial harems had political status and public careers, as 'highly educated' members of a 'complicated institution'.[3] Both of these concerns characterize the harem: the political nature of the home in an Islamic context corresponds with historical and postcolonial revisions of the harem, while the semi-naked female body resembles western portrayals of the harem popularized by Hollywood films like *Sinbad the Sailor* (1947) starring Douglas Fairbanks, Jr and Maureen O'Hara.

Unspeakable words define this text. This is done firstly by revealing what is normally hidden: when Raza and Bilquis Hyder's use of *takallouf* is made explicit, the meaning behind their outwardly polite communication is changed. And secondly, the unspeakable is encountered by engaging with the notion of the untranslatable symbolized as the exotic, the veil, the harem, the female body and the unpredictable female, all of which find an analogue in the veiled language of the Qur'an which is, according to Frithjof Schuon, veiled to such an extent that it becomes 'in places incomprehensible'[4] – a judgement which perhaps says as much about the reader as it does about the text.

Translatability

Wolfgang Iser asks how to define the concept of translatability, suggesting that, though 'we usually associate translation with converting one language into another' and that this translation usually involves some amount of cultural difference accompanying the language change, it may be 'more than a metaphor for cultural exchange'.[5] Iser argues that, where different languages and cultures come into contact, as in the colonial and postcolonial Indian subcontinent, 'the more a kind of translation is bound to occur'.[6] Iser sees translation as an enabling mechanism, because 'a foreign culture is not simply subsumed under one's own frame of reference; instead, the very frame is subjected to alterations in order to accommodate what does not fit'. For Iser, 'such a transposition runs counter to the idea of the hegemony of one culture over the other, and hence the notion of translatability emerges as a counter-concept to a mutual superimposing of cultures'.[7]

This optimistic view is not shared by postcolonial translation theorists Susan Bassnett and Harish Trivedi, who suggest that 'translation . . . rarely, if ever, involves a relationship of equality between texts, authors or systems'.[8] Their examination of the history of translation identifies changing trends in translated texts: they argue that Sir William Jones (1746–96) 'pioneered translations into English of Indian (specifically Sanskrit) as well as Arabic and Persian texts' and 'for some decades afterwards, the traffic in translation between the East and the West remained decidedly one-sided, from the East to the West'.[9] Using imagery of colonial land conquest, Bassnett and Trivedi describe how the 'Indian literary space was a vigorously contested terrain' where reception of and resistance to Western literary forms grappled until 'the resurgence of native traditions gave way to a hegemony of Western literary culture even as the British colonial dominance grew more entrenched all round'.[10] Selectiveness during translation, the 'common . . . temptation to erase much that is culturally specific, to sanitize much that is comparatively odorous',[11] suggests that translation was performed according to the needs of the colonizing power.

Despite maintaining that the act of translation is pure and free from hierarchy, Iser does engage with the idea of the Other, arguing that the translator exists in 'the space between [which] opens up the experience of otherness'.[12] The Other who is present at the moment when *takallouf* is introduced in *Shame* is an exoticized and eroticized female Other, embodied by Pinkie Aurangzeb, a woman who, though 'in her middle thirties' and 'several years older than Raza and Iskander', has 'a body worth lingering over' (pp. 104–5). Through the young male eyes of Raza Hyder, Pinkie appears complicit in her erotic representation, both because of how she uses her body, placing it 'excitingly on display, in a green sari worn dangerously low on the hips' and in her behaviour: Pinkie 'finds her pleasures wherever she can' (pp. 104–5). The green sari which functions to display the female body is set in opposition to 'the green dupatta' (p. 63) that allowed Bilquis Hyder to retain some relief from nudity in the bomb blast. Bilquis's scarf allows her to retain her social position: 'the dupatta of modesty had stuck to her body, fixed there by the congealed blood' – '"Never mind," Bariamma pronounced approvingly, when Bilquis was shaking with the shame of her revelations, "at least you managed to keep your dupatta on"' (pp. 64,76). The bomb, an act of violence reproducing images of colonial invasion, empowers 'denuded' (p. 64) Bilquis: stripped 'infant-naked in the street' (p. 63), she becomes the 'migrant . . . stripped of history' with her clothing representing 'continuity' and 'belonging'. Losing her clothes, 'Bilquis's past left her' (p. 64). The narrator inserts a reference to Partition at this point in the novel, to explain that 'in Delhi, in the days before Partition, the authorities rounded up any Muslims, for their own safety, . . . and locked them up in the red fortress' (p. 64). Partition, the last act of imperial rule, is envisaged as an analogous painful rebirth following a period of the scouring away of history: Bilquis is re-dressed 'top to toe' after 'returning to her senses' feeling 'the pressure of red stone against her skin' (p. 64). The colour green worn by Bilquis indicates the flag of the newly created Pakistan, making Bilquis's pain and her rebirth symptomatic of Partition, and Pinkie's exploitation in her green shawl another manifestation of that moment in history.[13]

If unveiling is analogous to translation, then its complex political significance is obvious. Both postcolonials and feminists ask the same questions about whose interests are served by unveiling, and the complexity of this idea is discussed by Lama Abu Odeh, who suggests that when in the 1970s most young women 'walked the streets of Arab cities wearing Western attire', they had to constantly negotiate a 'multilayered and highly complex' relationship with their bodies.[14] This was because 'the Western attire which covered their bodies carried with it the "capitalist" construction of the female body: one that is sexualised, objectified', while the postcolonial resistance to capitalism in those locations meant that 'these women's bodies were simultaneously constructed "traditionally": "chattelized", "propertized", "terrorized" as trustees of family (sexual) honour'.[15] The resulting comprehension of the female body was, according to Lama Abu Odeh, at once 'seductive, sexy and sexual' and 'prudish, conservative and asexual', held to a kind of ransom between opposing systems promising on the one hand the 'consumption of Western commodities' and on the other the 'threat of violence'. According to Fadwa El Guindi, feminists traditionally consider the veil with 'hostility'[16] yet at the same time, the act of unveiling, for Abu Odeh, brings its own oppressive demands in the form of adherence to Western capitalist modes of constructing the female body.

The idea that veiling is a necessarily oppressive practice is frequently contested by writers from within cultures where veiling is a common practice, who discuss the veil in a different way, considering veiling – as opposed to unveiling – as an act of independence, as what El Guindi calls a 'symbol of both identity and resistance'.[17] This view acknowledges that unveiling also appealed to imperialists. For, while in the colonial period in India, unveiling women was both an act of liberation, gaining the colonials humanitarian justification for their presence as they had become 'the liberator of Indian women',[18] it was also an act of conquest: undressing and knowledge of the previously unknown female body was part of the symbolism of conquering 'virgin' territory.

Indeed, as with Alloula's collection of Algerian harem postcards, disrobing could be used to further exoticize and eroticize the native woman, so that she becomes 'the sexual phantasm' that she is believed to be.[19] We can, then, understand Fadwa El Guindi's initial resistance to engage with either the word or the concept of the veil in a study on hijab – she writes, 'the veil is avoided as a subject of study because of what it stands for ideologically or for its association with Orientalist imagery'.[20] El Guindi defines her scholarly position in terms suggestive of translation: her text is written in an 'effort to bring about a fuller understanding'.[21] El Guindi suggests that veiling itself is 'a language that communicates social and cultural messages'.[22] Analysing this 'linguistic' act in a context which 'deprovincializes and de-exoticises it'[23] provides, rather than prevents, a translation of the veil as a symbol of the women who are veiled or unveiled, and of the stories and history of veils and veiling.

If veiling is an act of masculine or imperial domination, then the recurring images of the exotic harem and the veiled woman silence the female voice. Kristeva talks about 'the veil of language'[24] as if language itself prevents the communication of meaning because it functions as a veil. However, expanding on the paradox identified by Doane, that 'the veil acts to conceal, cover, hide and disguise, but – through its opacity it simultaneously conceals and reveals, both allowing and disallowing the gaze',[25] we might suggest that veiled language can reveal something even if it is rendered in a distorted form. The veil, of course, covers the mouth, symbolically preventing speech or communication, preventing translation. Unveiling, therefore, is an act of translation. *Shame* offers a response to the question of whether or not veiling prevents communication: here, women are veiled and segregated; women's stories are woven into shawls. Pinkie's shawl is a 'miraculous work [that] could only have been the product of the fabled embroiderers of Aansu, because amidst its miniscule arabesques a thousand and one stories had been portrayed in threads of gold' (p. 105). This fantastical item will be recreated by Rani Harappa when, like the threatened Scheherazade whose story is implied by a reference to the thousand and one stories (of *The Arabian Nights*), she will weave the stories that she is not permitted to voice – by the rules of *takallouf* – into a series of embroidered shawls, suggestive of the history of female storytelling and weaving where speech is prevented. Evoking the story of Philomela, Rani wove because she could not speak about her violent story.[26] The scarf has an opposite meaning when worn by Pinkie, who uses it not to 'speak' of male sexual desire, but to provoke it. She wears the scarf to heighten her sexual allure, while her husband sleeps in a 'condition of somnolent cuckolded dotage' (p. 105). Pinkie's home, too, is reminiscent of Western representations of the harem – note how she prepares for her party by 'allowing a servant girl to oil and braid her hair', and when surrounded by men her body is described as 'irresistibly vulnerable'. Pinkie's intended audience is male, but both in Philomela's and Rani's weavings, the intended audience of the story is female – namely, Philomela's sister and Rani's daughter, respectively. Women telling stories to women evokes a matrilineal progression of stories, or a telling of 'herstory', in opposition to the version of women's lives told by men. Rushdie is a male telling a version of women's lives, but he does so in what Justyna Deszcz has tentatively dubbed a 'feminist' mode of storytelling.[27] It might be said that a postcolonial mode of storytelling is at certain points analogous to a feminist narrative; both approaches provide a reworking of history from the position of a silenced subject.

Faithful or free

Rushdie's women are sometimes seen as 'problematic' and '[un]appealing'.[28] At the same time, though, they represent a political force, like those harem women, the most senior of whom exerted 'immense power in the kingdom'.[29] The notion of mystery and unpredictability, when considered in the context of language and translation, has origins, or perhaps an analogue, in the language of the Qur'an. The Qur'an is, by Muslims, considered to be 'the model par excellence of the perfection of language'.[30] However, according to some commentators, a certain sensibility is required in order to fully appreciate the text, because it appears 'to be a collection of sayings and stories that is more or less incoherent and at first approach in places incomprehensible'.[31] This is the case whether the text is read 'in translation or in Arabic'; the veiled language is a function of the sense and not the delivery. Schuon responds to claims that the text of the Qur'an provides few answers to its questions by suggesting that this complaint is a result of flawed reading.[32] By constructing an orientalist binary between Eastern and Western readerships, he is able to attribute these misunderstandings to assumed (and unsupported) cultural differences in reading styles: Western readers, claims Schuon, 'look in a text for a meaning that is fully expressed and immediately intelligible, whereas Semites, and Eastern peoples in general, are lovers of verbal symbolism and read "in depth"'.[33] This approach is at variance with Iser's suggestion that translation is a point of equal and mutual cultural contact. Schuon's assertion poses questions about to what extent the translatability of a text depends upon the culture of its readership, while demanding adherence to those orientalist binaries contained in the very core of his claims. Postcolonial theory challenges notions of translatability by engaging with the historical process of translation in colonized areas and by interpreting the choices made regarding translation in a colonized state, as Susan Bassnett and Harish Trivedi write:

> The strategies employed by translators reflect the context in which texts are produced. In the nineteenth century, an English translation tradition developed, in which texts from Arabic or Indian languages were cut, edited and published with extensive anthropological footnotes. In this way, the subordinate position of the individual text and the culture that had led to its production in the first place was established through specific textual practices.[34]

According to Bassnett and Trivedi's claims, then, what is deemed untranslatable may depend on who employs the translator. Other translation theorists take a purer, linguistic, approach to the idea of the untranslatable. For Wilhelm von Humboldt (1767–1835), the notion of the untranslatable was a paradox, as 'the more a translator strives for fidelity, the more deviant the translation becomes'.[35] Seeking fidelity, many translators attempt a translation which is 'faithful', 'literal' or 'equivalent'. As Cecilia Wadensjö observes, many translators respond to questions of translatability by using oppositions like '"faithful" versus "free", "literal" versus "figurative", "equivalent" versus "non-equivalent"' and so on.[36] But why should using methods to produce a 'faithful', 'literal' and 'equivalent' translation result in a 'deviant' translation as von Humboldt suggests? The answer must be that texts are inherently untranslatable. If the translator's fidelity results in a deviant translation, then by implication, a reliable translation could only be produced by using Wadensjö's alternative methods: those which are 'free', 'figurative' and 'non-equivalent'. To overcome this paradox, the target text produced should be a reproduction or reinterpretation instead of a strict translation of a text from one language into another, a rewriting rather than a translation, of the type which

Kristeva suggests is a property of intertextuality.[37] This rewriting would employ 'free', 'figurative' and 'non-equivalent' methods in order to produce a reliable reproduction of the source text.

Wadensjö is concerned with the reliability and the success of translations. She identifies two aspects which are traditionally considered in order to determine the success of a translation, or the translatability of a text: the first is how effectively 'a source text' can be converted into 'a target text'.[38] If translating the harem, this would mean, firstly, asking how reliably a harem woman can be interpreted by a Western European, and this involves finding out whether her clothes, relationships, occupation and the space where she lives can be rendered reliably in a culture that has misunderstood her for so long. Fatema Mernissi has argued at length that the harem has been fundamentally misrepresented in the West, in *Scheherazade Goes West* (2001): Mernissi is astounded by the journalists' 'grins' (2) in response to her recollections of the harem that for her is synonymous with prison but, for them, is evocative of a sinful paradise.

The second way to determine translatability is to find out whether or not the translation is able to reveal 'the hidden meaning(s) behind the original; the author's (or speaker's) actual intention(s)'.[39] This poses interesting questions about how far the translator can be trusted, as well as about how much control the author is judged to have over his text. Translations of the harem space may differ according to how much power is handed over to the reader. Responsibility for the interpretation of the text may be devolved from both the author and the translator, and instead may be given to the reader. This is Stanley Fish's argument: Fish's reader-response theory goes as far as to suggest that 'interpretive strategies', or the methods by which the text is understood, 'are not put into execution after reading' but that 'they are the shape of reading, and because they are the shape of reading, they give texts their shape, making them rather than, as is usually assumed, arising from them'.[40] If this is the case, then it is the reader who predetermines whether or not a translation is successful, and who retains control over the translatability of a text. This, of course, depends upon the notion that interpretation and translation are the same things. Cecilia Wadensjö infers that there is an unbridgeable gap between the two terms. She claims that translation is a more formal process (a 'mere medium of transmission'[41]), while interpretation requires an emotional investment on the part of the interpreter, who is understood to be playing a creative part in the production of a text, producing 'interpreter-mediated interaction' (this 'text' is usually a verbal and not a written text).[42] In this sense, the interpreter is equivalent to Fish's understanding of the reader. By devolving all interpretative power to the reader, Fish indirectly proposes that there may not be such a thing as a translation at all. If, as Fish suggests, 'notions of the "same" or "different" texts are fictions',[43] then the source and target texts cannot be compared or even distinguished.

Translating the harem

The difficulty of deciding on a reliable rendition of a text may be carried through into depictions of the harem in Western texts. The harem is generally depicted as either a demeaning or an empowering space for women, but it may be both of these things at the same time, as can be seen even in some of these opposing arguments. Sitara Khan apparently recognizes arguments that a harem space can be empowering for women, describing it as 'a "safe" area in which women can relax, be creative and supportive'.[44] Yet, Khan lists only limited activities which are enabled by this location: 'women can . . . henna their hands, oil their hair, have their bodies massaged, plot against their men – especially their husbands'.[45] According to Khan, women are empowered only to repeat demeaning tasks. Such conflicting accounts of the harem tend to cancel each other out to the point that the harem becomes untranslatable. Prevailing notions of the harem are dependent on the idea that this is a site of leisure and domesticity. But to see the harem as a domestic and parochial space leads, according to Leslie Peirce, to the mistaken belief that the harem 'is an Islamic manifestation of the Western notion of the public/private dichotomy'.[46] Catherine Cundy's reading of *Shame* makes reference to this 'Western notion'; Cundy suggests that because Bilquis's story of her father's cinema exploding is articulated in the enclosed, 'private' sphere of the women's quarters, and Rani Harappa's scarf depicting her husband's betrayal will only ever be seen by her daughter, the 'public/private separation inevitably undermines the authority of the women's stories'.[47] Rushdie is, of course, writing to a Western audience who share this sense, yet his depiction of harem spaces may also make reference to non-Western understandings of that space. Some readings of the harem space oppose the view that the private space is necessarily non-political. In *The Imperial Harem*, Peirce describes how feminist work has challenged the assumption that the home is a non-political space and 'emphasiz[ed] that the notion of a public/private dichotomy was historically created'.[48] Peirce argues that in Islamic law, the family is 'intrinsically political'.[49] The idea of the Muslim family as 'intrinsically political' is reflected in Rushdie's writing, where the home is often a site of power struggles – note, for example, how future prime ministers Raza Hyder and Iskander Harappa (fictionalizations of Zia Ul-Haq and Zulfikar Ali Bhutto[50]) become 'duellists' (p. 104) in the living room, and substitute romantic for political rivalries.

Given that so many contemporary scholars have aimed to reverse perceived notions of the harem as an exotic and erotic space begs the question: why? What is their primary aim? In the case of Alloula's examination of Algerian harem postcards in *The Colonial Harem* (1986) the main focus is the postcolonial aim of identifying the orientalism at work in the postcards. The aim of the colonial harem postcards was, Alloula suggests, to show purdah as both the repression and sexualization of the women photographed, in a 'phantasm of the oriental woman'.[51] Alloula claims that it is only the colonial gaze that transforms the harem into a sexual or erotic space and suggests that the Algerian photographs which he examines lift the veil of the women pictured solely to transform their harem space into 'a bordello [or] a brothel', causing 'dispossession through remuneration' controlled by 'an orientalism the presuppositions of which are no longer masked by the postcard'.[52] Entering the harem and lifting the veil, Alloula suggests, was an imperialist strategy to further exoticize the harem inhabitants by depicting them in 'various states of self-abandonment and lasciviousness' in what becomes a 'carnivalesque orgy' of awkwardly posed and sometimes undressed women surrounded by 'coffee and marijuana'.[53]

Shirley Foster's critique of the Western view of the harem, 'Colonialism and Gender in the East: Representations of the Harem in the Writings of Women Travellers', begins as a broadly feminist discussion, seeking to illuminate previously silenced female experience. This is achieved by explaining that instead of the harem being 'a site of sexual licence . . . charged with erotic significance', the harem was at least, in the beginning, 'a social space where women could gather and talk'.[54] The perception that this was an 'erotic' space, knowledge of which 'could be only voyeuristically obtained', derives from a masculine account of the harem, in which men desire knowledge (carnal or otherwise) of women. This is an exact reversal of the original rationale for the harem – namely, that it should be a space in which women are not so much known but rather are enabled to know: to read, write and learn. Foster supports her claim that the harem was not a secret space by explaining that it was easily accessible, at least to women – she points out that 'by the late 1840s a visit to a harem had become a regular item on the female tourist itinerary'.[55] Foster's concerns in this article are with the representation of gender and with the gendered experience of the harem; she claims that 'commentary engendered by harem sexuality and the institution of polygamy can be seen as an analogue for concerns about individual freedom and gender roles'.[56] She develops her argument by engaging with Judith Butler's discussion of gender as performance by describing the clothes worn in the harem as the basis for later cultural perceptions: 'because cultural values are written on the body, clothes and appearance are taken as indicators of value systems and social ideologies'. The conclusions drawn from these indicators are proven false by the reaction of harem women to European travellers' clothes – for instance, they perceive Mary Wortley Montagu's stays as 'a machine invented by her husband to lock her up'.[57] In this interaction, argues Foster, women of both societies believe the other, and not herself, to be the one imprisoned. According to Foster, the freedom afforded to women while wearing 'Persian women's costume' provides Montagu and her contemporaries with 'an alternative to the public/private dichotomy of European female existence'.[58] To summarize, the harem in Foster's account becomes a space where women can look out and from where they can speak about their opportunities and can impart knowledge, as opposed to the prevailing notion that it is men who are permitted to gaze inwards in order to take away knowledge of segregated women's lives.

Taking a different approach to that offered by Foster, the etymology of the term 'harem' is related to the geographical layout of the household and to the texts that have contributed to its current popular depictions in N. M. Penzer's study of the harem in 1936. The word 'harem' stems from the Arabic word *harām*, meaning 'that which is unlawful' and its opposite, *halal*, meaning 'that which is lawful'.[59] This dual and opposite etymological origin contributes to the depiction of the harem as a site of self-contradiction (at once empowering and limiting to its inhabitants). Both 'lawful' and 'unlawful' in origin, the harem is analogous to the uncanny as understood by deconstructionists. J. Hillis Miller describes deconstruction as 'a paralysis of thought in the face of what cannot be thought rationally: analysis, paralysis; solution, dissolution; composition, decomposition; mantling, dismantling; canny, uncanny'.[60] 'Deconstructive criticism', Miller suggests, 'moves back and forth between the poles of these pairs' or 'undecidabilit[ies]'.[61] Initially, the harem space was a stretch of land surrounding Mecca and Medina, which was a protected and sacred space where ordinarily permitted things were controlled and unlawful: Penzer describes how in this sacred space, the laws regarding language, dress and behaviour which were adhered to elsewhere in the region were not applicable, and instead, stricter rules governing all aspects of behaviour were enforced: a striking example of this is the rule that women were forbidden from talking to men in the street. Elsewhere, this rule applied only to young, unmarried women.[62] Because of this usage, Penzer suggests, the word began to take on further meanings such as holy, protected, sacred, inviolate, forbidden and so on. Ironically, though, it was the secular application of this word to the female living quarters (because this was their sanctuary) which accounted for the harem becoming almost exclusively associated with Islam.[63] Like the meaning of the harem, Miller suggests that all language is constructed from 'deep contra-dictions', and a 'tangle of repetitions'.[64] The connection of the terms *harām* and *halal* continues to this day, with *halal* signifying meat prepared according to Muslim law, and the image is exploited in *Midnight's Children* to connect the notion of something forbidden with the act of narration – note how Saleem Sinai pledges to tell the true history of his family rather than the more commonly known 'permitted parts of it, the halal portions of the past, drained of their redness, their blood' (p. 59). Stories like those from *The Arabian Nights*, Penzer suggests, created a shroud of secrecy around the harem, and as if replicating the flimsy veils that the harem women were believed to wear, the 'division between fact and fiction' became 'thin and ill-defined'.[65] Rushdie's *Arabian Nights*-influenced stories address that secrecy by engaging with the etymology of the word *halal* to deconstruct the opposite associations which emerged in the development of the usage of the words *halal*, *harām* and harem. Saleem comes to his conclusion that he will tell a 'haram' version of his family's story due to his experience as an uninvited observer in a harem space: he regularly hides in his 'mother's large white washing-chest' (p. 152). On one occasion, while 'hiding' among 'the comforting presence of enveloping soiled linen' in the bathroom, Saleem inadvertently sees his mother undressing, described in terms that replicate colonial notions of the phantasm of the naked female in the harem:

> My mother unwinds her sari! While I, silently in the washing-chest: "Don't do it don't do it don't do!" . . . but I cannot close my eye. Unblinking pupil takes in upside-down image of sari falling to the floor, an image which is as usual, inverted by the mind . . . O horrible! – my mother, framed in laundry and slatted wood, bends over to pick up her clothes! And there it is, searing my retina – the vision of my mother's rump, black as night, round and curved, resembling nothing on earth so much as a gigantic, black Alfonso mango! (pp. 161–2)

The eye becomes the colonial camera that sought to reveal such images of harem women in Alloula's postcard collection, for similar purposes of horror and titillation for Western observers. Entering the harem space – the bathroom, which temporarily becomes a private, secluded female space while his mother uses the toilet – enables Saleem's narrative. Coming face to face with a forbidden image allows Saleem to reconsider what a narrator can and cannot see: using the psychic gift which is brought to life by this incident, Saleem narrates past events and events that he would not witness without using telepathy. Thus, what was once forbidden or secluded (*harām*), becomes accessible (*halal*) after Saleem has entered the harem.

It is the notion of physical space that N. M. Penzer makes use of in order to deconstruct Western ideas about the function of the harem. Penzer's (1936) description of the harem building is an early example of ecocriticism which combines the physical landscape with the imaginary geography at work in texts about the harem. The 'division between fact and fiction' corresponds to both the location of the harem and the space of art: this space of art may be a room of one's own where there are resources, time and opportunity to write, or, it may be an imaginary location where different rules apply. Like the notion of a sacred, *harām* space where some things may be forbidden or restrained, this opposite, imaginary location may be one where law, which Anthony Julius suggests 'has no place in art', can be violated, because 'there should be no constraints upon the imagination'.[66] This is, of course, Rushdie's claim.[67] The harem becomes a trope for the free space of art, embodied by Saleem's narration, which lacks all the usual historical and spatial limitations that would normally hamper a character-focalizer. Penzer's early acknowledgement of what is now termed 'orientalism' also becomes a form of censorship in Julius's terms, but the explicit focus in this work is not an imaginary location, but a solid boundary which was difficult to define, that which marks 'the degree of separation' between the harem area and the male and public areas, or the selāmlik.[68] Penzer describes the rooms which would be constructed for a new favourite (or kadin). These rooms, suites, courtyards or kiosks (which were tower-like, room-sized extensions to windows) were 'left empty and fell into gradual decay' when a new favourite was chosen, as she would be given her own, newly built room.[69] Although the most powerful position for a harem woman was as 'sultan validé', or mother-in-law to the current sultan, achieved by being the wife or favourite of the sultan and giving birth to the first or oldest surviving male child, a sultan had very few wives or sexual partners.[70] The number of legal wives was limited to four, as in current Muslim sharia law derived from the passage in the Qur'an stating: 'marry women of your choice, two, or three, or four; but if you fear that you shall not be able to deal justly (with them), then (marry) only one'.[71]

Penzer adds to the debate on the clothing worn by the harem woman and describes the performative aspect of clothing in detail. Penzer claims that the harem woman was never seen 'in the same dress twice' by the sultan;[72] this enabled the harem woman to maintain her position of power and reserve. The veil and cloak that she wore, though, permitted a different type of independence, enabling 'clandestine meetings of wives with lovers', because behind their veils and cloaks, those wives were unrecognizable to their husbands.[73] Wearing the veil and the cloak created another imaginary geographical location: the rules governing the harem were transported with the woman's body. Carrying around her own sacred space, the harem woman's geography is flexible: though she is still contained and impeded by her veils she is also, in a sense, liberated. Penzer's reliance on geography to produce a reading of the harem is perceptible again in the presentation of the hierarchy governing the harem: the 'distinct position' of each woman in this hierarchy is perceived in almost geographical terms, where 'positions of power' were fought for with territorial determination because gaining that position could mean the difference between 'opportunity, luxury and riches', and less sought-after 'responsible jobs'.[74] Bariamma holds this position of ultimate power in *Shame* and dispenses her power in the form of social chastisement or acceptance.

Leslie Peirce engages with the geography of the harem differently. Peirce's study takes the Western notion of the public/private dichotomy and points to the misapplication of this structure to Eastern society as the source of the Western misunderstanding of the harem. Deploying Bernard Lewis's assertion that 'power relations in Islamic society are represented by spatial division more horizontal than vertical, in contrast to Western metaphors: instead of moving *up*, one moves *in* toward greater authority',[75] Peirce suggests that in the harem there is 'an inversion of dominant modern Western notions of the politically significant as "outer" or public, and the politically marginal as "inner" or private and domestic'. The harem, though a home and a domestic space, was 'the vortex' of the 'social, moral, and political order'.[76] Peirce engages with sociological and anthropological aspects of the harem, explaining that women were 'economically independent' and that they gained social power from 'exploitation of property'.[77] Yet, she suggests, this society where women were powerful was compromised by medieval Muslim religious leaders, who distorted 'Islam's original message of equality between sexes'.[78] Where women provided the most common 'metaphor for order',[79] a disordered or disruptive woman signified a disordered state.[80] The experience of the harem is described as a gendered one by Peirce, but in addition, there are differences between the experiences of young and older women: only young women were prevented from going to mosques or talking to men on the street,[81] as if freedom had something to do with fertility, sexual availability or desirability. This is another form of segregation: here, women are divided into two groups – those of sexually desirable young women and sober, undesirable or undesiring older women. Rushdie conflates this further segregation by creating sexually active and fertile older women, who live in self-imposed seclusion, in his portrayal of the Shakil sisters in *Shame*. In this way, Rushdie overturns the portrayal of secluded women again, producing characters who are powerful and sexually active, and who use their seclusion to empower their lives and to achieve their desires. Of four studies of the harem (by Foster, Penzer, Alloula and Peirce), Peirce alone engages with Islam and Islamic historical figures like Ayesha to find an explanation for the development of the contemporary notion of the harem as repressive.

In this sense, the harem is not seen as necessarily repressive in *Shame*, and liberation from seclusion is not always desired. As a result, Rushdie's depiction of the idea of liberation from the harem engages with 'liberation' as a term loaded with imperialist thinking that, in relation to the woman apparently confined in the harem, resembles the way that colonial powers in India championed the emancipation of women, outlawing sati (or Hindu 'widow-burning') in 1829. The abolition of sati was a preoccupation among writers of Rudyard Kipling's era when, as Bart Moore-Gilbert argues, 'it [was] recurrently used as a means to justify British rule in India by emphasising the relative enlightenment and humaneness of its cultural values'.[82] In anti-colonial backlash against changing laws, political groups in India fought to conserve sati and other anti-feminist ways of thought, including the promotion of purdah (defined by Sitara Khan as 'female veiling and seclusion'[83]). This anti-colonial measure can hardly be considered an enlightened approach, however.[84] Rushdie's disconnection from Islam (he says, 'I was brought up more or less without God'[85]) means that he is inevitably placed at a distance from the religious and cultural meaning of the harem in its local context. As an outsider he disagrees with female segregation, suggesting that 'no city which locks women away is ever short of whores',[86] while he recognizes and writes about the political value of the domestic space. The portrayal of the harem in *The Satanic Verses* and *Shame* is not, then, simply a reproduction of the colonialist's voyeuristic gaze and orientalist obsession with the harem, as described by Nicholas Harrison. Instead, in *Shame*, the female body – veiled or unveiled, inside or outside the harem – becomes a performance.

Naveed Hyder's wedding day is reminiscent of staged scenes in Alloula's *The Colonial Harem*: the 'women holding combs, brushes, silver-polish' are transformed into an approximation of a staged harem representation – note how at Naveed's exclamation that she won't marry her intended husband, 'all around her are women frozen by their delight into living statues . . . with petrified joy' (pp. 165–6). Naveed's name, meaning 'Good News', echoes the word 'Gospel';[87] she is, therefore, a symbol of Christianity inside the Muslim home, an internal colonizer. Her 'Christian' name dictates her action – Good News disrupts the structure of her wedding-day preparations and with it she shatters the myth of the obedient, Muslim daughter, becoming another of those disordered women who, as Peirce suggests, indicated a disordered state.[88] Though Good News Hyder is an encoding of Christianity, she is also an encoding of Islam. For Good News gives birth to 27 children, while the Prophet Muhammad's first wife, Khadija, is also unusually fertile: she has 6 children despite the fact that she was already 40 years old when they were married. These were Muhammad's only children apart from a boy who died in infancy with Mary the Copt, his slave and later his wife. Good News had a sibling who was still-born, who may be a reference to this boy child who died in infancy. Naveed's husband Talvar Ulhaq has powers of future divination, and gains social advantage by their marriage, suggesting a further connection between their relationship and that of Muhammad and Khadija, who also died leaving her young husband to outlive her and to become a significant political figure after her death. In the Bible, of the many female figures who have complicated stories of motherhood, perhaps the most comparable figure to Naveed Good News Hyder is Leah, the sister of Rachel who with her handmaid Bilpah forms a trio similar to Naveed, her sister Sufiya and their ayah Shahbanou. Leah had many children while Rachel could not conceive, and because of this, Bilpah was used as a surrogate mother, like Shahbanou's sexual relationship with Omar to protect Sufiya from a relationship for which her childlike mentality left her insufficiently emotionally prepared. Naveed is readable as a trope for both Christianity and Islam, and because of that she is untranslatable.

The use and meaning of Good News Hyder's name alters depending on translation: her name is Naveed, which in translation means Good News, yet she is called both: on her birth, she is introduced and her name is immediately restated and translated: 'Naveed, that is Good News' (p. 111). She is an embodiment of the doubleness of translation, inhabiting two languages and cultures concurrently. Yet, these cultures do not exert an equal force: she is referred to as Good News when she is in a position of weakness, but as Naveed when in control. Throughout her childhood she is 'Good News, plain-faced as a chapatti . . . Good News pummelling the ayah . . . Good News, exhausted by hair-pullery' (pp. 136–7), and this name is used for all passages relating to her wedding, motherhood and suicide.[89] She is Naveed when she refuses to marry her intended husband, Haroun Harappa: 'Naveed said firmly into the scandalized silence, "I won't marry that stupid potato"' (p. 147). She is Naveed when she takes over the conversation and demonstrates her authority over her ayah, stating: 'Marriage is power . . . . It is freedom . . . then who can tell you what to do?' (p. 155). For Naveed, marriage is not a process of entering the harem, but a method of getting out. Thus, she promotes a Western, nuclear family structure in opposition to the extended family living in the harem or zenana, and in this way performs her role as colonizer, which is signified by her name.

Beneath the veil

Opposing arguments about the meaning of the harem and its impact on women are repeated in discussions about the veil. Fadwa El Guindi disputes colonial and postcolonial practices of addressing the harem and the veil simultaneously, describing this approach as 'analytically unproductive'.[90] Though this argument is entirely valid in relation to anthropological study, the veil and the harem function in analogous ways in Rushdie's novels. The veil covering the mouth symbolically prevents speech and also perhaps physically hinders speech: the word 'purdah' means 'curtain', and that curtain can be 'literal or metaphorical'.[91] The argument that, in certain historical periods, veiling afforded women more freedom and independence, and therefore gave them a social voice not enjoyed by European women who were restricted in different ways, is contested by Sitara Khan's claims that 'purdah can be an excuse for debarring women from full socio-economic and political life, controlling women's space and movement', perhaps to 'ensure pre-marital chastity and post-marital fidelity'.[92] Again, this directly contradicts Penzer's suggestion that the veil was the vehicle for extramarital affairs.

Veiling in Islam is not, as it is often perceived to be, prescriptive.[93] Instead, veiling is an example of 'local customs' being 'incorporated into religious rights',[94] and may have developed from the Qur'anic instruction that 'Whenever you ask [the Prophet's wives] for any object, ask them for it from behind a curtain. That will be purer for your hearts and for theirs'.[95] There is a sense of fear at work in this attempt to contain the woman's body, as if there is something dangerous in the female body that may escape and seep into the outside (masculine) world and infect it. One of the reasons that it is suggested women are covered is to prevent men from being overcome with desire for them.[96] According to Daphne Grace, the veil 'acts to eliminate expressions of both difference within and unity of female identity; it both defines and disguises the individual self',[97] therefore lessening the complexity of her appearance and lessening the strength of women as a group, creating the perception that underneath those clothes is an idea of woman, which is simple, non-threatening and unremarkable. There are arguments to contradict the idea that veiling de-individualizes, including the suggestion that, like any other item of clothing, there is an element of choice over the style, fabric and colour of the veil. But is discussing the fashion choices available in veils really meaningful? Or does choosing the colour, pattern or fabric of the veil become a substitute for making a real choice about whether or not to veil? For Rushdie, veils are 'cloaks of invisibility', comparable to 'shrouds' (p. 262). Bilquis and Sufiya become like the shrouded dead bodies evoked by this image, when they are 'lost behind different veils' (p. 238). Those veils are also taken for granted: 'nobody questions women wearing veils' (p. 262).

Women's bodies become violent when unveiled. Bomb-attacked and naked Bilquis opposes the female suicide bomber on the aeroplane in *The Satanic Verses* who, under her 'loose black djelabbah' (p. 81) wears just 'grenades like extra breasts nestling in her cleavage, the gelignite taped around her thighs' so that 'the arsenal of her body' (p. 81) creates a woman who is 'not so much the bomber as the bomb' (p. 74). This woman is 'insensible to her own beauty' (p. 78) and will destroy this beauty when she ignites the bomb. She is a literalization of the Western dream of the 'sex-bomb', but while the Western dream is bound up with minimal clothing (clad in a bikini, evoking the origin of the term bikini, named after the Bikini Atoll nuclear bomb test site[98]), the Eastern sex-bomb is bound up with maximum clothing: veiled and covered in explosive material, making her twice as explosive, both sexually and politically. She is feared but desired, and this is a contradictory type of fascination with the danger underneath the veil: is female empowerment desired through unveiling in this narrative, making this a feminist statement? Or is the destruction of a beautiful and powerful femininity desired, which is the inevitable result of the explosion? In the Algerian war of independence, the veil became, as Daphne Grace writes, 'a symbol of resistance to colonisation, of emerging nationhood, and traditional values'[99] when Algerian women became suicide bombers by concealing bombs beneath their veils, in the same way as in India, anti-colonials supported traditions of purdah and sati in order to prevent the growth of imperial sympathy. Frantz Fanon has acknowledged the power of the veil in the context of resistance to colonial control, in his essay, 'Algeria Unveiled'. In *The Satanic Verses*, the eventual explosion of this female body-turned-bomb is a rupture which disturbs historical sense, leaving Gibreel and Saladin to struggle with metamorphoses caused by their impossible survival. It is at the same time, because of the eroticization of the female bomber's body, a burst of what Kristeva calls 'jouissance (female sexual pleasure)' which takes part within that rupture which for Kristeva can only be inhabited by the female.[100] This is a rupture which is elsewhere experienced in the extremes of bodily sustenance, banquet and famine, in *Shalimar the Clown*. And in *Shame*, this feminine potency takes the form of a monstrous woman, Sufiya Zinobia, although 'the whole essence of Woman denies' the possibility that 'a Beastji somehow lurked inside Beauty' (p. 159), Sufiya is feminine: describing the 'severe classicism of her features' and her 'small' size, the narrator claims to avoid (while evoking) comparisons to 'an Oriental miniature' (p. 137). The female bomber is desired and 'insensible to her own beauty' (p. 78), and Bilquis's bloodied and bomb-blasted nakedness is what attracts her husband: 'the bold fellow just liked what there was to see' (p. 65).

There may be many forms of danger hidden underneath the woman's veil. As a child, Sufiya displays shocking violence, tearing the heads off 'two hundred and eighteen turkeys' and pulling 'their guts up through their necks with her tiny and weaponless hands' (p. 139). Because of her unusual brutality, the character becomes a fairytale: we see within her 'the beast inside the beauty. Opposing elements of a fairy-tale combined in a single character' (p. 139). Indeed, 'her transformation [through marriage] from Miss Hyder into Mrs Shakil' (p. 172) echoes Robert Louis Stevenson's famous account of the transformation of Dr Jekyll into Mr Hyde, continuing her containment within fictional narratives. Perhaps as a result of her seclusion in fiction, 'Sufiya Zinobia turned out to be, in reality, one of those supernatural beings, those exterminating or avenging angels, or werewolves, or vampires, about whom we are happy to read in stories, sighing thankfully or even a little smugly while they scare the pants off us' (p. 197). Naming this chapter on Sufiya's fairy-tale monstrosity 'The Woman in the Veil' is an indication that veiling and seclusion contributed to Sufiya's psyche. But the assumed reader of this chapter title is necessarily the Western reader, for whom a woman in a veil is shocking. A subheading in the chapter clarifies the narrative position on the effect of veiling: Sufiya's murderous rampage is a departure from the realist novel and presented in the form of a frightening fairytale, entitled 'The woman in the veil: a horror story' (p. 216). In this way, the text reinforces the idea of the power held by the veiled woman in resistance to colonial representation. After she is suspected of committing murders, Sufiya is held captive in a coma by her husband and father, ostensibly for her protection. The narration of Sufiya's cartoonish escape through a 'Sufiya-Zinobia-shaped hole in a bricked-up window' (p. 242) retains the structure of a fairytale:

> There was once a wife, whose husband injected her with knock-out drugs twice daily. For two years she lay on a carpet, like a girl in a fantasy who can only be awoken by the blue-blooded kiss of a prince; but kisses were not her destiny. She appeared to be spellbound by the sorceries of the drug, but the monster inside her never slept, the violence which had been born of shame, but which now lived its own life beneath her skin; it fought the narcoleptic fluids, it took its time, spreading slowly through her body until it had occupied every cell, until she had become the violence (p. 242).

In *Shame*, what lies beneath the veil is not simply a dangerous woman, but also (at certain times) a male body. When Omar, Bilquis and Raza Hyder flee Pakistan to escape a metaphorical book-burning, they are disguised under 'head-to-toe cloaks of invisibility, veils' (p. 262). In this case, the male body, and one of those the ex-president (or ex-'dictator' (p. 261)), is hidden under the guise of the veiled female. When Raza and Omar are 'obliged . . . to put on the humiliating black shroud of womanhood' (p. 68), their bodies are translated into female bodies.

The treatment received by Omar, Bilquis and Raza Hyder during their 'veiled' bus journey 'south and west' (p. 267) questions how far the veil really offers the professed protection to women that it should, as the mobile manifestation of their sacred, harem space. Seeing Omar's large frame climb 'aboard the last of the buses of their flight', the driver says, 'even the transvestites are going into purdah now', provoking 'a racket of wolf-whistles, dirty laughs, obscenities, ululations' and hands pinching their bottoms (p. 268). The veil becomes as flimsy as the material it is made from, and Omar 'is sure that someone will tear' them away, leaving them 'done for, trapped', vulnerable and helpless. Bilquis's female voice causes 'a hush of embarrassment in the bus' (p. 269) and the veil regains its protective power. However, the notion of sanctuary afforded by those clothes is rendered conditional: only desirable female bodies are protected against molestation by the veil; large, untypical and unattractive women may not be guaranteed the same protection. Men retain the power to unveil women and to abuse them: when women appear too big or old or ugly through their purdah, men try to remove their clothes so that they become visible and can be controlled, mocked and touched.

Daphne Grace engages with the practice of male veiling, which is often referred to as a way to equalize veiling and prevent it from being discussed in purely feminist terms. When Rushdie's male characters are veiled, they are silenced, 'they scarcely speak' (p. 267). They fear for their lives, 'cowering in the shadows' in 'fear and despair' (p. 267). They are in disguise, evading mob rule, much like the male author in hiding during the height of the fatwa tension. Beyond the veil is, though, not just a female body or instead a male body but also a dead body. Note how the brothel madam in *The Satanic Verses* speaks her last words 'from behind her drapes', and when the prostitutes throw back:

> The black hangings they [see] a dead woman who might have been fifty or a hundred and twenty-five years old, no more than three feet tall, looking like a big doll, curled up in a cushion-laden wickerwork chair, clutching the empty poison-bottle in her fist (p. 388).

This dead female body opposes what Bram Dijkstra has claimed is the symbolic meaning of the dead woman: the 'icon of virtuous femininity'.[101] Instead, this dead brothel madam who has committed suicide is the horror of the female body, the female diabolic, which Elisabeth Bronfen claims may have arisen from 'the Greek *diaballo* – meaning to translate as well as to split, cause strife and difference, reject, defame, deceive'.[102] Even in death, the female body is symbolic of 'strife', deception and defamation. More interestingly, though, it represents translation: by unveiling the brothel madam, the prostitutes become aware that she was dead, and thus release the associations of the female diabolic, the *diaballo* who can be translated; this instance of unveiling exemplifies translation.

The veil is depicted as a boundary, and beyond this boundary is an object: a female body or something else. This 'object in its veil' as opposed to either 'the veil' or 'the veiled object' is what Walter Benjamin identifies as 'the beautiful'.[103] In the context of *Shame* and *The Satanic Verses* the beautiful can be defined as the desirable female body, and it poses a complex question, as 'the idea of unveiling becomes that of the impossibility of unveiling'.[104] Desiring the geographical space, colonial invaders also desire this female body: 'a dominant metaphor of colonialism was that of rape, of husbanding 'virgin lands', tilling them and fertilizing them and hence 'civilizing' them'.[105] Sara Suleri describes how in the past, 'the 'femininity' of the colonized subcontinent has provided Orientalist narratives with their most prevailing trope for the exoticism of the East'. Suleri suggests that even in trying to argue against Orientalist representations of the East, 'the common language of imperialism . . . perpetuates itself through what seeks to be an opposing methodology, suggesting that the continued equation between a colonized landscape and the female body . . . causes considerable theoretical damage to both contemporary feminist and postcolonial discourses'.[106] In colonial India, rape and disfigurement of the female body has been used as a 'rhetorical weapon' in court cases, where the 'colonial dynamic is metaphorically represented as a violated female body that can be mourned over with sentimentality's greatest excess'.[107] During the Partition of the subcontinent, the female body was disfigured and abused with terrifying brutality: 'nearly 75,000 women . . . had been raped and abducted on both sides of the border at Partition'.[108] The female body became the medium for protest. The combined image in Raza Hyder's escape of the threat to the veiled female body posed by aggressive men who treat them like 'whores' (p. 269), and of book-burning when stories are set in flame – in *Shame*, stories are 'sparks' that 'will start a fire' (p. 261) – is at work in the disfigurements inscribed on the (female) body by violent protesters during Partition: 'Apart from the rapes, other, more specific kinds of violence had been visited on women. Many were paraded naked in the streets, several had their breasts cut off, their bodies tattooed with marks of the 'other' religion'.[109] Men's inscribing their hatred on the female body, though it might unveil the female body and make it into a political emblem, is a reworking of the existing text of the female body. This is a bodily act of translation. If unveiling is translation, then revealing the female body in this brutalized way is a translation, but perhaps one which conveys the translator's ideology instead of the meaning of the text.

The curtain

The presentation of the female body through veiling allows for different interpretative possibilities. As Khan observes, 'purdah is a Farsi word meaning curtain',[110] which is the name chosen for 'the most popular brothel' in *The Satanic Verses*.[111] As Antonia Fraser indicates, the mask is the prostitute's uniform, 'the badge of her profession',[112] hence 'purdah' for Rushdie's brothel. Rushdie, it seems, wants to suggest that to enter the brothel is to pass beyond, or through the veil or curtain of silence – his brothel is a place of speech: customers' gossip reveals secrets with 'the absolute indiscretion of their tongues' (p. 377). The brothel is a female-dominated space, where women can speak, and translate what is ordinarily untranslatable. The prostitutes who work in this brothel undergo a flawed process of translation: abandoning their names and identities in a bid to earn more money by performing a fantasy role, they each assume 'the identity of one of Mahound's wives' (p. 381), performing something unspeakable. In this translation process, though, they grow 'so skilful in their roles that their previous selves began to fade away' (p. 382). At that time, 'it was customary for a whore, on entering her profession, to take the kind of husband who wouldn't give her any trouble – a mountain, maybe, or a fountain, or a bush – so that she could adopt, for form's sake, the title of a married woman' (p. 382). In this brothel-as-harem, the body is translated – or given away – and independence is lost along with the voice, as the prostitutes desire to 'turn themselves into the oldest male fantasy of all' (p. 384): subservient wives, a result of the 'translation' from 'the youngest whore' (p. 380) into 'Ayesha', 'the oldest, fattest whore' into 'Sawdah' (p. 382) and so on. The original is lost in the process of translation like the texts manipulated by colonial translators who omitted the more 'odorous' aspects.[113] At the same time, the identity transformation of the prostitutes engages with 'the concept of a high-status original' which was believed to be superior to the translation.[114] Imperial translators attempted to produce a superior translation by effacing the language or imagery of the original, but Rushdie's prostitutes are weakened by their translation: they become silent: 'they had grown so accustomed to their new names that they couldn't remember the old ones. They were too frightened to give their . . . assumed titles, and as a result were unable to give any names at all' (p. 390). Because of the flaws produced in the prostitutes' translation, this renders their lives untranslatable, so the opportunity provided by their unveiling was lost in their performance of character roles. The brothel in *The Satanic Verses* becomes a performance which repeats orientalist images of the harem. The connection between the postcolonial state and the brothel is reinforced by a moment in *Shame* when Iskander Harappa dubs the General Assembly of the United Nations a 'harem of transvestite whores' and its members 'eunuchs' (p. 179), perhaps in imitation of Gandhi's suggestion that parliament was like '"a sterile woman and a prostitute": the first because it could never enact a law according to its own judgement and the second because it continuously shifted its allegiance from one set of ministers to another, depending on which happened to be the more powerful'.[115] Iskander Harapper's outburst is characteristic of the kind of language that punctuates *Shame*, the kind of 'bad language' borne of translation that will be explored in the subsequent chapter.

3

Translation as Transgression: Bad Language

Roman Jakobson's categories of contemporary translation theory are 'intralingual' translation, a rewording of signs in one language with signs from the same language; 'interlingual' translation, or the interpretation of signs in one language with signs from another language (translation 'proper'); and 'intersemiotic' translation, or the transfer ('transmutation') of signs in one language to non-verbal sign systems (from language into art or music).[1] This chapter engages with the processes of intralingual translation at work in Rushdie's novels, *Shame* and *Midnight's Children* and *The Satanic Verses* where retellings of narratives of Indian independence and migration form the texts' key themes. *The Satanic Verses* is a migration story, and *Midnight's Children* and *Shame* explicitly address the moment of Indian independence from colonial rule, Partition, and the effect of those events on the postcolonial subject. In this way, the novels are receptacles for intralingual translations of an earlier, dominant colonial version of Indian history including the moment of independence and its effects on both India (addressed in *Midnight's Children*) and Pakistan (as told in *Shame*). Because it is accompanied by further social and geographical division decided on purely linguistic lines, the process of transition from colonial subject to postcolonial citizen, imagined especially in *The Satanic Verses*, is depicted in a moment of incomplete or improper linguistic translation, resulting in 'bad' language. This is then figured literally in slang, obscenity and silence.

As well as forming a compelling theoretical framework from which to read the novel as a whole, intralingual translation occurs as a phenomenon within the novels, when characters have to rephrase or retell their stories in order to conform to specific linguistic regulations. In *The Satanic Verses*, Salman the Scribe tests his prophet Mahound's knowledge and connection to God by altering the prophecies slightly, by selecting synonyms, and ultimately raises the question of doubt, which is for Rushdie the opposite of faith. In *Shame*, the active use of obscene language leads directly to violence, so the specific words chosen have physical manifestations. In *Shame*, the concept of *takallouf* governs linguistic freedom to the extent that insults, which are required to be understood literally instead of figuratively, frequently end in death and murder. The act of interlingual translation (translation from one language to another) also provides a subject matter for the novels; in *Midnight's Children*, for example, when Bombay state is divided on linguistic lines, Saleem Sinai performs a hasty translation that saves him from becoming a victim of the brutal language riots but which, he believes, decides the bloody fate of many others who come from a different linguistic background.

Midnight's Children and linguistic territories

Pivotal to narrator Saleem Sinai's recasting of the history of Indian Independence is his part in the Bombay language riots – or, at least, as a juvenile character he believes this to be the case. It is the narrator's preoccupation with a moment of unfortunate translation – when he recites for Marathi language demonstrators a poem intended to mock the Gujarati language – that punctuates his subsequent retelling of the story of post-1947 India and Pakistan, and the story of his life. The language riots are described by Catherine Cundy as a 'site of conflict in the novel'.[2] A 'site' of conflict is an appropriate description, because the riots started after the division of India into states and territories based on language:

> Kerala was for speakers of Malayalam . . .; in Karnataka you were supposed to speak Kanarese; and the amputated state of Madras – known today as Tamil Nadu – enclosed the *aficionados* of Tamil. (*Midnight's Children*, 189)

Saleem's linguistic territory is even more complicated than this administrative reorganization, though: first, his geographical territory, the state of Bombay, had been ignored during the process by an oversight meaning that the language marches seemed legitimately to have the power to decide which was the dominant language: Gujarati or Marathi. Secondly, Saleem speaks English with many of his neighbours and with his family, in the fashion of his father's mock-Oxford accent. And in addition, Saleem is beginning to experiment with silent, non-linguistic forms of psychic communication, at which he discovers he is growing adept: ignored by his young neighbour and tormentor Evie, he says,

> I realize I don't have to ask her, I can just get inside that freckled mouth-metalled head and find out, for once I can really get to know what's going on . . . I find myself pushing, driving, forcing my way. (190)

Saleem's psychic transgression into Evie's thoughts causes her to push him away from her mentally and physically: Saleem learns, 'when you go deep inside someone's head, *they can feel you there*' (192). Evie's reaction is an acknowledgement of the moral transgression that Saleem has performed because of the evocative language she chooses when she shouts: 'GET OUT GET OUT GET OUT . . . GET OUT TO HELL!' (191). She pushes him down the hill, where he trespasses (or transgresses) into the disputed territory of the 'impassioned throng' (191) of language marchers. The language marches described in *Midnight's Children* convey the historical events which led to the partition of Bombay State in 1960. Aparna Dharwadker refers to the language riots in Bombay in demand for a separate Maharashtra in the early 1950s: 'the formative idea behind the state of "Maharashtra" was that it would be the home of the Marathas. The demand for the state led to months of language riots between Marathi and Gujarati speakers in Bombay'.[3] Thus, the language marchers themselves seek a transgression of boundaries:

> The Samyukta Maharashtra Samiti ("United Maharashtra Party") which stood for the Marathi language . . . demanded the creation of the Deccan state of Maharashtra, and the Maha Gujarat Parishad ("Great Gujarati Party") which marched beneath the banner of the Gujarati language . . . dreamed of a state to the north of Bombay City, stretching all the way to the Kathiawar peninsula and the Rann of Kutch (189).

At the same time, they tempt and taunt others to transgress the boundaries they desire and the temporary boundary they create with their combined bodies: 'Methwold's Estate was cut off from the city by a stream of chanting humanity' (189). When Saleem is thrust into their midst, the marchers taunt him, urging him to 'speak some Gujarati!' (191), which to these Marathi speakers would be an act of linguistic transgression. Saleem responds with the only Gujarati he knows: 'a rhyme designed to make fun of the speech rhythms of the language: Soo ché? Saru ché!/Danda lé ké maru ché!' which translates as 'How are you? – I am well! – I'll take a stick and thrash you to hell!' (191). This transgressive taunt, 'a nonsense; a nothing; nine words of emptiness' (191), saves him, as it is a welcomed act of transgressive translation, allowing him, somewhat, to gain the favour of the Marathi protesters, who take up the chant until it becomes a battle song. The song becomes transgressive because of its meaning when translated: it is the translation that reveals the Marathi speakers' attitude towards Gujarati and provides the linguistic groups' violent battleground. However, such linguistic transgression does not go unpunished: Saleem is aware that, as he says, 'to the tune of my little rhyme the first of the language riots got under way, fifteen killed, over three hundred wounded', so as a consequence of linguistic transgression, Saleem was responsible for violence which ultimately led to the partition of the state of Bombay.

Midnight's Children relates the event of Indian Independence, described by Syed Manzurul Islam as 'a migrant's event' which reveals the significance of the 'location of the writer'.[4] This is what gives the novel its hybrid narration: as Syed Manzurul Islam describes, though the events surrounding 15 August 1947 are apparently narrated by a character experiencing their results, they are narrated from the position of the migrant writer located in 'London, 1981'.[5] In *Midnight's Children*, language is on the point of reaching the hybrid climax that Rushdie anticipates: Islam suggests that the portrayal of Saleem's progressive grandfather Aadam Aziz as a 'half-and-halfer' is 'precisely the condition from which the subject of the postcolonial nation emerges'.[6] There are references to hybrid language throughout the novel, including the intriguing image of Saleem's 'Anglepoise-lit writing' (38). Syed Islam concentrates on the linguistic significance of the image, defining the phrase 'Anglepoise-lit writing' (and Saleem's narrative style) as: 'a highly literary style – characteristic of European modernism and its post – with its penchant for meta-fictive commentary, oblique narrative angle, temporal circularity and digression'.[7] Islam goes on to abbreviate this definition into the term 'self-reflexivity', a description which equals the work of the Anglepoise lamp, a uniquely individualistic type of lighting which lights up only the small, restricted area of desk or writing materials in its scope. The phrase also seems to imply Anglophone or Anglophile literary writing alongside the notion of writing by lamplight.

That *Midnight's Children* was awarded the Booker of Bookers (1993) and the subsequent Best of the Bookers (2008) may indicate the continuing relevance of novels that express ideas about hybrid language. Translation, though, is still performed with difficulty in the novel: in order to tell his story (in other words, to translate it for his readers) Saleem must transgress linguistic boundaries (by causing language wars) and the boundaries of societal propriety – flouting the laws of halal in order to tell a 'haram' version of history retaining all of its 'redness' and 'blood' (59). The requirement that the storyteller transgresses may be due to the narrative form, which is 'epical', having an 'affinity with the Indian oral genre of the "sea of stories"'.[8] There may be less scope for translation within the bounds of a novel that relies heavily on its relationship to an established Indian literary form. This is in fact the point: if Rushdie 'deliberately set out to emulate

Mahabharata' (Islam 1999: 125), this was in order to present the constraints placed upon the hybrid narrator, caught between, as Syed Manzurul Islam puts it, Bombay, '15 August, 1947' and 'London, 1981'.[9]

This dual focus on Bombay and London has an impact on much postcolonial South Asian literature, even if the London is sometimes a distant or imagined one. Writing in English has been described by many writers in formerly colonized countries, notably Ngugi wa Thiong'o, as problematic and even treacherous. In this sense, English is itself 'bad' language. For Rushdie, though, writing in English is not symbolic of the colonizer's power; writing in the language of the former colonizer permits a rewriting of the English language. It is perhaps in this spirit that Rushdie's controversial choice to include only English-language texts in his edited collection, *The Vintage Book of Indian Writing, 1947–1997*, should be taken. The collection doesn't suggest that only English-language writing is of literary value; instead, it represents the extent of the revision of English literature that has taken place since the end of British colonial rule in India, a fundamental part of the reason for such a collection, bound in that historical moment. *Midnight's Children* represents a very non-English storytelling style (one that is as *unsaxogrammatical* – perhaps more accurately, *un*-Anglo-*saxogrammatical* – as Rushdie's later retelling of *Hamlet* in the short story 'Yorick' exemplifies); it is a text that is the epitome of 'bad' language if this is a term that can be designated to texts that don't follow accepted grammatical rules: audacious sentences of more than a page in length have been noted by many reviewers.

'Bad' language in *Midnight's Children* and *Shame*

Rules over how to tell a story correctly, over what can and cannot be said, over slang, obscenity and blasphemy form the core to both *Midnight's Children* and *Shame*, where for both novels, the obscene becomes the performative: swearing and other 'bad' language (like translation) enacts retribution. Likewise, in *The Satanic Verses* Salman the Scribe is told his mistranslations will not go unpunished, in what Rushdie once described as an eerie prediction of the fatwa, which was pronounced in response to what can also be described as Rushdie's 'bad' language: the misnaming of Muhammad and the retelling of stories held to be 'obscene' by some. When characters swear in Rushdie, they engage in long and elaborate outbursts of obscenity. Little Mir Harappa frames his obscene tirades with politeness: he addresses Rani Harappa, the target of his words, politely as 'Rani Begum', before apologizing for the swearing in which he is about to indulge: 'no point you blaming me for this. Blame your husband . . . Excuse me, but . . .' (96). His demeanour is formal and proper: he arrives on horseback and is accompanied by a dozen armed horsemen who, however, dismount and then loot the house. The narration of this episode exposes the contrast between, on the one hand, Mir as 'a proud equestrian figure', who is determined to salvage his honour, calling his comments 'justifications' and asking of Rani's husband, 'does he think he can insult me in public and get away with it?' and on the other hand, his words and actions: swearing and looting. Little Mir's insults are repulsive, but at the same time, obscure and ridiculous; he calls Iskander Harappa: 'that bullock's arsehole'; 'pizzle of a homosexual pig'; 'sisterfucking bastard spawn of corpse-eating vultures'; 'sucker of shit from the rectums of diseased donkeys'; 'murdering rapist of his own grandmother'; 'nibbler of a crow's left nipple'. Mir's insults seem to have no relevance to his particular grievance, which is his accusation that 'when [Iskander] took that whore from me he took my honour' (96–7). Absurdly for someone feeling dishonoured by the 'theft' of a prostitute, one of the accusations levelled at Iskander is that he is immoral because he has sex with prostitutes (and that he is the son of a prostitute): Mir says:

> His great father locked up his wife and spent every night in the brothel . . . a whore disappeared when her fat stomach couldn't be explained by what she ate, and then the next thing Lady Harappa was holding the baby even though everyone knew she hadn't been screwed in a decade . . . like father like son. (97)

In apparent support for her friend Rani, Bilquis Hyder frames a response to these accusations with terms of endearment like 'sweetie' and 'darling'. In contrast to Mir's insults, which are graphic and metaphorical, Bilquis's accusations (which she claims she delivers in order to 'defend' her 'friend' Rani) are specific and detailed. She describes how Iskander visits belly-dancer shows, international hotel swimming-pools where 'the naked white women go', cock-fights, bear-fights, snake-and-mongoose-fights and that he goes to the red-light district with movie cameras. She accuses him of indulging in alcohol, gambling, opium and of adultery with 'women in their waterproof figleaves'. She describes the event provoking Mir's attack in more detail, claiming that 'Isky pulled his cousin's juiciest little French tart from right under his nose, at some big cultural event' (97). Though the detail provided by Bilquis's list of crimes may be more hurtful, she circumvents the bad language of the insult because she does not swear, and claims to be providing the information to help her friend, so her comments are more difficult to classify as insults. Mir's less specific insults conform to

Andersson and Trudgill's suggestion that swearing 'should not be interpreted literally'.[10] Note that *Shame*, too, should not be interpreted literally: it is not 'a realistic novel' but 'only . . . a sort of modern fairy-tale', so, the narrator suggests, 'nobody need get upset, or take anything I say too seriously' (69–70). The difference between Mir's and Bilquis's insults is to do with the performative, 'the utterance which allows us to do something by the means of speech itself', which is opposed to the constative, 'the classical "assertion", most often conceived as a true/false "description" of the facts'.[11] The performative is discussed by Derrida, in response to J. L. Austin's claims that a performative utterance 'produces or transforms a situation'.[12] It might be said that Mir's insults are performative, in this case, and that they produce the context for looting the house, which, without such hostile and obscene language, would not be justifiable by the events in the narrative because they would not follow logically. Derrida disputes the power attributed to the performative by Austin and asks whether a performative statement could 'succeed if its formulation did not repeat a "coded" or iterable statement'.[13] Taking Mir's swearing and looting as an example, then, the act of 'justifying' (Mir calls the insults he delivers 'justifications' for his behaviour) and thereby prompting the looting of Rani's house by uttering the performative insults would not be successful if Mir and his followers did not reproduce the 'coded' statements – arriving armed on horseback, maintaining an aggressive demeanour, going inside Rani's house uninvited and so on – which successfully formulate the performative.

Other incidents of swearing in the novel correspond with plot events more straightforwardly. When Iskander Harappa is detained in prison by Raza Hyder, the insults directed at Hyder begin with ridiculous and distasteful images, calling Hyder a 'seducer of your grandmother's pet mongrel bitch' and a 'diarrhoeic infidel who shits on the Qur'an'. Then, however, Iskander accuses Hyder of being the 'seller of your daughters at low prices to the bastard offspring of pimps' (225). Raza Hyder has two daughters, and one of these is Sufiya Zinobia, who marries Omar; Omar does not know the identity of his father, and the three Shakil sisters equally claim to be his mother. These are women who were called 'whores' (14) by their father on his deathbed, and the combination of these factors lends some relevance to the insult. The narrator strengthens the connection between these insults and events by commenting that the red 'betel-juice' spittle 'spattered from top to bottom' in the room during the outburst of abusive language made it look 'as if a herd of animals had been slaughtered in there' and specifically, those slaughtered animals are imagined as 'turkeys', the animal slaughtered by the emotionally unstable Sufiya in great numbers.

As a result of his swearing, Iskander is imprisoned, considered 'a menace to the country' (225), and accused of 'arranging for the murder of his cousin, Mir Harappa'. Colonel Shuja comments: 'just look where bad language will get you' (226). As well as causing his arrest, Iskander's bad language enables him to take control of his imprisonment; he awaits the death penalty, and when he believes he is going to die, begins to say his prayers in 'beautiful Arabic' (237). This 'good' language is interrupted: Colonel Shuja suggests that he is not facing imminent death after all, but instead, must sign a full confession to receive clemency. Rather than submitting to the proposed confession text, Iskander chooses to retain linguistic power by swearing fiercely: 'the obscenity of his language inflicted stinging blows, Shuja felt them piercing his skin'. The use of language to cause humiliation and anger in someone who holds power in this situation is described as 'a kind of suicide':

> When Iskander yelled, "fuck me in the mouth, pimp, go suck your grandson's cock," that was it, it didn't matter that Shuja was not old enough to have a grandchild, he stood up very slowly and then shot the former Prime Minister [Iskander Harappa] through the heart. (237–8)

Rushdie is not alone in using swearing and obscene expressions as a reaction to the postcolonial aftermath of imposed language and linguistic divisions. Like *Shame*, where fluctuating political power is presented as being determined by the use of bad language, Ziad Doueiri's film *West Beirut* is an example of a postcolonial (film) text concerned with the effect of societal upheaval, which uses 'bad' language as a way to measure change.[14] Beirut is presented as a society held together by tentative linguistic codes: the film's main protagonists, Tarek and Omar, attend the French High School of Beirut, where Tarek's teachers suggest to him that the French 'created your civilization and your constitution' and that French education 'is the only way out of your primitive customs'.[15] In linguistic rebellion, Tarek repeatedly misspells the word 'Monsieur' as 'Meucieux' (a slang spelling and pronunciation) and 'Mes Yeux' (my eyes – perhaps a meaningful misspelling suggesting that the young man endorses a different perspective from the one being taught to the class). It is at this point that the massacre signalling the beginning of the civil war occurs. From this moment onwards, obscene or offensive language is used repeatedly by characters in response to their precarious situation: a woman shouts at her neighbour in outrage at his crowing rooster: 'Goddamn it, . . . damn rooster, . . . have him shut the fuck up. . . . May Allah spread pain all over you'.[16] An argument between Tarek and a taxi driver in the street is punctuated by insults: 'motherfucker', 'faggot', 'cocksucker': this language appears to lead directly to the outbreak of gunfire. Omar's father attempts to save his family from the violence by forbidding what he defines as 'obscenity': theatre, cinema, rock and roll and any mention of sex, as he believes that 'music about sex is the work of Satan'. Indeed, Omar echoes his father's sentiments, when he tells Tarek that their problems are a form of retribution for voyeurism: he says, 'all my problems started when I let you peep at Leila' (his young Aunt). Like Rushdie's brothel in *The Satanic Verses*, the 'whorehouse' in *West Beirut* is the only neutral territory where 'there's no East and West', and it is this place that Tarek believes can save Beirut, as if the celebration of that forbidden, 'obscene' sex and rock and roll can, in contrast to the opinion of Omar's father, strengthen and fuse the two religious factions back into one harmonious city, because as the brothel Madam suggests, 'a bed has no religion'. Linguistic 'obscenity', then, is seen as empowering people to overcome civil war, in the film.

There are further examples of the empowering properties of 'bad' language in *Shame*; during the height of his power, Iskander Harappa consciously uses language according to the demographic make-up of his audience in order to maintain power, and this means that at times, he uses 'obscene' language as a political tool. Although as a rule Iskander 'expunged from his public, urban vocabulary his encyclopaedic repertoire of foul green village oaths', when 'campaigning in the villages he allowed the air to turn green with obscenity once again, understanding the vote-getting powers of the filth' (125). The use of swearing for political reasons is a common use of 'bad' language acknowledged by Lars Andersson and Peter Trudgill, who claim that 'politicians can use swearing in official situations, and when they do, they certainly attract attention. They will be cited and they will appear on the news so they had better have something intelligent to say in connection with the swearing'.[17] This use of swearing is an example of the 'covert prestige' afforded to the speaker by their bad language, as Andersson and Trudgill describe: 'there must be some positive values connected with all this bad language. . . . so-called bad language is often associated with toughness and strength' which is 'highly valued among quite a number of people'.[18] The law of *takallouf* prevents Raza Hyder from censuring Iskander's swearing and forces him to ignore his 'anger'. *Takallouf* is the law which obliged people to pretend that

> words meant no more than they said . . . a form of tongue-tying formality, a social restraint so extreme as to make it impossible for the victim to express what he or she really means, a species of compulsory irony which insists, for the sake of good form, on being taken literally. (104)

Takallouf is described as a 'starch' (105) and 'sophistication that permitted obscenity and blasphemy' (106). Raza's anger may be a product of 'the layers of social artifice and aspiration' that 'bad' language attempts to cut through, according to Robert Adams.[19]

In other circumstances, swearing is equally permissible in *Shame*; one such circumstance is the event of childbirth, the only time when 'filthy language . . . is permitted to ladies' (89). However, the precise 'filthy language' used by the woman in labour is a mystery; at no point does it appear on the printed page: though this is presented as an example of the legitimate use of 'bad' language, its absence from the text suggests that it is not 'permitted' after all. *Midnight's Children* may provide an answer to this puzzle; when narrator Saleem Sinai suggests that the usual way to tell a family history is to tell a 'halal' version of events, made up of the 'permitted parts' (59) only, perhaps he implies that even with his desire to tell a full story, some of the 'redness' and 'blood' (of which ladies' swearing during childbirth is surely an example) must be left out. Thus, distasteful language is censored because it is 'haram', forbidden and unlawful. Language which is unlawful according to a religious practice is blasphemous language. Blasphemous language includes terms prefaced by the word 'bloody' in a Christian context, as Andersson and Trudgill explain when providing a history of the term as a swear word.[20] The OED refutes this connection, suggesting that 'there is no ground for the notion that "bloody", offensive as from associations it now is to ears polite, contains any profane allusion or has connexion with the oath "'s blood!" [or, "Christ's blood"]'. However, this 'notion' has passed into the common perception of the etymology of the term 'bloody', and is therefore a valid sense of the use of this term in Rushdie's writing. This provides a connection between the 'halal' story which excludes the 'bloody' parts in Islamic family histories and a Christian version which would similarly recognize that which is 'bloody' as something obscene and forbidden.

Blasphemy and 'bad' language in general are connected: Andersson and Trudgill cite Edmund Leach's suggestion that much of the language held to be 'obscene' (in the context of the English language) has a blasphemous 'religious' origin, and the remainder are concerned with 'sex and excretion' or 'animal abuse',[21] three categories into which Little Mir Harappa's insults fit comfortably. The term 'blasphemy' refers to 'profane speaking of God or sacred things' and 'impious irreverence' as well as speaking 'against anything held "sacred"'. The term is also used interchangeably with 'slander' and 'defamation' (OED). The sense of 'blasphemy' as something connected to a legal term like slander provides a further means of punishing blasphemy outside that assumed by its religious sense, where punishment may be deferred until after death. Anthony Julius's definition of 'transgression' addresses the concept of the obscene: the four essential meanings of transgression are, according to Julius,

> The denying of doctrinal truths; rule-breaking, including the violating of principles, conventions, pieties or taboos; the giving of serious offence; and the exceeding, erasing or disordering of physical or conceptual boundaries.[22]

Blasphemous words and deeds are punished in Rushdie's *Midnight's Children*, *Shame* and *The Satanic Verses*. In *Shame*, Rani Harappa calls Omar a 'fat pigmeat tub' (94) invoking the offensive term 'pig' which like pork, 'is a four-letter word' in Pakistan (70). Because she ignores advice to 'dip [her] tongue in water' (93), Rani's blasphemy is punished by the looting of her house by Little Mir Harappa, which is accompanied by the first instance of extended swearing in the novel. Likewise, Farah's first words in the novel are 'a casual blasphemy' (43), a fact of which the reader is frequently reminded, and for which Farah is repeatedly punished in ways that make language inaccessible to her: she is hypnotized and rendered dumb, then forced into marriage which effaces her name and takes away her independent voice, so that on her return to the town of Q. she 'spoke to no one . . . except to order food and supplies in the shops' (55).

Cultural translation and blasphemous eating

Because *Shame* is apparently not 'a realistic novel', the narrator is permitted to indulge in blasphemous asides, like the joke about God carrying out the instructions of a series of political leaders (Ayub Khan, Yahya Khan, Zulfikar Ali Bhutto and Zia Ul-Haq), and asking them, 'why don't people seem to love me any more?' (112). Religion, then, and blasphemy with it, *Shame* suggests, has flexible boundaries and is subject to the political power but not a moral order. In a postcolonial context, these boundaries are defined by the response to colonial powers. Homi Bhabha suggests that Rushdie's repeated use of the word 'blasphemy' in *The Satanic Verses* is 'not merely a misrepresentation of the sacred by the secular; it is a moment when the subject-matter or the content of a cultural tradition is being overwhelmed, or alienated, in the act of translation'.[23] Harish Trivedi is one prominent Translation Studies academic who has reacted strongly to Bhabha's use – or 'usurpation', even 'abuse' in Trivedi's words – of the term translation. In a 2005 essay titled 'Translating Culture vs. Cultural Translation', Trivedi describes emotively the notion of 'cultural translation' – what he sees as, literally, swift cultural change due to altered circumstances – as something that should not be confused with 'translation'. Trivedi has assumed that Bhabha's notion of translation, used when discussing *The Satanic Verses*, is consistent with Rushdie's use of the term when he suggests that as migrants, he is among many 'translated men'. However, Bhabha approaches the text from a textual, literary framework, which is not equitable with Rushdie's assessment of his own biography. Bhabha's sense of translation should be seen in relation to the translation process going on within the narrative: Gibreel Farishta's translation of South Asia past and present, and the retelling of stories ('satanic verses') reputedly erased from the Islamic texts; Bhabha explicates Gibreel's 'migrant's dream of survival', not Rushdie's, as Trivedi has claimed.[24] Translation as subject matter within the literary text is, I would suggest in response to Trivedi's fears, perhaps less likely to render translation 'dead and buried'.

In a post-Partition context, what may once have been distasteful or impolite to a section of the community in India (e.g. using a term like 'pig' or 'pork') has become a blasphemous utterance with an associated enforceable law in Pakistan: in Karachi, Rushdie 'wrote a teleplay adaptation of Edward Albee's *Zoo Story* for the new government-operated television station, but it was censored for containing the word pork'.[25] References to pork in the play include the hamburgers used to gain influence over the landlady's dog, which are deemed unsayable, though references to pork in *The Zoo Story* do not contradict its connotations in Muslim culture, as the meat is so repulsive that even the dog refuses it. Setting up the environment in which the story of *Shame* takes place, the narrator refers to this early censorship experience, describing 'the TV chief who once told me solemnly that pork was a four-letter word' (70).

In *The Satanic Verses*, the actress Pimple Billimoria is unable to act because of the disappearance of co-star Gibreel, and in her state of sudden contradiction, she utters blasphemies: her words are 'such a torrent of obscenities' (13) that like those obscenities apparently permitted to the woman in labour, they cannot be repeated on the page. Here, inaction (Gibreel's) causes blasphemy (Pimple Billimoria's), but elsewhere in *The Satanic Verses*, it is the acts themselves that are blasphemous. Gibreel performs a blasphemous act when he eats pork in explicit defiance of God: 'he had lost his faith. . . . he loaded his plate with . . . the pork sausages from Wiltshire and the cured York hams and the rashers of bacon from god-knows where; with the gammon steaks of his unbelief and the pig's trotters of secularism' (29). This act is swiftly followed by retribution in the form of 'a punishment of dreams' (32). The origin of the rule banning the consumption of pork in Islam implies a belief in a vengeful God who punishes undesirable personality traits: 'in folkloric terms, eating the meat of the pig is said to contribute to lack of morality and shame, plus greed for wealth, laziness, indulgence, dirtiness and gluttony'.[26] Contemporary commentary gives a long list of health risks associated with eating pork, to back up the religious rule:

> Pork consumption has been proven to be harmful to human health, contributing to a litany of diseases, and physical ailments. . . . some medical reasons are high blood pressure, headaches, stomach disorders, painful joints, laziness, and lethargy. Pork meat is also host to a number of parasites and worms, namely: Paragonimus, and the sucking worm Clonnrchis Sinesis. There is also the danger of infestation by the infamous and extremely harmful trichina worms that live and breed in swine's flesh and which are reported to infect one out of every four humans who ingest its poisonous meat.[27]

The quotation on the morality of eating pork is all related to consumption and food, especially 'greed', 'indulgence' and 'gluttony'. Other characteristics assumed to have an association with overeating that are included in the statement, such as 'dirtiness' and 'laziness', are characteristics referred to by Rani in relation to Omar Khayyam Shakil in *Shame*. Along with calling him a 'fat pigmeat tub', she says: 'what a shameless type he must be, to carry all that tummy about' (80). Gibreel's consumption of pork is performed according to these undesirable traits: he 'began to eat as fast as possible, stuffing the dead pigs into his face so rapidly that bacon rashers hung out of the sides of his mouth' (30). He overindulges, and if he is punished, it must surely be punishment for his gluttony as much as for what he has eaten. Other characters provide examples of indulgence for which they believe they are punished: Mahound suggests that his wife's death is punishment, 'a kind of vengeance . . . upon the innocent' for 'the repudiation of the Satanic verses' (124). Saeed believes that his wife's cancer is his punishment (not hers), 'because [he] lusted after Ayesha' (233). In *Midnight's Children*, Saleem believes that he communicates with angels: this blasphemous thought is punished by his father, with 'a mighty blow on the side of [his] head' (165) rather than divine retribution.

Acts of communication: The satanic verses

Neither Mahound nor Saleem Sinai could be said to be entirely responsible for their blasphemous acts: both receive communication from an external source, whether this is God, the devil or psychic abilities. Their words may emanate from another source, a source resembling the poet's muse. Either a muse or a God, is responsible for the communications received by the poetic and the prophesying characters in *The Satanic Verses*. Mahound's description of his angelic communication is like that of a poet describing how he finds the inspiration to write: he is provided with the messages that he seeks; he says: 'it feels to me, most times, as if he comes from within my heart: from within my deepest places, from my soul' (106). In one of the novel's most frequently cited episodes, Ayesha, the youngest wife of Mahound, suggests that his revelations are engineered in order to win arguments: 'your God certainly jumps to it when you need him to fix things up for you' (386). Mahound's voices and revelatory experiences are not depicted as wanton corruption, however; the presence of the muse suggests the creative talents of the human writer or speaker as well as a more mystical source of inspiration. In Saladin's London, Jumpy Joshi secretly writes poetry and claims that his writing has its source in 'inner voices' (186). In Jahilia, Baal elevates the whores at the expense of God, when refusing to cooperate with the law that wants to punish him in the name of the Lord: 'I am Baal. . . . I recognize no jurisdiction except that of my Muse; or, to be exact, my dozen Muses' (391). In creating a successful business, Baal is prepared to sacrifice his beliefs, claiming that, 'where there is no belief, there is no blasphemy' (380). If God is merely a Muse, then revelation is actually creativity, and all poetry is as authoritative as scripture, or, scripture is simply a work of poetry. Religion is presented as a man-made phenomenon, so that the only God who could exist is the one who is imagined by the individual. However, the muse of a character in a novel must, of course, be the author.

Shame: Intrusive narration

The authorial narrator of *Shame* is intrusive and his narration includes events that are apparently unconnected to the plot. Malise Ruthven suggests that the 'characterisation, metaphor and narrative' of *Shame* are 'perpetually undercut by playful interjections by the author which subvert the suspension of disbelief'.[28] This subversion permits Rushdie to retain a satiric tone while apparently telling a fairy tale. The authorial narrator interrupts the narrative to describe the differences between the text as it stands, as 'a sort of modern fairy-tale' (70) and the text that would have existed 'if this were a realistic novel about Pakistan' (68), in which case, the narrator claims that he 'would not be talking about Bilquis and the wind' (68). Instead, the novel would include the narrator's 'youngest sister . . . studying engineering in Karachi'; 'covert, subterranean water pumps to steal water'; 'the subtle logic of an industrial programme that builds nuclear reactors but cannot develop a refrigerator'; 'genocide in Baluchistan'; 'anti-Semitism'; 'smuggling, the boom in heroin exports, military dictators, venal civilians, corrupt civil servants'; and 'bought judges' (69–70). The narrator claims that had these things been the subject of *Shame*, 'the book would have been banned, dumped in the rubbish bin, burned' (70). Thus, the narrator, from a point outside the 'fairy-tale', circumvents censorship by discussing what cannot ordinarily be discussed in what Catherine Cundy terms narratorial 'asides'.[29] The resulting uncensored text cannot so easily be controlled because this passage is apparently unrelated to the characters and events (or the subject) of the novel. Ato Quayson describes narrative as being constituted by 'characters', 'a story', 'setting' and 'a narrator who is the vehicle of all the other elements'.[30] This relationship is complicated when the narrator describes events external to the text, and questions the status of his characters, claiming: 'you can imagine how depressed I am by the behaviour of Omar Khayyam Shakil. . . . what kind of hero is this? . . . How is one to account for such a character?' (142). The authorial narrator makes the connection between the narratorial asides and the plot in a statement which defines the novel as satire and makes it difficult to mistake the relevance of the corruptions referred to by the narrator in previous asides:

> How does a dictator fall? There is an old saw which states, with absurd optimism, that it is in the nature of tyrannies to end. . . . well, I mustn't forget I'm only telling a fairy-story. My dictator will be toppled by goblinish, faery means. "Makes it pretty easy for you," is the obvious criticism; and I agree, I agree. But add, even if it does sound a little peevish: "*You* try and get rid of a dictator some time." (257)

In relation to characters' swearing and blasphemy, then, the narrator, though expressing apparent distaste, is distrusted by his readers and considered an '*Outsider*' or '*Trespasser*' because of his '*foreign language*'. Like the translator whose translation, according to Lefevere, 'readers decide to accept or reject' (Lefevere 1992: 5), this narrator is suspected of speaking with a '*forked tongue*' and telling nothing '*but lies*' (28).

It is the blasphemous or offensive language used to discuss the prophet figure Mahound in *The Satanic Verses* that has been cited by some as giving the most offence, including the construction of the character's name: 'here he is neither Mahomet nor MoeHammered; has adopted, instead, the demon-tag . . . the

Devil's synonym: Mahound' (93). The extent of the narrator's responsibility for the blasphemies and obscenities of the characters is complicated by intrusive narrators who express apparent dismay at the behaviour of characters. In this sense, the narrator performs a kind of censorship by watering down the effect of characters' actions with punitive narratorial commentary.

The intrusion of the narrator occurs as an aside to the events in the text, while a further level of censorship is explored within the events described, and these acts of censorship are very different from the intrusive narrator's pensive judgements. Instances of censorship within the events of the novel take a predominantly physical form. Perhaps this is in part due to the restriction on the language and thought of characters imposed by *takallouf*, which prevents those characters from making judgemental interpretations of each other's speech, and instead channels their censorship towards the physical. When Haroun Harappa's offensive newspaper article 'was reprinted in Newsweek . . . the authorities back home had to intercept the entire shipment of that subversive issue and rip out the offending pages from every copy' (147). Film is censored in the same fragmentary (and not entirely reliable) manner: the 'chief film censor' enjoyed watching 'special compilations of the juiciest bits excised from incoming foreign films' (125). Other art forms are censored by substitution, to allow their performance: a production of *Julius Caesar* in modern dress and including the assassination of a Head of State was only permitted to go ahead once the uniform of Caesar was replaced with (British) Imperial regalia, which turned the play into a 'patriotic work depicting the overthrow of imperialism by the freedom movement of Rome' (241). Omar's brother Babar has his diaries censored: they are 'returned to his family with many of their pages missing' as 'tattered remnants of . . . brutalized volumes' (128).

In *Shame*, censorship is used to uphold corrupt political regimes: Raza Hyder's instruction to imprison the 'subversives' who wrote about him in newspapers is refused – 'General Raddi said . . . "Mr President, we do not believe such an action would be wise"' (261) – and this revocation of censorship is the beginning of the dictator's 'fall'. This episode has a historical counterpart: Ali Eteraz claims that General Zia (the political figure on whom the character of Raza Hyder is based, according to Goonetilleke[31]) was 'responsible for a whole breed of blasphemy laws being enacted' including:

> The Pakistan Penal Code (PPC) and the Criminal Procedure Code [which] were amended, through ordinances in 1980, 1982 and 1986 to declare anything implying disrespect to Muhammad, *Ahle Bait* (family of the prophet), *Sahaba*

(companions of the prophet) and *Sha'ar-i-Islam* (Islamic symbols), a cognizable offence, punishable with imprisonment or fine, or with both.[32]

The 'connections hinted at in print' that Raza Hyder could not subdue become 'sparks [that] will start a fire' that leave Raza Hyder 'a crushed figure' (262). The physicality of censorship is likewise present in *The Satanic Verses*, where Eugene Dumsday escapes the hijacked aircraft by losing his tongue:

> Shouting hysterical incoherencies . . . in the grip of his waking nightmare he drivelled on and on until . . . the woman, came up, swung her rifle butt and broke his flapping jaw. And worse: because slobbering Dumsday had been licking his lips as his jaw slammed shut, the tip of his tongue sheared off . . . Eugene Dumsday had gained his freedom by losing his tongue; the persuader succeeded in persuading his captors by surrendering his instrument of persuasion. (79)

Eugene later has his tongue rebuilt from his buttock, which is imagined as a form of cannibalism: 'wouldn't fancy a mouthful of my own buttock meat myself' (418). The cannibalistic eating of human buttock meat resonates with the experience of the old woman in Voltaire's *Candide* whose 'one buttock' was removed, along with one buttock of each woman in the starving fortress, to provide 'a delicious meal' for the soldiers, who had already eaten two eunuchs.[33] Rushdie has in fact been described as a 'late twentieth-century Anglo-Indian Voltaire'[34] because of the censorship of his work, and this description equally applies to the similarity of brutal bodily alterations depicted by the two writers. Because of his writing, Voltaire was exiled from Paris, but for his, Rushdie received a death sentence in the Fatwa.

The Satanic Verses predicted this death sentence with what Rushdie has termed eerie foreknowledge; Salman the Scribe (sometimes seen as a double for the author) is told, 'your blasphemy, Salman, can't be forgiven. Did you think I wouldn't work it out? To set your words against the Words of God' (374). Rushdie writes, 'it's true that some passages in *The Satanic Verses* have now acquired a prophetic quality that alarms even me'.[35] Here, Rushdie could be seen to invite censure upon himself, thus lending support for Ruth Parkin-Gounelas's claim that 'the activity of the artist is . . . better compared to suicide than creation' (Parkin-Gounelas 2001: 198). Parkin-Gounelas's claim is based on Maurice Blanchot's argument that,

> All forms of symbolization such as language are dependent on the replacement and disappearance of the object named or symbolized. Language means that

> the thing named can be detached from its existence and "suddenly plunged into nothingness"; language is thus a form of "deferred assassination".[36]

Lacan writes, 'the symbol manifests itself first of all as the murder of the thing'.[37] Once the thing is named by language or symbolized, what it names and symbolizes is murdered. Salman the Scribe 'named or symbolized' the author, and the 'deferred assassination' implied by the replacement of the author by the character portrayed is made explicit in Rushdie's text by the threat that his 'blasphemy . . . can't be forgiven'. Rushdie's text suggests that the author is complicit in his own death; that, like Salman the Scribe who blasphemously alters the transcribed word of God (like a transgressive translator), when the author writes, he knows that he must die in order for his text to be read. Barthes' suggestion that 'the birth of the reader must be at the cost of the death of the Author'[38] is accepted by Rushdie, who complies with this need while writing. To Blanchot's argument, Parkin-Gounelas adds:

> The material presence of language (its acoustic properties, or its presence as ink and paper) can be seen as an attempt to supplement or disguise this originary lack, the destruction of the thing. . . . In seeking to recover that which it had to destroy in order to come into existence, literature, like language, perpetually repeats the paradox of its own death.[39]

In other words, the explicitness of the symbolization of Salman the Scribe threatened with death for blasphemy as the inevitable death of the author possesses so strong a 'material presence' that perhaps this is an effort to survive 'the destruction of the thing' that is the death of the author. By including a character called Salman the Scribe, the author is constantly referred back to and thereby resurrected by the text which after having been read, carries out his death. The fatwa text, though, does not name the writer who should be punished by its edict. The writer is the anonymous 'author of the book entitled *The Satanic Verses*', and even this identifier is further anonymized by the end of the fatwa text to simply 'the author of the book'. Similarly, Malise Ruthven's *A Satanic Affair* is explicitly 'about a book and some of its readers' and 'not about Rushdie'.[40] It is almost as if the Ayatollah's refusal to name Salman Rushdie in the fatwa text has caused Rushdie's later anonymity. Likewise, Rushdie writes about his period in police protection following the fatwa: 'my own name was never used. I learned to answer to other names. I was "the Principal"'.[41] If the author is not named by the text which demands his death, then, contrary to Salman the Scribe whose death is demanded in the novel, the author, absent from the fatwa text, has already died; when, for Barthes, 'this disconnection occurs, the voice loses its origin, the author enters into his own death, writing begins'.[42] His text has become what Barthes strives for: 'a multi-dimensional space in which a variety of writings, none of them original, blend and clash'[43] – something controlled by the reader in the world of the text after the death of the author.

The fatwa, Rushdie argues, is invalid, as it 'contravenes fundamental principles of Islamic law; and since it was issued without the faintest pretence of any legal process'.[44] In fact, the fatwa can be further disputed, as Malise Ruthven claims that 'the Islamic laws of blasphemy . . . only applied to Muslim lands'.[45] Shabbir Akhtar suggests that the punishment for blasphemy according to Sharia law is not the death penalty, but that this is the punishment for apostasy: he claims that the Qur'an and all schools of Sharia law endorse 'capital punishment for public recantation coupled with active opposition to the House of Islam', and that 'particularly in Indian Subcontinental contexts, a man's *izzat* (roughly speaking, honour) is thought to be at stake if a family member converts to another faith. There is immense social pressure to disown the apostate, if not to kill him or her'.[46] Rules surrounding what can and cannot be spoken or written tend to be governed by laws of slander and libel. The libel law is defined as 'any published statement damaging to the reputation of a person. In [a] wider sense, any writing of a treasonable, seditious, or immoral kind. Also, the act or crime of publishing such a statement or writing' (OED). Slander refers to 'the utterance or dissemination of false statements or reports concerning a person, or malicious misrepresentation of his actions, in order to defame or injure him; calumny, defamation' but also, 'a source of shame or dishonour; a discreditable act; a disgrace; a wrong' (OED). This second sense provides an explanation for the treatment of writers in *Shame* and *The Satanic Verses*, including the poet who 'had been hung upside-down by the ankles and beaten' until he 'had the poetry shaken out of him' (28, 158) and the writer Baal who was 'sentenced to be beheaded' by Mahound, who sees 'no difference' between 'whores and writers', both being 'people [he] can't forgive' (392).

Beheaded and beaten writers are censored by being silenced in Rushdie's texts, and this image is best examined in the character of Bilquis, who is an example of Bhabha's decontextualized 'subject-matter or . . . content of a cultural tradition'.[47] Bilquis is transplanted from a small family into an extended household with an 'enormous stock of relatives' with a language providing 'a quite specific name for each conceivable relative' all living together in a mixed-gender 'wicked bedchamber' (75). Bilquis is 'overwhelmed, or alienated, in the act of translation'[48] and is thereby censored: she is 'trapped in a language' and her 'tongue was silenced' so that she 'virtually never spoke' (75). Silenced, Bilquis acquires 'the triple reputation of sweet-innocent-child, doormat and fool' (75), characteristics which combined with her dumbness make her signify the doll or dummy that to Julia Kristeva is transposable with the body of a text: Anna Smith describes Kristeva's argument that ventriloquism 'becomes a vital device, for in the form of transposition, it allows the writer a provisional strategy for throwing her voice across the veil of language'.[49] This transposition may be what Kristeva describes: the substitution of a text for speech, which makes language accessible, unveiling it as Bilquis was unveiled when a bomb 'tore the clothes off her body' (63). Or, this transposition could be the one that occurs during translation; the primary OED definition of 'translation' is 'transference; removal or conveyance from one person, place, or condition to another', and the definitions of 'transposition' are, the 'removal from one position to another; transference' and also, 'translation into another language'. Roger Ebbatson suggests that female silence at the moment of translation is a form of resistance: 'in [Rupert Brooke's] South Sea poems the colonial woman resists the pressure to speak or give herself up to the poet in a subaltern silence that blocks and chokes off the narrative drive for mastery'.[50]

Silence is a form of protest for the disenfranchised female in *Midnight's Children*, too: Saleem Sinai's grandmother, known as the Reverend Mother, hides 'behind a deafening wall of soundlessness' (53) because her protests did not prevent her husband from allowing the poet in hiding, Nadir Khan, to shelter in their basement. This apparent silence provides the means of communication via ventriloquism that Kristeva refers to: if the woman is silenced by 'the veil of language', she must refuse to speak within its structures, and instead, learn to speak by 'throwing her voice', thus remaining apparently silent while forcing the text containing the female subject to speak for her. The Reverend Mother's silence becomes a powerful physical force which announces its presence loudly and heavily among the other members of the family: her body 'was swelling, month by month. The unspoken words inside her were blowing her up . . . Mumtaz had the impression that her mother's skin was becoming dangerously stretched' (59). Bilquis, though silenced, follows Kristeva's instructions even more directly: she asks questions of the other women, those who do choose to speak within their masculine linguistic structure (or, from behind 'the veil of language' which constitutes their 'zenana' (75) or secluded female living quarters). Thus, the answers provided by these other women say what Bilquis wants to say without her having to speak: she asks Rani, for example, about the practice of men beating their wives, and the answer provided is an exclamation that Bilquis might have uttered, but doesn't need to, because she has been able to throw her voice like a ventriloquist, and Rani's is the mouth that speaks for her: 'oh, yes, . . . how they all hit! Tharaap! Tharaap!' (76). Bilquis is considered lucky because her husband Raza Hyder 'was a good man who did not beat his wife' (76). Her abstinence from being beaten renders her even further separated from the language, in Kristeva's terms, because Kristeva 'believes that for matter to become "porous" rather than devouring, language must pulverise the female body' (Smith 1996: 188). Both Bilquis's and Rani's stories are only articulated within restricted spaces, and their separate experiences of hysteria may be due to their silenced or restricted expression, after Dianne Hunter's claim that: 'hysteria can be considered as a self-repudiating form of feminine discourse in which the body signifies what social conditions make it impossible to state linguistically'.[51] Kristeva and Clément's study of women and religious rules provides support for this statement; they suggest that though the woman in an Iraqi Sufi community 'has the right to scream, to stammer, or to sing, it is forbidden [for her] to articulate'.[52] This is a different kind of restriction: though the speaker is not silenced, still she says nothing. Rushdie is sensitive to such gradations of censorship; he writes: 'every story one chooses to tell is a kind of censorship, it prevents the telling of other tales' (p. 70). In such examples, it becomes clear that, as Stendhal claims, 'language was given to man to conceal his thoughts', and not to convey them.[53] As Robert Adams suggests,

> Social intercourse provides examples of language used to suppress, rather than express, ideas. The high pressure talker pours forth an unbroken stream of irrelevant detail, not out of an urge to say something, but to prevent something, anything, else from being said.[54]

Both silence and wordiness may thus be used to circumvent censorship. Censorship may also be circumvented by a process of selective translation. Nicholas Harrison suggests that languages have different properties of concealment: the French language, he suggests, acts as 'a kind of veil' in colonized Algeria, veiling the Algerian's 'own voice'.[55] However, Harrison suggests that veiling is not necessarily an example of 'constrained or disguised identity', but instead may be a way to 'construct beauty'.[56] This corresponds with Walter Benjamin's definition of beauty as the 'object in its veil' as opposed to either 'the veil' or 'the veiled object'.[57] Thus, a non-native language can be used as a veil to reconstruct the self and to provide a platform for speech which may be prohibited in the native language. If this speech is performed in order to 'construct beauty', then translation is a positive and enabling mechanism. Other examples of translation into the French language suggest that this may instead be a process of 'constrained or disguised identity', however: 'the French edition of *The Satanic Verses* was released . . . in a pseudonymous translation, using an anagram of [the author's] name'[58]; as a translation process this could not be a more overt attempt to constrain or disguise identity. There is a further element of translation at work in the text: 'at no point . . . does Rushdie refer to the prophet Muhammad by name, nor the city of Mecca, nor to the Sheria law, nor anything directly concerned with Islamic faith' (Walsh, cited in Appignanesi and Maitland 1990: 26); instead, he translates these terms into Mahound, Jahilia and their associated law and religion. By translating the Qur'an and its origin into a 'novel of postwar cultural migrations and diasporas', Yunus Samad suggests, Rushdie 'performs the subversion of its authenticity' through an 'act of cultural translation' that 'relocates the Koran's "intentionality" by repeating and reinscribing it'.[59] This is not the same as writing an allegorical text – the allegory generally relies upon the use of an extended metaphor to produce a reference, whereas Rushdie's revision of the beginning of Islam is precisely that: a rewriting in a new context, a 'cultural translation' that produces a new text rather than alluding to an original. Bhabha has called Rushdie's 'cultural translation' a 'mistranslation'.[60] Indeed, if Rushdie attempted to circumvent censorship by translating his story into a different cultural context, then he failed to avoid censorship as he was subsequently given a death sentence. Perhaps this failure to avoid censorship can be described as a 'mistranslation' or a bad translation, as the 'bad language' was not fully translated into a new cultural context in a way that it would become unrecognizable to its source context. On the other hand, making the 'bad' language unrecognizable in its target context may be a more accurate example of a 'mistranslation'.

Slang and the migrant's double vision

For some, including some of Rushdie's detractors, slang is the equivalent of linguistic transgression, the equivalent of the bodily image of 'malignant cells which destroy vocabulary', according to Andersson and Trudgill.[61] In fact, David Crystal suggests, there are merely 'islands of identifiable usage' of formal

English, and that at all other times, speakers of standard English use informal language, including what would be termed 'slang'.[62] The common disgust at the use of slang is why, Ruthven suggests, Rushdie's depiction of Mahound (who has been compared to the Prophet Muhammad) was so shocking to some readers. Sardar and Davies suggest that Rushdie's writing 'about the Prophet Muhammad and the events of his life' is produced 'to abuse, mock, malign, throw contempt and score ideological points. Why else does the author,' they ask, 'use such language?'.[63] Ruthven writes that, though others have combined 'sexual impropriety' and the Prophet Muhammad in the same text, this has only been done using 'polite academic discourse whereas Rushdie's language is that of the street'.[64] Ruthven's claim reverses linguistic expectations: ordinarily, academic discourse would be more highly regarded and its findings taken more seriously than those of slang or 'street' language. Perhaps it is the power of slang that makes it so threatening, then; Andersson and Trudgill suggest that slang has a very positive function; that is, 'to make your speech vivid, colourful and interesting'.[65] Goonetilleke claims that in *The Satanic Verses*, the unreliably reported incident of the 'satanic verses' may lead 'orthodox interpreters' to 'try and unwrite their story'.[66] This may be taken further, to propose that Rushdie's version of an emerging religion compiled in 'argots and street language'[67] may unwrite the existing version, which (especially as Islam is a religion of learning) is preserved in polite, academic discourse. In *Shame*, the effect of the combination of 'polite' and 'street' languages (here, specifically for comedic purposes) is transformative: 'comedy enters [the] bloodstream, effects a permanent mutation' (130). Rushdie cites changing language as a key concern of good novels: 'those which attempt radical reformulations of language, form and ideas, those that attempt to do what the word *novel* seems to insist upon: to see the world anew'.[68]

Homi Bhabha addresses those literary conservative fears about 'mutations', 'reformulations' and seeing the world 'anew'. He suggests that it is only nationalist discourses that attempt 'to produce the idea of the nation as a continuous narrative of national progress'.[69] Instead, he claims that 'nations, like narratives, lose their origins'. Like Rushdie's language, constructed from puns, renamings and hybrids, Bhabha points to the 'ambivalence of language' which forms 'the discourse of the nation'.[70] According to Bhabha, when the ambivalence of 'colonial discourse' is disclosed, it 'disrupts its authority' with 'a double vision'.[71] Language which disrupts authority may be considered transgressive or obscene; this corresponds with Robert Adams's description of swearing as a tool, a linguistic device used as a method of trickery, in his assessment of the practice of swearing in baseball games:

> Direct personal insult is only the upper register of a larger duplicity that's involved in making one's opponent unexpectedly play two games at once, or a second instead of a first. Even with a minimum of speech, the simple acts of interruption, distraction, erratic timing, and irrelevant impulse may be acts of disconcerting aggression against an opponent and his game.[72]

Making 'one's opponent' (the colonized, perhaps) 'play two games at once' forces their double vision, if colonial discourse can be expressed as a kind of 'duplicity'. This double vision, Bhabha suggests, is in *The Satanic Verses*, 'the migrant's'.[73]

More recent postcolonial theorists have questioned Bhabha's term, noting its 'inflexibility and partiality', and claiming that 'cultural identity' is constructed through a process of '"aggregation" instead of the rigidly dualistic fusion implied by hybridity'.[74] This more flexible relationship creates a space between languages in which transgressive language can operate without necessarily being tabooed, whereas a hybrid may itself be seen as taboo. Andersson and Trudgill cite Leach's argument that things which are 'contradictory or anomalous in some way are often tabooed'[75] in order to make a further connection between the double vision that causes hybrid language and 'bad' or transgressive language. The migrant's double vision may be 'the truest eye',[76] so when presented with a new version of the life of Muhammad, written in a hybrid slang, their keen eye may be strongly influenced. Robert J. C. Young cites Bakhtin's claim that 'hybridity delineates the way in which language, even within a single sentence, can be double-voiced'.[77] As if this 'double-voiced' quality of language can endow the words spoken with double the strength, volume or clarity, Young suggests that hybrid languages become the most powerful, because 'they preserve the real historical forms of cultural contact' and suggest 'a different model from that of the straightforward power relation of dominance of colonizer over colonized'.[78] In *Midnight's Children*, the power gained by the double-voiced individual who was born at the moment of Indian independence (and is thus in possession of an even greater share of this power, according to the narrative) is demonstrated by Saleem Sinai when he claims that 'it is possible to create past events just by saying they occurred' (443). It is this power of hybrid language that Rushdie claims when he refers to Indian writing in English as 'twice-born'.[79] He goes further, and suggests that 'English has become an Indian language', and that 'the East is imposing itself on the

West, rather than the other way around'.[80] Rushdie discusses this linguistic change symbolically in geographical terms:

> The map of the world, in the standard Mercator projection, is not kind to India, making it look substantially smaller than, say, Greenland. On the map of world literature, too, India has been undersized for too long. Fifty years after India's independence, however, that age of obscurity is coming to an end. India's writers have torn up the old map, and are busily drawing up their own.[81]

This stance has probably encouraged critical responses that engage with the idea of translation as transnationalism, for example, Homi Bhabha's conjecture that the terms 'transnational' and 'translational' are fundamentally connected when cultures come into contact.

4

Translation and Form: The Short Story

By examining Rushdie's short stories in *East, West* and the parallel which I suggest exists between them and Goethe's three translation types, this chapter shows that the short story form might be more inherently suitable for translating the stories of places, ideas, people and times. This chapter compares Rushdie's short stories from the three sections of his *East, West* collection (titled 'East', 'West' and 'East, West') with Goethe's definition of three types of translation in his *Book of West and East* (*West-Őstlicher Diwan*) published in 1819, to suggest that Rushdie's three sets of short stories correspond with these three definitions of translation.

Because translation is, as D'Alembert suggests, 'such a complex matter'[1], translation theorists provide broad definitions of what translation is and what a translator does. These definitions present new ways to read texts which are not translations in the strict sense of being a kind of duplicate of an existing text presented in a different language. Rushdie's short stories are not translations of the same narratives already written in a different language, but rather, translations of existing stories according to the definitions of translation proposed by theorists like Lefevere, who suggests that a translation may be, broadly, 'a foreign text' represented 'in one's own culture'.[2]

If a translation is, as Lefevere claims, 'a text that represents another',[3] then Rushdie's texts represent, in the 'East' section, Eastern stories for Western and postcolonial readers, because the geographical location of these stories is the East, and the tales and myths that inform these stories are Eastern ones, whether they refer to stories from *The Arabian Nights*, the Qur'an or (Colonial) popular myth. In the 'West' section, the translations represent Western stories for Eastern and postcolonial readers by revising such mainstays of Western literature as *Hamlet*, *The Wizard of Oz* and (perhaps a dubious fiction) Christopher Columbus and his 'discovery' of America, in stories set in European locations. The 'East, West' section is more complicated: here, Eastern and Western stories are presented together in the stories of migrant people who use bilingual dialect. These are postcolonial stories for Western and Eastern readers. The tension created by translations of stories from the East to the West and the West to the East resembles the similar struggle between translations created in colonial India where, as Susan Bassnett and Harish Trivedi suggest, 'the Indian literary space was a vigorously contested terrain, with the impulse for an eager reception of the new Western modes of literature being counterpointed by a tendency to resist such influence, often through reasserting the older indigenous forms of Indian writing'.[4]

In his *Book of West and East*, Goethe suggests that 'there are three kinds of translation'.[5] The first type 'acquaints us with foreign countries on our own terms'.[6] This type of translation is produced in a 'simple prosaic' form, which Goethe suggests is the most appropriate, because it allows us to be surprised by 'foreign excellence in the midst of our national homeliness, our everyday existence'.[7] This type of translation is used by Rushdie in the 'East' section of his *East, West* short story collection. 'Foreign' stories are presented to Western readers in simple prose which allows the reader more easily to consume unfamiliar words, concepts and images in a narrative form which resembles the familiar short story or fairy tale, and involves recognizable character types and personal narrators who more readily provide access to 'foreign' locations and concepts.

'Good Advice is Rarer than Rubies' is a story about migration, and the myth of the desire of South Asians to emigrate from the East, to the West. The loss of this fantasy of England when Rehana's immigration application is unsuccessful causes her advice expert to cry, 'But this is tragedy! . . . Oh, how I pray that you had taken up my offer! . . . It is spoilt, all spoilt' (p. 15). At the same time, the story uses popular Western mythology about the East, informed by the imagery and storytelling devices of *The Arabian Nights*. The first image which replicates the formulae of *The Arabian Nights* is the construction of the story's main character who resembles the dramatically beautiful women who populate those stories, and whose environment evokes the mystery surrounding those women: 'the dawn bus, its headlamps still shining, brought Miss Rehana to the gates of the British Consulate. It arrived pushing a cloud of dust, veiling her beauty from the eyes of strangers until she descended' (p. 5). The use of Arabian Nights symbolism enables the Western reader to engage with an unfamiliar culture from a position of some familiarity, even though this familiarity is based on a collection of fairy tales which was originally presented in Edward Lane's English translation as evidence that 'the Arabs' were 'far more gullible than educated

European readers' and as evidence of the strangeness of people who reputedly 'did not make the same clear distinction between the rational and the fictitious'.[8] This tactic makes the collection accessible to the target Western audience, translating a foreign text after Goethe's definition of the first type of translation, in a manner that 'acquaints us with foreign countries on our own terms'.[9]

This story conforms to Goethe's formulation of the first type of translation in linguistic terms, too. The text is presented in 'simple prosaic' form, in short passages constructed from sentences which echo the bold statements of fairy tales: for example, 'Miss Rehana told the driver it was a beautiful bus, and he jumped down and held the door open for her, bowing theatrically as she descended' (p. 5). The explicit theatricality of this gesture is usually absent from a fairy tale, but the princess-like image is instantly recognizable. Goethe suggests that using simple prose is the most suitable method of allowing the reader to absorb 'foreign excellence in the midst of . . . [their] everyday existence'.[10] In addition, foreign phrases and objects inserted into the text are translated or defined in simple terms. The migration 'advice expert' Muhammad Ali shouts after the applicant Rehana who is ignoring his advice, 'what goes of my father's if you are?' (p. 12). This odd construction is immediately clarified by the 'translated' idiom in parenthesis, so the reader learns that this phrase means, 'what was it to him' (p. 12). The same approach is used to define unfamiliar objects, like the 'bus's "front mud-guard"' which is immediately identified as 'the bumper' (p. 13) in a translation which, despite its brevity, reveals much about the differences between bus travel in the UK and South Asia, British buses are protected from bumps and South Asian buses are protected from swelling mud. Other unfamiliar terms are translated by their full contextual explanations, like the 'lala' who is described as guarding the gates of the British consulate 'in a gold-buttoned khaki uniform with a cockaded turban' (p. 5), immediately clarifying the identity of this character. In this way, the foreign word, though immediately startling and unfamiliar on the page, is brought to full clarity with the kind of 'fluency' which, according to Lawrence Venuti, is conventionally required of the translator.[11] Roger Berger claims that Anglophone African short stories produce location the same way, instead of through 'cartographic' descriptions of landscape.[12] Berger suggests that in this way the short story differs from the Anglophone African novel, where 'cartographic' landscapes are commonplace, and serve to 'repossess the appropriated land'.[13]

The simple prosaic method of presenting foreign objects and words continues in the second story in *East, West*, 'The Free Radio'. The narrator describes the employment of Ramani the rickshaw-wallah in careful detail; his customer the 'thief's widow' has to 'pay for the ride' in the rickshaw which is big enough to hold her and her 'five kiddies', although the effort leaves Ramani 'puffing hard' and 'the veins . . . standing out on his legs' (p. 21). Grammatically, the story is presented in less familiar language; constructions like the narrator's assertion that 'must-be she had decided already to put her hooks into Ramani' (p. 21) and the thief's widow's addressing the narrator as 'mister teacher sahib *retired*' (p. 24) are clear in meaning to the reader from a different culture, but retain the foreignness of their original context, which again permits access to the foreign 'on our own terms', as Goethe describes.[14] Because these non-standard grammatical choices are presented in the speech of characters or in the narrative of an unreliable character-narrator, the reader can more easily adapt to their 'foreignness' than he or she would if faced with a more confrontational authorial narrator.

Like the storyteller delivering oral narrative to members of his community, this narrator expresses personal involvement in the narrative, which informs the presentation of the characters in his story, as he introduces Ramani as a 'stone-head' (p. 19), and his love-interest the thief's widow as 'a truly cheap type' (p. 21). His storytelling style is similarly unreliable due to his personal involvement in the narrative: the development of the plot is dependent on the narrator's choices; he says, 'for a time . . . I closed my eyes to this affair of Ramani and the thief's widow, because I had done all I could and there were many other things in the town to interest a person like myself'. Some of these 'other things' are equally distasteful to the narrator, including the forced sterilization taking place in a caravan: the narrator 'heard rumours of what was happening in the caravan but . . . closed [his] ears' (p. 24). Again, this narrative style is reminiscent of *The Arabian Nights* where the narrator Scheherazade's presence and her vulnerability alter the reader's engagement with the stories: the narrator's predicament becomes just as important as that of the characters whose stories are told.

A careful description of the sterilization programme is another method of allowing readers access to the foreign culture on their 'own terms'. Historical and political contextual information about the armband-wearing young men of the 'new Youth Movement' who recruit people for sterilization 'in national interest' (p. 26) at 'the time of the State of Emergency' (p. 24) is worked into the narrative as a set of clues for the reader to follow to become more familiar with the location and observe how the culture influences what is otherwise a commonplace story of inappropriate romance. Far from being a myth, the free radio given to men in return for their patriotic act of sterilization is presented as factual by the narrator, who describes how this sometime common scheme is, unbeknownst to Ramani, now 'a dead duck, long gone, . . . *funtoosh*' (p. 26).[15] For months, in anticipation of his free radio, Ramani would 'put one hand up to his ear as if he were already holding the blasted machine in it, and he would mimic broadcasts with a certain energetic skill' (p. 27).

The radio, perhaps because of its solid predecessor, which was according to Ramani, 'some years back' presented to 'Laxman the tailor' following his operation (p. 26), is real despite its absence. Ramani's 'high, ridiculous falsetto' performance of 'playback music' and All-India Radio news announcements causes his neighbours to believe that 'it was really on its way, or even that it was already there, cupped invisibly against his ear as he rode his rickshaw around the streets of the town' (p. 27). Hollywood (or Bollywood) fame, though, is mythologized in the story. After learning that he will not receive a radio in return for his sterilization, Ramani transfers his hopes to film stardom, proclaiming, 'I am off to Bombay, where I will become a bigger film star than Shashi Kapoor or Amitabh Bachchan even' (p. 30). Ramani's luxurious lifestyle in preparation for fame takes place at a geographical distance from the rest of the story and outside the view of the narrator. Perhaps for this reason, it is doubted: in reference to the fairy tale about the boy who cried wolf, the authenticity of his fake radio causes the narrator to doubt a success which may well have been real, remembering 'the huge mad energy which he had poured into the act of conjuring reality, by an act of magnificent faith, out of the hot thin air between his cupped hand and his ear' (p. 32).

It is a different type of faith from Ramani's magnificent, creative faith that the third story in the 'East' section, 'The Prophet's Hair', is concerned with. The relics of the Prophet Muhammad evoke a fearsome power in a family who are compelled to disclose their true feelings while in possession of the relic, but the subsequent state of conflict is the reason behind their involvement with crime gangs, theft and violence. Islamic and Arabian Nights references combine in the recurring dual imagery of Paradise and bloody violence. The story begins in 'a yard wet with the blood of a slaughtered chicken' and the violent assault of a young man called Atta, who was 'beaten within an inch of his life' (p. 35). His 'torn and bleeding' body was found on the banks of the 'gardens of Shalimar' at dawn, by 'a flower-vendor [who] was rowing his boat through water to which the cold of night had given the cloudy consistency of wild honey' (p. 35).

Even more than the other stories in the 'East' section, this story owes its structure to *The Arabian Nights*. The story of the battered man found by the flower seller ends abruptly and the flower vendor 'plays no further part in our story' (p. 36). Instead, the narrative is taken up by Huma, the sister of the beaten man. Her attempt to hire a thief is structured with a new, separate beginning, like each successive Arabian Nights story. This layer of narrative begins like a separate tale: 'the story of the rich idiot [in reference to her brother Atta] who had come looking for a burglar was . . . common knowledge in those insalubrious gullies' (p. 37). And again, like those Arabian Nights women, Huma has 'exceptional beauty'. The magical happenings in this story do not resemble the fairy-tale magic of *The Arabian Nights*, though. The story begins in 'a winter so fierce it could crack men's bones as if they were glass'; this extreme cold is presented as a magical 'spell' (p. 35) as much as a seasonal one. Religious miracles take place in a magic realist context which invites the reader to question why religion (and specifically, Islam) is allowed such power in a culture that its containment in a relic can cause men to feel that they are bursting, 'as though, [as Huma and Atta's father experiences] under the influence of the misappropriated relic, he had filled up with some spectral fluid which might at any moment ooze uncontrollably from his every bodily opening' (p. 45). The owner of this relic reveals unsavoury truths about his unhappiness in marriage and 'the existence of a mistress' (p. 45), and orders his daughter into purdah before 'constructing a great heap of books [excluding only the Qur'an] in the garden and setting fire to it' (p. 46). Sexual deviance, female seclusion and book burning are Western myths about Islam, repeated here and presented as desperate behaviour which results in the death of Huma, Atta and their father and causing their mother to be 'driven mad by the general carnage' (p. 56). Western myths of Islam are called into question by this story, because of the dissolution of the family as a result of the sudden imposition of what apparently constitutes religious devoutness. In this way, the story does what Ashcroft, Griffiths and Tiffin suggest is the function of postcolonial literature and produces a 'subversive' text.[16]

To return to the linguistic aspect of the short stories, Andre Lefevere claims that 'a translation should . . . sound "foreign" enough to its reader for that reader to discern the workings of the original language that expresses the language game, the culture of which the original was a part, shining through the words on the translated page'. Lefevere refers to a reader who is able to read both the language of the original and of the translation, and this is why he suggests that readers rarely exist nowadays who are able to, and who possess the desire to, 'read original and translation side by side', and 'appreciate the difference in linguistic expression as expressing the difference between the two language games'.[17] Interestingly, Lefevere goes on to say that 'this is a type of translation no longer practised in our day and age, simply because the audience for it has almost ceased to exist'.[18] Postcolonial writing challenges these assumptions. In fact, allowing the 'culture of which the original was a part' to shine 'through the words on the translated page', or the page of the postcolonial short story, is exactly what Rushdie does. This is especially apparent in passages of dialogue in his short stories, energized by foreign words like 'ji', 'bivi' and 'sahib', and made 'foreign' by the frequently '*unsaxogrammatical*' (p. 65) sentence structure. This is not something that Rushdie does alone, though he was the first to use the concept of the empire 'writing back',[19] and openly addresses the ways that language can empower postcolonial writers to produce an English which sounds foreign to the former colonizers.[20] Berger suggests that the postcolonial short story (with reference to the Anglophone African short story) aims to produce a new English language, citing Chinua Achebe's insistence that the English language is able to carry the weight of his African experience, although it will have to be a new English, altered to suit its 'new African surroundings'.[21] Paul Brians suggests that in *Things Fall Apart*, Achebe does this by privileging the language of the Ibo characters:

> The language of the novel is simple but dignified. When the characters speak, they use an elevated diction which is meant to convey the sense of Ibo speech. This choice of language was a brilliant and innovative stroke, given that most earlier writers had relegated African characters to pidgin or inarticulate gibberish. One has the sense of listening to another tongue, one with a rich and valuable tradition.[22]

The use of 'foreign' language, narrative structure and imagery is a particular feature of the postcolonial short story. This is what makes the postcolonial short story so similar to translation. And Ian Reid suggests that the colonial and postcolonial period was particularly relevant to short fictional forms; he says that, 'the tensions and transitions between different forms of coloniality have done much to shape the history of the modern short story'.[23]

Goethe's second type of translation is one that reproduces colonial covetousness, in which 'the translator . . . tries to appropriate foreign content and reproduce it in his own sense'. This involves the adaptation of 'foreign words' to the translator's 'pronunciation', as well as an equal adaptation of 'feelings, thoughts, and even objects'.[24] This type of translation is apparent in the second, 'West', section of Rushdie's short story collection, where English and American stories, characters and mythologies are adapted into a new, postcolonial idiom.

The 'West' section begins by selecting a pillar of Western literature to deconstruct: the story 'Yorick' revises *Hamlet* by providing a kind of prequel to the play, installing Yorick as its main character. Like the postcolonial who revises history, or as Rushdie puts it, 'remak[es] the past, reinventing it for their own purposes',[25] this story's narrator proposes that Shakespeare's Prince Hamlet 'is quite mistaken in believing the ghost's name to be Hamlet too', and that in fact the king's name was 'Horwendillus' (p. 65). This challenges the legitimacy of the original story by suggesting that it is based on a questionable history. It also engages directly with *Tristram Shandy*, evoking another subversive and fragmented text in order to challenge the ultimate colonial, canonical literary figure. Then, making use of the notion of an Oedipal relationship between Hamlet and his mother, Rushdie constructs a primal scene where a young Hamlet witnesses his parents having sex and misinterprets his father's 'grunting, roaring' and 'falling wildly upon the lady' who 'sobs and flails', 'squeals and shrieks' (p. 75) as attempted murder. Hamlet's voyeurism is punished: his father 'thrashes him, & lashes, & then thrashes once again' (p. 76) awakening in the child 'dark dreams of revenge' (p. 76) and the result in this retelling is Hamlet's orchestration of his father's murder. By rewriting *Hamlet*, Rushdie is performing Goethe's second type of translation, in which 'the translator . . . tries to appropriate foreign content and reproduce it in his own sense'.[26] Rushdie's use of archaic language and antique objects is an example of this translation method in practice. The narrator reconstructs the seventeenth-century writer's workshop by listing the items which would have been found inside and around it in the manner of a museum inventory: 'strong vellum' created by 'ancient-time papersmiths', 'letter-boxes, desk drawers, old trunks, the most secret pockets of courting lovers, . . . attics, cellars' (p. 63). The purpose of this collection of antique objects is not the restoration of the story, though, but the 'annihil[ation]' and 'destruction' of it (p. 63).

Though this story is narrated from the perspective of somebody who finds evidence of flaws in the historical accuracy of Shakespeare's *Hamlet* and who is removed from the story by 'multicoloured generations' (p. 83), the narrative borrows seventeenth-century textual practices including the use of ampersands in place of the word 'and', as well as frequent capitalization and italicization. In addition, the conversations which motivate the plot are presented in script format to more closely echo the original play while professing to recast dominant interpretations of characters and plot. By falsifying the history behind the play, the story seeks to overturn Shakespeare's canonical power and recast the canon from a postcolonial position, questioning dominant readings of history. Yet, conversely, by making such close reference to *Hamlet*, the original story is also authenticated: as Lefevere suggests, the original lends authority to the translation: 'if you produce a text that "refers to" another text, rather than producing your own, you are most likely to do so because you think the other text enjoys a prestige far greater than the prestige your own text might possibly aspire to. In other words, you invoke the authority of the text you represent'.[27] Because this story is a type of translation, it relies on the original (which therefore must be a text of value) in order to maintain its legitimacy. Traditionally, though, the translation would hold the original story in high regard instead of distorting it; because of this, the distortion of *Hamlet* and the rubbishing of its history implies that this translation too is a questionable narrative. In fact, the narrator admits in the final part of the story that 'Yorick' is 'a COCK-AND-BULL story' (p. 83), which as Rocio Davis points out, adds a further dimension to the retelling of this story, as it is produced 'in the style of *Tristram Shandy*'.[28] From another perspective, by reducing 'Yorick' to a 'cock-and-bull story', the previously accepted authority of the original is reinstated: this poppycock fiction does not shake the canonical status of the original like it might have done if the story was more fully supported by its narrator. Postcolonial comedy and fantasy, as Graeme Harper suggests, 'become . . . sites for challenging or confirming identity, of recognizing or attempting to negate cultural hegemony, of appropriating imposed forms of social or artistic engagement'.[29] The genre of the text which proposes this challenge ('cock-and-bull' or not) may not matter. In the end, *Hamlet*'s solidity has been questioned not by a sustained scholarly act but by 'a COCK-AND-BULL story', further questioning the stability of its foundations.

The second story in the 'West' section tackles a more modern but equally powerful fiction: 'At the Auction of the Ruby Slippers' rewrites *The Wizard of Oz* and along with it, the myth of the Hollywood film industry. In contrast to the fairy tale and filmic magic of the original, this story employs science fiction and magic realist elements to construct a brutal economic auction process where 'guards at the exits crack their bullwhips idly' (p. 92) and 'memorabilia junkies' are electrocuted by the 'state-of-the-art defence system' which reacts indiscriminately to any contact with the case containing the ruby slippers. The common science fiction trope of using coloured skies to immediately evoke an alien landscape is adapted to the auction room, where movie stars have visible auras which have been 'developed in collaboration with masters of Applied Physics', of 'platinum, golden, silver, bronze' or 'livid green, mustard yellow, inky red'. If a non-movie star should 'collide' with these auras, he or she is 'knocked to the floor by a security team' (p. 88). The Hollywood mainstay *The Wizard of Oz* is a contemporary equivalent of *Hamlet*, a fiction that has become an institution representing an unquestionable story of undoubted legitimacy and fame. Rushdie writes about this film in his essay 'Out of Kansas', suggesting that the dominant fiction to emerge from this film was, in fact, not the one played out on the screen, but the illusion about its production: 'behind-the-scenes tales show us, sadly, that a film that has made so many audiences so happy was not a happy film to make'.[30] After Shakespeare, Hollywood is the second influential Western fiction to be deconstructed by Rushdie's translation of the story into a fierce commodity and a process of exchange, where money can buy anything, because, 'thanks to the infinite bounty of the Auctioneers, any of us, cat, dog, man, woman, child, can be a blue-blood; can be . . . *somebody*' (p. 103).

The third dominant Western fictional form addressed in the 'West' section is the fiction inherent in Western or Colonial history. Questioning the historical truths on which colonial history was built, 'Christopher Columbus & Queen Isabella of Spain Consummate their Relationship (Santa Fé, AD 1492)' addresses the idea of the 'discovery' of America. The idea that an individual has the capability to 'discover' or create an already populated continent is a form of perception that allowed modern colonialism to flourish. Though the story translates Columbus's life story and his struggle to secure funds for his expedition, at the same time, the narrator employs the contemporary rhyme, which states: 'in fourteen hundred and ninety two' Columbus sailed 'the ocean blue' (p. 107). The invocation of this rhyme flags up the revisionary aspect of the story instead of presenting the story as a historical tale, similar to the museum aspect of 'Yorick'. The purpose of this rhyme is also called into question by its use in this context: such inane rhymes are taught to school children so that they unquestioningly ingest the ideas that those rhymes convey, accepting the notion that in 1492, one man named Christopher Columbus discovered America. Adapting 'foreign content' to 'his own sense' (as is the formula of Goethe's second translation method), Rushdie presents Columbus as a migrant, stating that 'foreigners forget their place (having left it behind)' (p. 108) and thereby transplanting contemporary migration and postcolonial issues into a fifteenth-century context.

When Rushdie writes about *Hamlet* and Christopher Columbus in the West stories, and about the Prophet Muhammad in the East story, he 'produce[s] a text that "refers to" another text, rather than producing [his] own', because of the 'prestige' enjoyed by the original.[31] These three stories have similar aims: to use the authority of the original stories (leaving aside the fictionality of those stories for the moment) in order to endow the revision of those stories with some of that prestige, as Lefevere suggests when he claims that a translation borrows the prestige of the text it translates. At the same time, though, these are original stories rather than, for example, an Urdu translation of *Hamlet*, or an English translation of the Hadith, the text which describes the Prophet Muhammad's life. Because of this, the accepted prestige and authority of those original stories is called into question, as is the reader's preconceptions about those stories, including, for example, the notion that Christopher Columbus discovered America or that Shakespeare was the best writer ever to have lived and Hamlet the ultimate tragic hero.

According to George Steiner, translation is 'that which gives language life beyond the moment and place of immediate utterance or transcription'.[32] Rushdie provides the stories that he refers to with 'life beyond the moment and place' of their original telling or transcription; in this way, the method of his storytelling causes the new stories that he tells to become translations. Because translation can lift language – or the story – from its original context, the text which has been translated becomes disconnected from its time and location, and both the original and the translated text are legitimized and made portable by the translation process. At the same time, the original is legitimized by its perceived value and need, which is indicated by the fact that a translation has been produced.

The third type of translation is one which Goethe calls 'the highest and final one'.[33] This is 'the one in which the aim is to make the original identical with the translation, so that one should be valued not instead of the other, but in the other's stead'.[34] This method of representation involves the translator becoming 'closely' attached 'to his original', abandoning the 'Universe of Discourse'[35] of the target 'nation'.[36] Instead of shaping the text to the taste of the reader, this type of translation requires that 'the taste of the multitude must first be shaped to accept it'.[37] This more radical type of translation allows revisions to be made to existing ideas of literature and the text, and to literary canons, and in this sense, it is very close to the purpose of postcolonial literature. This mutual blending of literary forms and reader expectations is the type of writing used in Rushdie's third section, titled 'East, West', in acknowledgement of the harmonious blending of national literatures, or Universes of Discourse.

The 'East, West' section of the collection begins with a story entitled 'The Harmony of the Spheres'. This is a title which refers to the underlying aim of the three stories in this section, which is to discuss the conjunction of East and West in a harmonious partnership. This conforms to Goethe's third type of translation, a harmonizing process, where there is no dominant audience for whom the translation is created, and there is no dominant narrative form, or 'Universe of Discourse'[38] to which the writer is compelled to adhere. The story is concerned with the suicide of a young writer called Eliot Crane, whose mood swings between wild laughter and 'deep depressions' (p. 128) are imagined as hemispheres of the Earth or of the brain which cannot be made to function in harmony. Crane's delusions involve alien invaders who 'had sneaked into Britain when certain essential forms of vigilance had been relaxed' (p. 127), signalling the concern with postcolonial migration and more earthly types of illegal 'alien'. Eliot Crane perhaps combines the bleak poetry of T S Eliot and his contemporary Hart Crane whose writing was more optimistic, yet who committed suicide. This story is also concerned with fiction: Eliot Crane's delusions were not all fictional: his affair with the narrator's wife was not a fantasy. This revealed truth causes the 'collapse of harmony' (p. 146) as the more comfortable fiction – where the narrator's wife was faithful and his friend's disturbing ideas delusional – is proven false.

'Chekov and Zulu' is titled in reference to the two Star Trek characters, whose names are used to disguise the identities of diplomats, though Sulu's name has been incorrectly transcribed in the manner of bilingual language adaptation. The language used throughout this story is the language of the bilingual, who mixes languages and grammars together to create something new that is not quite English. The story begins with a conversation employing both English and Urdu words, and constructed from non-standard grammar:

> "Adaabarz, Mrs Zulu. Permission to enter?"
>
> "Of course, come in, Dipty sahib, why such formality?"
>
> "Sorry to disturb you on a Sunday, Mrs Zulu, but Zulu-tho hasn't been in touch this morning?"
>
> "With me? Since when he contacts me on official trip? Why to hit a telephone call when he is probably enjoying?" (p. 149)

This blending of languages and grammars is done in abandonment of the 'Universe of Discourse'[39] of the target 'nation',[40] in order to force the reader's dialectal taste to change shape in order to accept a new syntax, in compliance with Goethe's third translation method.

The particular names chosen for the characters connect literature (Chekov) and Africa (by the mistranscription of Sulu into Zulu) in a way that implies a concern with colonial and postcolonial literature. *Star Trek* promoted an ideal and equal future where cultures, races and continents on Earth had no perceptible differences (in the face of further away aliens), and the native languages of the crew were only present in their accents because all spoke fluent English. The story uses this harmonious linguistic and cultural space as a point from which to translate, and the *Star Trek* mission to overcome hostile aliens is translated into the diplomats' mission to overcome terrorism in South Asia. *Star Trek* becomes a metaphor where 'Beam me up' (p. 166) becomes the escape code, employed in order to help the diplomats cope with their dangerous mission which appears less threatening when translated into a fantasy.

The final story in the 'East, West' section, and the final story in the collection, is 'The Courter', which, like the opening story ('Good Advice is Rarer than Rubies') deals with issues of migration and the myth of the desire of South Asians to emigrate to the UK. The location of this story is London, though, in opposition to the first story where Rehana purposely failed her emigration test so that she could remain in Lahore. In 'The Courter', Mary the ayah, 'a tiny sixty-year-old Indian lady with her greying hair tied behind her head in a neat bun' explains her 'unpredictabl[e]', 'myster[ious]' 'heart trouble' as 'homesickness' (p. 208). East and West are made explicit in this story: 'it was England that was breaking her heart, breaking it by not being India. London was killing her, by not being Bombay. . . . her heart . . . was being pulled both East and West' (p. 209).

Translated fictions are both Eastern and Western in this story – Scheherazade, Marilyn Monroe and the Flintstones are the fictional backdrop for the migrated family, and these combine to influence the child narrator with both locations. The thorough combination of locations causes something that if not harmonious exactly, at least allows the narrator to 'come and go', offers 'choices'. This is a complicated offer, though, and in the end, the narrator states: 'I do not choose between you. . . . I choose neither of you, and both. Do you hear? I refuse to choose' (p. 211). Lefevere contests 'the persistent notion that translation is mainly a matter of dictionaries and grammars'.[41] Instead, he claims that 'translation can be studied as one of the strategies cultures develop to deal with what lies outside their boundaries and to maintain their own culture while doing so – the kind of strategy that ultimately belongs in the realm of change and survival, not in dictionaries and grammars'.[42] Postcolonial literature – and especially Rushdie's fiction – suggests that survival is also a matter of dictionaries and grammars.

Berger claims that it is only linguistics which allows Anglophone African short story writers to represent their landscapes: 'a sense of place – however problematically – is first invoked by the speech-act elements framing the texts', instead of by writing descriptively about the landscape. These speech acts, Berger continues, include 'cover illustration and design' which 'contribute a sense of place to these stories, even though this sense of place is curiously based on a rather stereotypical and monolithic image of Africa – an image that many African short stories indirectly attempt to subvert'.[43]

'The Firebird's Nest'

Rushdie's more recent short story, 'The Firebird's Nest' (originally published in 1997 in *The New Yorker*), discusses sati or Hindu widow burning, something that was once a practice and has now gained the status of a colonial myth. The story engages with the mythology that has grown out of this discontinued practice:

> There are cracks big enough to swallow a man.
>
> An apt enough way for a farmer to die: to be eaten by his land.
>
> Women do not die in that way. Women catch fire, and burn. . . .
>
> Yesterday, . . . a woman in a red and gold sari, a fool, ignited in the amphitheatre of the dry waterhole. The men stood along the high rim of the reservoir, watching her burn, shouldering arms in a kind of salute; recognizing, in the wisdom of their manhood, the inevitability of women's fate. The women, their women, screamed. (pp. 45, 47–8)

The story also shares a resemblance to the Bluebeard fairy tale, which was written by Charles Perrault, but has had numerous retellings. In 'The Firebird's Nest', the young wife is taken to the foreign 'kingdom' of Mr Maharaj, a 'prince [who] has become plain Mr Maharaj' but who in his 'country residence' 'is still the prince' (p. 47). Mr Maharaj, like Bluebeard, has a palace, but 'it crumbles, stinks. In her room, the curtains are tattered, the bed precarious' and like Bluebeard's young wife, she is left here alone: 'he installs her, vanishes, without an explanation. She is left to make herself at home' (p. 52). Bluebeard's series of dead wives and the money that they bring is a hidden secret in the original fairy tale, but here the idea is acceptable: a 'pretty young girl' marries 'an old fool' because 'the old fellow will have settled for a small dowry . . . in a long life there may be more than a single dowry. These things add up' (p. 50). The fairy tale structure is also explicit, as if it is the idea of fiction itself which is at question:

> Here Mr Maharaj is still the prince, and she his new princess. As though she had entered a fable, as though she were no more than words crawling along a dry page, or as though she were becoming that page itself, that surface on which her story would be written, and across which there blew a hot and merciless wind, turning her body to papyrus, her skin to parchment, her soul to paper. (p. 47)

The first character perspective is that of the white, western female, whose ideological perspective is broadly feminist, 'she is a woman of modern outlook and does not like it, she tells [her husband], when he speaks this way, herding her sex into these crude corrals, these easy generalisations, even in jest' (p. 48). The second is the upper-caste Indian male who represents the traditional Indian orthodoxy which would have created and maintained the cultural practice of sati, sometimes as a method of colonial protest.[44] At the same time, this character represents the 'brown sahib'[45] who cooperated with colonial structures to change Indian law and society; this character is after all of a wealthy class who has benefited from global travel, education and business. The third perspective is that of the subaltern, as discussed by Dipesh Chakrabarty, who says that, 'struggles and debates around the rather tentative concept of multiculturalism in Western democracies have often fuelled discussions of minority histories' including 'subaltern social groups and classes,' such as, former slaves, working classes, convicts, and women'.[46] Subaltern histories or '"minority histories" can . . . end up as . . . instances of "good history"' – a 'good history' is 'supposed to enrich the subject matter of history and make it more representative of society as a whole'.[47] This is because, as Neil Lazarus claims, 'the disenfranchised sectors of the society' are 'typically an *overwhelming* majority of the population'.[48] In 'The Firebird's Nest', the subaltern group is represented by the men and women living in the rural village visited by the upper-caste Indian and his white, Western wife. The women living in this village, subalterns, are still victim to sati, here presented as an obscured image defining the women's lives. By engaging with the subaltern in Chakrabarty's terms, Rushdie's short story provides a different platform for discussing the postcolonial subject and the way that their life is bound up with translation than his novels, which are usually populated with dominant histories of the rich and powerful. Because of the three characters present in 'The Firebird's Nest', this story bridges (or harmonizes) the three categories and translation types of 'East', 'West' and 'East, West'.

Lefevere argues that 'translation is a channel opened, often not without a certain reluctance, through which foreign influences can penetrate the native culture, challenge it, and even contribute to subverting it'.[49] This is one of the aims and results of postcolonial literature, permitting it to affect literary canons, as Ashcroft, Griffiths and Tiffin suggest:

> The interaction of english writing with the older traditions of orature or literature in post-colonial societies, and the emergence of a writing which has as a major aim the assertion of social and cultural difference, have radically questioned easy assumptions about the characteristics of the genres we usually employ as structuring and categorizing definitives (novel, lyric, epic, play etc.). Our sense, not only of that which ought to enter the canon, but also of what could be given the name "literature", has been altered by writers incorporating and adapting traditional forms of imaginative expression to the exigencies of an inherited english language.[50]

Indeed, Susan Lohafer claims that 'the definition of story' employed by short story theorists 'seemed to lie in the origins of culture, the morphology of folktales, the oral tradition'.[51] As well as the challenge to Shakespeare's position in the literary canon offered by 'Yorick', stories like 'Chekov and Zulu', 'The Free Radio' and 'Good Advice is Rarer than Rubies' incorporate linguistic and structural forms from oral narrative and from non-standard English language both by asserting the 'social and cultural difference' suggested by Ashcroft, Griffiths and Tiffin and by 'incorporating and adapting traditional forms of imaginative expression to the exigencies of an inherited english language'.[52]

Rushdie's *East, West* provides a channel for the penetration of cultures even in the title; the comma in the title resembles a bridge across which this influence may travel. The specific form of the title of *East, West* contributes to the way that the collection is structured and the way that East and West are connected. Rushdie talks about how he selected this title in a 1994 interview. He says that 'the most important part of the title was the comma. Because it seems to me that I am that comma – or at least that I live in that comma'.[53] To compare Rushdie's choice with the similar meaning but completely different construction of Goethe's title enables further interrogation of the two texts. The title of *The Book of West and East* presents the West first and the East second, contrary to Rushdie's title. The insertion of the word 'and' between the two locations forces their total separation and portrays independent and ultimately opposite states of mind and locations.

Of course, Goethe's title is the one chosen by his translator, and in fact, his original title is constructed in a very different way. The original title is *West-Őstlicher Diwan*, which can be translated in various ways, but most notably connects the words meaning 'west' and 'east', though 'Őstlich' can actually mean 'east', 'eastwards' and 'oriental'.[54] Then 'Diwan', for instance, has various senses in English. The divan is an Oriental council of state, a council in general or a court of justice or council chamber.[55] These senses of the word invite a postcolonial reading of the title, suggesting connections to new regimes, legal systems and ideologies, imposed by colonial governments. Other postcolonial concerns, especially with regard to geography and boundaries, are addressed by the sense of the word meaning 'a room having one side entirely open towards a court, garden, river, or other prospect'.[56] This image of an open fortress evokes a sense of conquered land and flourishing colonials who want to keep an eye on, but have no real need to secure, their borders from submissive 'natives'. Other exotic representations of this word include the sense of 'a name sometimes given to a smoking-room furnished with lounges, in connexion with a cigar-shop or bar'. Images of luxurious rooms where smoking takes place as an event in this way are common in colonial representations of the harem. The more textual senses of the term 'divan' from which the original title of Goethe's text was actually derived include the meanings, 'a brochure, or fascicle of written leaves or sheets, hence a collection of poems', and 'a Persian name for a collection of poems . . . a series of poems by one author, the rimes of which usually run through the whole alphabet'.[57] This second sense is more interesting in relation to the short story form and the structure of a collection of short texts. The collection of poems referred to in this definition, arranged alphabetically, speaks to the teeming structure of *The Arabian Nights*, and with Rushdie's orderly organization of his nine stories into three sections, each containing three stories. In comparison with these senses of the word 'Diwan' in the original title, the term 'book' appears straightforward and has few relevant alternative senses, perhaps the only one worth mentioning is the religious sense of the 'Book', which might endow this text with a religious, ideological meaning by suggesting that it employs and compares the way that Eastern and Western religious texts are read.

Rushdie's conforming to Goethe's three types of translation in the three sections of his short story collection, 'East', 'West' and 'East, West', seems to suggest that the short story form is the ideal form for translation. The short story form is a unique form, which Benjamin suggests is compelled by memory: the storyteller and listener are connected by 'the listener's . . . interest in retaining what he is told'. All stories, he suggests, are connected by the reader's memory: 'one ties on to the next, as the great storytellers, particularly the Oriental ones, have always readily shown. In each of them there is a Scheherazade who thinks of a fresh story wherever her tale comes to a stop'.[58] Benjamin privileges the short story form, suggesting that 'what distinguishes the novel from the story (and from the epic in the narrower sense) is its essential dependence on the book'.[59] It was, he goes on to say, the growth of capitalism and control of the press which led to the decline of storytelling and the short story form.[60] In 'The Storyteller', Walter Benjamin suggests that every 'real' short story

> contains, openly or covertly, something useful. The usefulness may, in one case, consist of a moral; in another, in some practical advice, in a third, a proverb or maxim. In every case the storyteller is a man who has counsel for his readers. . . . Counsel woven into the fabric of real life is wisdom.[61]

Berger suggests that there is a different audience for the Anglophone African short story than for the novel: 'the Anglophone African short story, unlike the novel, is addressed – not to outsiders but to an African reading and listening audience' and 'unlike the novel – is much more accessible to a general reader in Africa. It tends to appear in magazines [and it] . . . tends to be written and published *in* Africa'.[62] Because of this, the Anglophone African short story 'provides a model for a new kind of postcolonial text'.[63]

Rushdie's collection of short stories follows Goethe's definition of the three types of translation theory precisely, according to the three sections of the collection. Other postcolonial short stories fit into these three categories just as easily, however. Roopal Monar's story 'Bahadur' is a challenging text linguistically; Monar combines languages in order to 'appropriate foreign' (colonial) language and 'reproduce it in his own sense'. In accordance with Goethe's second translation mode, this creates a text which challenges canonical forms of literature and speaks with a very new voice:

> This Bahadur couldn't read and write at all people say, but he gat more commonsense than most estate people who uses to wuk in the backdam from soon-soon morning until six o'clock in the evening, when cricket and night beetle does croak inside the cane field, by the beezie-beezie and the blacksage bush corner. [64]

Like the linguistic challenges posed by Monar's writing, Ben Okri's writing is also rich with those 'foreign . . . feelings, thoughts, and even objects' required to conform to Goethe's second translation type, like the 'tapster' in 'What the Tapster Saw', whose 'renowned herbalist' friend was 'harassed by the demands of his many wives' and 'kept chewing bundles of alligator pepper seeds and dousing his mouth with palm-wine'.[65] However, Okri's writing does not provide easy references or translations for its reader; instead, it abandons the 'universe of discourse' in order to create what Goethe suggests is required for the third, the 'highest and final' translation type, where 'the aim is to make the original identical with the translation, so that one should be valued not instead of the other, but in the other's stead'. Applying this formula to postcolonial literature, this type of text attempts to equalize the relationship between colonial and postcolonial literatures, so that the 'translation' – literature produced by writers native to formerly colonized regions – may be read instead of the colonial writings concerned with the same location. Steiner suggests that, 'in one sense, each act of translation is an endeavour to abolish multiplicity and to bring different world-pictures back into perfect congruence'.[66] This resembles Goethe's third sense of translation, in which he describes an 'identical' relationship between the original and the translation. It also resonates with the third, 'harmonizing' section of Rushdie's short story collection. Steiner goes on to say that,

> In another sense, [translation] is an attempt to reinvent the shape of meaning, to find and justify an alternative statement. The craft of the translator is . . . deeply ambivalent: it is exercised in a radical tension between impulses to facsimile and impulses to appropriate recreation. . . . the translator "re-experiences" the evolution of language itself, the ambivalence of the relations between language and world, between "languages" and "worlds".[67]

If Rushdie's and other postcolonial short stories follow translation formulae in such a straightforward way, can it then be inferred that the short story is the optimum medium for literary translation, the literary form with the richest resources for translation theory to explore, that there is something about the short story form that makes it inherently translatable?

Rushdie's longer fiction presents obstacles to translation. In *The Satanic Verses*, Gibreel Farishta is prevented from delivering God's message to his Prophet due to religious doubt. In *Shalimar the Clown*, translation is disrupted by desire and hunger, symbolized by the evocative spices of Kashmir, and their equal effect on the gluttony of a young dancer and the sustained anger of her rejected lover and his terrorist group. In *Midnight's Children*, language barriers and wars complicate translation, and in *Shame*, translation is prevented by female veiling and seclusion. There are certain parallels between the characters and their stories in Rushdie's novels, and those in his short stories, which imply that it is indeed the short story form which allows those similar narratives a space for translation which is denied their counterparts in novels. One example is the similarity between the narrator of 'The Courter' and Saladin Chamcha in *The Satanic Verses*, both of whom migrated to England as teenagers. Chamcha loses his linguistic certainty and feels that he is victim to bilingual influences which betray his Indian identity. On the aeroplane following a trip to Bombay, on waking from sleep he interprets his Bombay English dialect as 'his traitor voice' (p. 34). He anglicizes his name from Salahuddin Chamchawala to Saladin Chamcha and develops a distaste for Indian food, calling it 'this filthy foreign food' (p. 258). In contrast, the narrator of 'The Courter' regrets the loss of his linguistic uncertainty: he returns to his childhood home in London in an attempt to find 'Mixed-Up', the porter from 'some Iron Curtain' (p. 179) location (again making him uncertain) whose state of semi-muteness and mixed-up control of language helped the young narrator (who had a far superior command of English) to feel that he had become integrated into his community.

Another example is the similarity between the stories of inappropriate romance in 'The Free Radio' and *Shalimar the Clown*. In 'The Free Radio', the unconventional relationship between Ramani the rickshaw-wallah and the thief's widow is presented in the simple judgemental diction of the unreliable narrator, but ends in apparent success and harmony when Ramani is groomed for stardom and is able to support his new family. In *Shalimar the Clown*, though, Boonyi and Shalimar's relationship is initially scandalous because, similarly to Romeo and Juliet's feuding families (whose story provides an 'original' for which Boonyi and Shalimar's relationship is a 'translation'), the couple come from different religious communities. Once the village accepts their relationship as progressive and positive, though, the tragic aspects of *Romeo and Juliet* are rewritten into Boonyi and Shalimar's story. Both lovers are brutally killed as a result of their desire for revenge rather than through love for each other. Because the *Romeo and Juliet* story is distorted, this results in untranslatable desires which can only be fulfilled by the revenge motive.

After talking about the 'harmonious' space of the short story as a literary form where there is an opportunity for successful translation, and the idea that the short story is the ultimate text to use to demonstrate translation theory, questions remain over whether this is really such a good thing. Is the apparent success of translation in the short story form necessarily a positive thing, if the result is that a successful translation gives the misleading impression of the successful and harmonious postcolonial subject? Maybe the failed translation is what was important and valuable in the longer texts where translation was impossible. If so, does this mean that the short story form has become a tool of the postcolonial writer as much as it was a tool of the colonial writer enabling the dissemination of ideological material much like other short forms like fairy tales and fables? Instead, interpreting the success of translation in the short story more optimistically, perhaps the use of this form indicates a new canonical voice and a space for the often disregarded narrative form of the short story, bringing with it elements of oral narrative and other short forms of literature, in the same way as postcolonial writers have forged a place for non-standard English and bilingual voices in a body of work that will constantly challenge dominant literary forms, genres and definitions.

5

Kashmir and Paradise: Translating History

When translators translate, they can change the way that a location or a time is perceived by the reader. They can also influence the receiving culture by exposing them to the unfamiliar images and ideas conveyed in the translated texts, ideas which can be perceived as a threat, as Victor Hugo noted when he wrote that 'when you offer a translation to a nation, that nation will almost always look upon the translation as an act of violence against itself'.[1] *Midnight's Children* and *Shalimar the Clown* both represent Kashmir in a new way. They retell the history of a time and a place, translating local stories of Kashmir in order to question dominant histories of the region which focus on terrorism (or, depending on your point of view, freedom fighters) and a civil war of attrition. Rather than presenting one straightforward new version of history, though, Rushdie's texts question the legitimacy of historical representation altogether. This is enacted textually by the use of narrative structure which situates Kashmir in the present moment and evades the sense of an ending that Kermode suggests compels all Western narratives (and their readerships).

In this chapter, I turn again to the most frequently addressed problem of translation studies: the idea of the inherent superiority of the original. But in this chapter, I discuss the ways in which Rushdie's effort to translate not just Kashmir's history but also the historical mode itself offers a way out of this bind: it might be impossible to rewrite Kashmir's history in a way that comprehensively undermines the original (colonial) version of that history, because any new history will inevitably be seen as supplementary, as of secondary status. But if the historical mode of representation is itself the subject in question, no sense of chronological hierarchy is established. Rushdie rethinks, rewrites, translates the idea of history when, in *Midnight's Children* and *Shalimar the Clown*, Kashmir is presented as an ever-present moment, somehow divorced from history. Rushdie's rewriting of Kashmir is, then, an indirect translation which is alert to the potency of a colonial legacy. This legacy – supported by historical representation as a Western mode[2] – prevents retellings from existing independently of that colonial history. Translating the historical mode, then, also points to the way that postcolonial texts declare their independence from their colonial heritage.

Problems with history

This chapter will interrogate the way that Salman Rushdie conveys a history of Kashmir in *Midnight's Children* and *Shalimar the Clown*. *Midnight's Children* can be read as a literary history of the Partition of India and the periods immediately before and after. At the time of its publication, readers wanted *Midnight's Children* to be recognizable as history – they resented its 'incompleteness' or 'inadequacy' as if it failed to fully meet their aspirations of the text because its historical representation was not complete or precise.[3] Finding the novel lacking as a history, these readers' reactions emphasize that, however much a literary text is focused on history, it still does something fundamentally different from historical writing. In addition, though, such a reader reaction offers proof that *Midnight's Children* is an unusual narrative: though engaging with history, it is not a literary history, and this is obvious to its popular readership. Instead, the text plays with the historical form in order to convey the present moment of Kashmir, and this representation of the immediate present emerges through an acknowledgement of previously existing histories. *Midnight's Children* invokes Kashmir as a symbol of the longed-for past and future; *Shalimar the Clown* more directly addresses the Kashmir of the same historical period: Boonyi and Shalimar are young lovers who leave Kashmir, and Boonyi's daughter, named India by her adopted mother and Kashmira by her real mother, uncovers her family history while attempting to find her connection with Kashmir.

In an essay from his collection, *Imaginary Homelands*, Rushdie has called Kashmir 'one of the most beautiful places in the world'.[4] The Kashmir valley 'set jewel-like in the northern hills'[5] is valuable for both its beauty and its context. This 'paradise on earth'[6] remains a physical paradise in part because of the surrounding mountains and desert, but in post-1947 South Asia, Kashmir is part of an ongoing struggle with bordering India and Pakistan, both nations claiming that Kashmir should rightfully belong within their national boundary. Its isolation, though contributing to its beauty, gives Kashmir the level of autonomy that means it can maintain its independence through the ongoing violent struggle that has turned it into a 'vandalized Kashmir'; as Rushdie writes with some sadness: 'Paradise has been partitioned, impoverished and made violent'.[7] Rushdie's fiction conveys his preoccupation with the contrast between Kashmir as beautiful yet violent even in work where Kashmir is a peripheral location, and in some ways this increases the sense of its permanent impact on the stories that happen elsewhere: in both *Shalimar the Clown* and *Midnight's Children*, Kashmir haunts all of the other locations. This strategy culminates in an indirect retelling of Kashmir's history.

Kashmir appears at the beginning of *Midnight's Children* as the location of Aadam Aziz's loss of faith:

> Aadam Aziz hit his nose against a frost-hardened tussock of earth while attempting to pray. Three drops of blood plopped out of his left nostril, hardened instantly in the brittle air and lay before his eyes on the prayer-mat, transformed into rubies. . . . at that moment, as he brushed diamonds contemptuously from his lashes, he resolved never again to kiss the earth for any god or man. (10)

The region is prominent again at the end of the text: 'proposing a marriage', Padma insists that 'there is the future to think of', and that 'the honeymoon is to be in Kashmir' (444). That future in Kashmir, though, 'shall never' be reached – 'Kashmir will be waiting', but not for the narrator Saleem, who will 'die with Kashmir on [his] lips' (462). Only a fanciful 'optimism' (444) can generate a sense of that place for dying Saleem. For India/Kashmira in *Shalimar the Clown*, this optimistic longing is for Paradise; because in her imagination, 'the terms *Kashmir* and *Paradise* were synonymous' (4). India/Kashmira has constructed an imaginary Kashmir in an idealization of that location, somewhat reminiscent of colonial engagements with colonized landscapes in that it is based on desire and intuition, not facts. Kashmira's longing is for her mother and her homeland, and the two desires become intertwined. Susan Stewart combines two definitions of longing pertinent to Kashmira's experience – those of homesickness and of 'the fanciful cravings incident to women during pregnancy'[8] – to further her discussion of pregnancy as an 'elsewhere'. Thus motherhood and homesickness are imagined as equivalent states of desire, an equivalence made literal for Kashmira as postcolonial migrant. Conjoining motherhood and homesickness in a postcolonial context invites a reading of the pregnant body as a symbol of postcolonial migration in *Shalimar the Clown*. For Kashmira's mother Boonyi, Kashmir also at one time represented a desired happy ending: Kashmira is named after the home to which Boonyi so longs to return, saying that to return to Kashmir 'is the only thing [she] now want[s] in the world' (210). In *Midnight's Children*, this is where Kashmir is always situated: in the uncertain past and in the impossible future. To tell a history of Kashmir is impossible in this text, because to attempt to rewrite the region's history even as a disturbed Paradise would be to attempt to convey a certainty that the ongoing instability of the area belies. Despite this, though, the texts convey Rushdie's desperate need to rewrite the representation of Kashmir that persists in the popular imagination following the decolonization of India, which was the direct instigator of civil war in the region. Instead of translating the colonial history of Kashmir by writing a new postcolonial literary history of the region, Rushdie translates the historical mode of telling itself. Rather than telling a history of Kashmir, Rushdie tells a story of the present of Kashmir, of the now, and it is this telling of a present moment in place of a history of Kashmir in both *Midnight's Children* and Rushdie's *Shalimar the Clown* that is the focus of this chapter.

Rushdie engages with a number of specific historical events in his presentation of Kashmir. Instead of retelling these historical events in a new history of Kashmir or even a literary history, though, they are rendered current or incomplete. According to H V Hodson, Kashmir was one of the two states (along with Hyderabad) most likely to become independent at the end of British rule (or to become independent dominions of the commonwealth).[9] An ongoing sense of independence is key to Rushdie's presentation of the region, contemplated from the 1919 of *Midnight's Children* in Amritsar onwards, at which point Kashmir is understood to be an independent princely state and 'not strictly speaking a part of the [British] Empire' at all (33). When that independence needs to be more rigorously asserted, Rushdie's narrative too takes up the call of 'Kashmir for the Kashmiris', placing it in the mouth of the traditionalist (and the ageless) boatman, Tai, and silencing those words in 1947 with a rifle shot attributed to the memory of the orders of 'RE Dyer' (37), the Brigadeer Reginald Dyer, whose troops carried out the Jallianwala Bagh massacre in Amritsar in 1919. *Midnight's Children*, then, does engage with and re-present a number of specific historical events that are commonly presented in telling a history of Kashmir. First, the novel conveys the region's independent tradition and its intention to retain that separation after India's independence from British colonial rule. And secondly, it describes the region's distance from yet its connection with the Amritsar massacre of 1919, which is told by the Kashmiris present at that massacre as well as those who, though absent, were killed in the spirit of it. In an interview, Rushdie claims to make explicit engagement with 'the period between'47 and'77 – the period from Independence to the Emergency' in *Midnight's Children* (Reder 2000: 18). *Shalimar the Clown*, too, presents this historical period in Kashmir, and the years afterwards in which the valley battles famine and terror and struggles to appease its sorrows in cups of 'salty pink [Kashmir] tea' (65). The famine in the Pachigam of *Shalimar the Clown* occurs in Summer 1988 amid JKLF (Jammu and Kashmir Liberation Front) militancy.

However, both texts have trouble in telling these historical events. On the literal level, *Midnight's Children* intends to retell those events in a manner that quantifies the extent of Kashmir's involvement in the final stages of colonial rule in South Asia and its aftermath, and this is achieved by the awareness of context: between the Amritsar massacre and the death of Tai the boatman is a 'far away . . . World War in progress' (39). *Shalimar the Clown* juxtaposes the Second World War with Kashmir during Partition in order to equalize these histories. This is done in part by replicating images of a sudden lack of food and by changing the food symbolism which signified both regions from feast to fast. Wartime Europe is transformed from a previous state of plenty, at least for the wealthy, depicted as 'a glass of cognac beside . . . morning coffee and a tepid brioche' (140). This turns into widespread want, symbolized by 'tasteless black bread' (141). In Kashmir, the 36- and 60-course banquets are replaced by hunger when war meant that: 'a statewide famine was a real possibility' (300). Thus, the end of colonial rule is presented from the point of view of what Rushdie refers to as 'Indian experiences of it'.[10]

So why is it that neither text can straightforwardly retell history, that Saleem Sinai cannot tell a straight history, that he is 'buffeted by too much history' instead of buoyed and propelled by it? History is traditionally constructed in a particular fashion, and it has a habitual way of telling the things that it finds out, as Foucault discusses:

> For many years now historians have preferred to turn their attention to long periods, as if, beneath the shifts and changes of political events, they were trying to reveal the stable, almost indestructible system of checks and balances, the irreversible process, the constant readjustments, the underlying tendencies that gather force, and are then suddenly reversed after centuries of continuity, the movements of accumulation and slow saturation, the great silent, motionless bases that traditional history has covered with a thick layer of events. . . . Beneath the rapidly changing history of governments, wars, and famines, there emerge other, apparently unmoving histories: the history of sea routes, the history of corn or of gold-mining . . . .[11]

To understand and categorize these things, they have been organized into series, systems and criteria. However, according to Foucault, certain historical disciplines have been turning away from 'vast unities like 'periods' or 'centuries' to the phenomena of rupture, of discontinuity'.[12] For Foucault, there is a conflict between 'seeking, and discovering, . . . discontinuities', and reliance upon 'stable structures'.[13] Stable structures imply the kinds of certainties that the colonial project relied upon and that the postcolonial subject seeks to undermine.

Perhaps the answer to the question over why Saleem Sinai (and by extension, Rushdie) is unable to tell a straight history is that the past must retain its uncertainty in postcolonial tellings of history, because to write a fixed and certain history is to represent a particular view, one that is just as partial as a colonial history. As Leela Gandhi points out, 'a variety of postcolonial commentators have argued that "history" is the discourse through which the West has asserted its hegemony over the rest of the world'.[14] History may not be an appropriate medium for a postcolonial retelling, if this is the case. Saleem Sinai is well aware of the storyteller's (or the historian's) partiality: 'memory's truth', he admits, 'selects, eliminates, alters, exaggerates, minimizes, glorifies, and vilifies' and 'in the end it creates its own reality' (211). It is, he says, the 'temptation of every autobiographer' to believe that 'since the past exists only in one's memories and the words which strive vainly to encapsulate them, it is possible to create past events simply by saying they occurred' (443). There is a sense of postcolonial engagement with the idea of legitimate histories in the suggestion that 'no sane human being ever trusts someone else's version [of history] more than his own' (211). But the healthy scepticism when considering other people's versions of history is overpowered by the awareness that this is a narrator who has already admitted that he might 'distort everything – . . . rewrite the whole history of [his] time in order to place [him]self in a central role' (166). The difficulty in telling a straight history might also be caused by narratee Padma, who insists on a future in Kashmir that is impossible. Similarly, India/Kashmira in *Shalimar the Clown* longs for Paradise when she imagines her future in Kashmir. Kashmir is in both texts situated in the uncertain past and in the impossible future. So, to tell a history of Kashmir as disturbed Paradise is impossible in either text, and instead, Rushdie tells a story of the present of Kashmir, of the now.

Retelling as translation

For translation theory, Rushdie's retelling of the history of Kashmir for a new postcolonial audience is a type of translation because to translate, in a postcolonial context, is to retell a story or a history (or a present moment), rewriting for a new context or audience, in the sense of Roman Jakobson's definition of intralingual translation[15] and Andre Lefevere's assertion that a translation is 'to represent a foreign text in one's own culture', where the 'foreign' may be, of course, the foreign language, but also the 'foreign' as something made distant or unfamiliar by historical, political, cultural or other differences.[16] In comparing history with translation, Tejaswini Niranjana claims that 'translation is belated, always comes after the original, is always a supplement. But the "original" lives on only in translation'.[17] In living on, the sense of the inherent value of the original is rekindled – this is something that cannot be acceptable from the perspectives of postcolonial studies and postcolonial translation theory: these disciplines are always aware of the ideological motivations behind histories and therefore, translations must question any 'original' version of history and the idea of an inherent superiority of any text. If both histories and translations rely on the superior value of an original, then neither history nor translation is adequate. Instead of rewriting the history of Kashmir from a postcolonial perspective, these texts do something more complicated, and present the present, the now of that past-Paradise. This is because there is no certain sense of an ending if a history is to be truly questioned and retold: the past must retain its uncertainty in postcolonial and subaltern tellings of history, because to write a fixed and certain history is to represent a particular view, perhaps one that is as partial as a colonial history.

Tejaswini Niranjana combines history and translation in her reading of history according to Derrida and Benjamin. Niranjana suggests that for Derrida, history is rendered arbitrary by the opposition of nature and culture.[18] If history is constructed from arbitrary relationships, then it does not represent cause and effect, so it is impossible to construct history scientifically, or rationally, in an effort to represent the history of Kashmir in a way that is preferable to previous colonial versions. Even a translation, of the intralingual type – a translation that functions within a language, to retell a story from a new perspective or for a different audience – couldn't produce a valid history of Kashmir. Niranjana contrasts this with Benjamin's suggestion that there is an '*afterlife* of art works', to argue that 'history "follows" nature [rather than existing as in a synchronous relationship with a nature/culture opposition], and translation, which comes from the afterlife or sur-vival of a work, displaces the work into the realm of history, revealing therefore its instability at the "origin"'.[19] So, to translate is to render the original unstable, because the translation renders the original historical, and a history is necessarily unstable. Instead of producing an unstable narrative, Benjamin suggests that history can be written in a different way that demonstrates 'the art of experiencing the present as the waking world to which that dream which we call the past in truth relates'.[20] This method acknowledges the limitations and instabilities of history by expressing the past as a dream.

Continuing the comparison between translation and history, Niranjana notes the problem with 'intertwining . . . "translation" and "history"' and cites Derrida's proposed solution: 'Derrida has often spoken of the need to *reinscribe* the notion of history by revealing its discontinuous and heterogeneous nature'.[21] In a literary history, a discontinuous and heterogeneous nature may be conveyed by the form (or structure) of the text: the literary text can refuse linearity and disrupt the sense of an ending. Foucault writes that 'it is a long time now since historians uncovered, described, and analysed structures, without ever having occasion to wonder whether they were not allowing the living, fragile, pulsating "history" to slip through their fingers'. He refers to this as a 'structure/development opposition'.[22] Not quite an opposition between structure and development, but a conflation of the two modes is at work in Rushdie's presentation of the history of Kashmir. The art of telling a history is 'to give it shape and form' and 'shape and form', for Saleem Sinai, equates to 'meaning' (461). The form, or structure, is the meaning of Rushdie's history of Kashmir. The kind of development that Foucault sees in the living and pulsating history is here what calls into being those structures that for Foucault work in direct opposition.

Even if the text tries to do something different with history, to make much of narrator Saleem's intention to break the tradition of telling 'the halal parts of history' (59), it might be impossible to do so, because any history is constructed within these limitations. Foucault questions the legitimacy, or possibility, of ordering and structuring a history, saying that although 'we may wish to draw a dividing-line; . . . any limit we set may perhaps be no more than an arbitrary division made in a constantly mobile whole. We may wish to mark off a period; but have we the right to establish symmetrical breaks at two points in time to give an appearance of continuity and unity to the system we place between them?'. [23] This evokes the notion of history as arbitrary, to suggest that the demarcations used to comprehend history are arbitrary, and acknowledges the limitations of historical representation in general. Foucault's approach to history has been read as an intent to 'break.. off the past from the present and, by demonstrating the foreignness of the past, relativize.. and undercut.. the legitimacy of the present'.[24] *Midnight's Children* seems to do the opposite, to delegitimize the present by connecting it to an uncertain history. Madan Sarup sums up the approach of a Nietzschean historian who 'begins with the present and goes backward in time until a difference is located. Then s/he proceeds forward again, tracing the transformation and taking care to preserve the discontinuities as well as the connections'.[25] In direct contrast to a traditional view of history, which might seek to explain the present by its source in the past, the discontinuities, or the 'gap[s] between the past and the present' are left 'unexplained'.[26]

There is a split between "genealogical" and "traditional" forms of historical analysis:

> Whereas traditional or "total" history inserts events into grand explanatory systems and linear processes, celebrates great moments and individuals and seeks to document a point of origin, genealogical analysis attempts to establish and preserve the singularity of events, turns away from the spectacular in favour of the discredited.[27]

Rushdie's histories also work against linear processes, yet they do posit grand explanatory systems and celebrate great moments and individuals – it's just that the moments and individuals are different moments and individuals from those ordinarily celebrated. The 'discredited' histories favoured by a 'genealogical' approach to history might be subaltern histories, or they might be Saleem's stories, and the problems associated with an unreliable narrator. Coincidentally, genealogy, or family history, is the method by which Saleem tells the history of Partition and of Kashmir. A family history is able to dominate a more generic history: 'the hundred daily pin-pricks of family life . . . alone [can] deflate the great ballooning fantasy of history and bring it down to a more manageably human scale' (345). Similarly, *Shalimar the Clown* can be read as a family history: the novel opens by defining the character India/Kashmira as 'the ambassador's daughter' (3) who 'had no mother' (4) and whose 'father's death' leaves her haunted by both the memory of 'Shalimar from Kashmir' and her desire to reach that Paradisiacal location (11). For India/Kashmira, history is created by filling in the gaps and finding out about her family history. For Saleem Sinai, family history is an already well-known tale that he, as narrator, carefully discloses. And, just as genealogy favours an understanding of 'historical beginnings as lowly, complex and contingent' which 'reveal the multiplicity of factors behind an event and the fragility of historical forms' and where 'there can be no constants, no essences, no immobile forms of uninterrupted continuities structuring the past',[28] a fragmentary and multiple history of the birth of a fractured nation and its inhabitants is told by Saleem. In *Shalimar the Clown*, though, the method of telling history is different – India/Kashmira is not a narrator, so she is not a producer of historical representation, fragmentary and complex, fragile and lowly or otherwise. Instead, India/Kashmira is the reader's connection with the present moment: she represents the now while Saleem is haunted and ravaged by it. India/Kashmira as a focalizer doesn't know her own history and is thus stranded in the present moment of the narrative. The detachment of India/Kashmira as a focalizing character occurs in a short passage dominated by the inanimate focal object of a car, given to India by her father a few days before his assassination, a 'silver luxury speed-mobile with bat-wing doors' (12). India/Kashmira feels that this car is 'potent, wrong' (12). This is the last emotion which she expresses in this scene: once she is inside the car, although she is the focalizer in terms of the presentation of physical space to the reader, she no longer has an emotional impact on the image: inside the car the character's senses are blocked, and the narration becomes an objective placing of images, evoking a strong sense of emptiness or gaps in narration:

> The handsome driver, Shalimar from Kashmir, remained on the sidewalk, diminished into an insect in her wing mirror, his eyes like shining swords. He was a silverfish, a locust. Olga Volga the potato witch stood beside him and their dwindling bodies looked like numerals. Together they made the number 10. (12–13)

Once inside the car, India's desire and her position as a focalizer is repressed by the emotionless husk of the car, and it is also disrupted in terms of geographical space: she sees Shalimar standing on the pavement only through a mirror, and therefore sees his distortion and reflection, his opposite, as well as seeing his body as a reflection of herself: she looks into the mirror, but sees Shalimar instead of her own image. This scene suggests the mirror described by Kristeva when telling the story of her patient Didier, who dreamt that he saw his sister's face in a mirror instead of his own, and chose this mirror (where he became his sister) instead of the alternative offered, which was to retain his own face, even though this meant falling into a void through his open window.[29] Kristeva describes Didier as suffering from a phantasmatic inhibition which rendered him unable to tell a story and claimed that 'Didier could thus be considered a symbolic emblem of contemporary man – an actor or consumer of the society of the spectacle who has run out of imagination'.[30] Shalimar's and India/Kashmira's communities are locations of spectacle, populated by actors and consumers: India/Kashmira overeats in Los Angeles restaurants served by beautiful unsuccessful actors; Shalimar is from the Kashmir village of Pachigam, where,

> At times of celebration people liked a bit of a drama to watch but there was also a demand for those who could prepare the legendary wazwaan, the Banquet of the Thirty-Six Courses Minimum. . . . the villagers of Pachigam were the first to

> provide a rounded service which offered both sustenance for the body and pleasure for the soul. (61–2)

If a history of Kashmir cannot be told, then telling Kashmir's future is also impossible, as predicting the future is traditionally dependent on the certainty of the past, but is in these texts left to depend upon an uncertain past. This is why the present moment – the now – is everything.

Kashmir is itself imbued with a sense of constancy, described in *Shalimar the Clown* as 'Kashmiriyat, Kashmiriness, the belief that at the heart of Kashmiri culture there was a common bond that transcended all other differences' (10). This sense of constancy of place, this fixedness, questions the possibility of rendering a history of that place. Constancy is symbolized in *Midnight's Children* by the constant references to 'ice-blue Kashmiri sky' (143) in the eyes of the characters who have left Kashmir, as if their gaze is constantly fixed on Kashmir. The colours with which Kashmir is painted are as bright and vivid as those in a fairy tale, but in *Shalimar the Clown*, the comfort of fairy tale is missing: visitors to the fairy-tale Paradise are overwhelmed by the sensory onslaught from these colours:

> women . . . looked through you with their ice-blue eyes their golden eyes their emerald eyes their eyes of creatures from another world. They floated by you on the lakes wearing their scarlet headscarves their burgundy their cobalt headscarves concealing the dark or yellow flame of their hair (99).

For Kachhwaha, this is too much and the result is sensory confusion: 'he saw sounds . . . he heard colours. He tasted feelings' (100). For those who leave, to return is to regret the lost Paradise, and to fail to reach a happy ending. The ideal end for Boonyi is imagined as communal eating: 'at Firdaus's table they would enjoy the happy ending of . . . meals together' (220). Her desires are unsatisfied, though: instead of achieving a return to childhood with a happy family reunion, Boonyi discovers that she has been rejected: 'she was being punished. She was being judged in dumb show and ritually ostracized' (221–2).

Kashmir's histories, and translating World War Two in *Shalimar the Clown*

Rushdie's presentation of Kashmir can be compared with other historical presentations of the location. One dominant portrayal of Kashmir in standard modern histories is a representation of the economic concerns that accompanied the final stages of colonization, of Partition and of the years afterwards. Ian Talbot suggests that 'Partition left most industrial development in India, and separated Pakistani raw materials from their markets'.[31] He goes on to confirm that 'it was not until December 1947 that an agreement was reached on Pakistan's share of the cash balances. The bulk of this (Rs 550 million) was held back by the government of India as a result of the hostilities in Kashmir following the former Princely state's controversial accession to India. It was only paid on 15 January 1948 after Gandhi's intervention and fast which led to his assassination'.[32] In comparison, Rushdie's Kashmir has an answer to crop failure and famine. In *Shalimar the Clown*, fasting and starvation characterize war in Kashmir. The political and religious divisions imposed on the Kashmir village in *Shalimar the Clown* mean that crop failure is dependent upon the farmer's religion. The crop failure, like a biblical plague left behind in colonial bibles, is seen as a judgement: 'the end of the world is coming because [the] apples are too bitter to eat' (297). These doomsday bitter apples complement the other uses of the image of rotten apples. Rotten apples represent the displaced Hindu population of Kashmir: 'three hundred and fifty thousand pandits, almost the entire pandit population of Kashmir, fled from their homes and headed south to the refugee camps where they would rot, like bitter fallen apples, like the unloved, undead dead they had become' (296). Rotten food symbolizes death, as does the generai state of food availability due to the very limited crops which were successful: 'right now I'm so sick of honey and peaches I might even prefer to starve' (300), says Firdaus. Peaches and honey evoke the foods of paradise, they are like nectar and manna, and honey is described in the Qur'an as emblematic of the pure, joyful productivity of nature:

> Your Lord has inspired the bees: "Set up hives in the mountains and in trees and in anything they may build. Then eat of every kind of fruit and slip easily along your Lord's byways." From their bellies comes a drink with different colours which contains healing for mankind. In that is a sign for people who meditate.[33]

Rejecting these foods creates a sense of lost Paradise: with the division of a harmonious people during the Partition of India, Kashmir, the novel suggests, is no longer Paradise, and instead has become a godless place where families reject God-given honey in favour of suicidal thoughts of self-starvation: 'maybe we won't live long enough to reach the point of starvation . . . what a stroke of luck! We can choose from so many different ways to die!' (300). The displaced Hindu population as a result of wartime famine and violence evokes the Jewish population displaced during the World War II, of which Max Ophuls, the American ambassador who falls in love with newly-wed Boonyi, is one. The Jewish experience in the World War II is removed and reconstructed, to retell that prominent historical event in a contemporary, South Asian context. Thus, the historical moment has been translated. If, as Kristeva suggests, 'every narration is made up, *nourished* by time, finality, history, and God',[34] then both the history of Kashmir and its fiction is sustained by the food that nourishes the narrator. Narrative form is constituted by the food and the history which it digests, as the body is constituted of – rather than simply being fuelled by – the food consumed by it, according to Marx (who was therefore the first to suggest that 'you are what you eat'[35]). *Shalimar the Clown* suggests that the history of Kashmir is bound up with its fiction and mythology, as is Europe's. These historical retellings are polluted with romantic entanglements. Max's career in political espionage is structured by a series of romantic conquests and affairs: 'the greatest contribution Max Ophuls made to the Resistance was sexual . . . he was the man who seduced the Panther, Ursula Brandt' (163). Shalimar's civil war actions (or acts of terrorism) were similarly based on his plan to take a lover's revenge on Boonyi for her adultery: 'his own goals were personal as well as national, and would not be denied' (258). This explicitly connects romantic desire with the production of history. In this way, romantic desire and historical documentation are compelled by the same hunger and longing for an ending.

Though the presentation of the foods available during economic decline in *Shalimar the Clown* may not refer to the same historical period as that referred to by Ian Talbot, the comparison remains important because of the stark opposition of feast and fast. This brings up an interesting question: are historical novels or literary representations of history only permitted to engage with historically valid events and symbols? Is literature, like history, forbidden from making anachronistic connections? Or can literature be as intertextual with historical events and symbols as it can with literary texts, bringing in anachronistic references which contribute to meaning? Perhaps allowing anachronism in literature offers an answer to the problematic portrayal of a literary history of Kashmir's failed Paradise, and the sense that in both *Midnight's Children* and *Shalimar the Clown*, the desire for an ending is defeated by the non-linear structure of the novels.

Because the desire for an ending is defeated there is no ending, and therefore, there is no certain history, and the Kashmir that is that constant state, a Paradise or a ruptured Paradise, cannot be written down: Kashmir cannot be possessed as it would be in an authoritative history. All of the history of Kashmir regarding the partition of India and the questions related to its accession to one or other side, and the violence accompanying those events, is rendered false and questionable. Kashmir remains not-possessed. Therefore, the history that is related in history books doesn't relate to Kashmir at all. If that's the case, is there a form in which Kashmir's history can be told? Is it even possible to describe kashmiriyat? In other words, how is it possible to render the now of Kashmir?

When Boonyi gives away her baby daughter in order to return home and in an effort to retain her Kashmiriness, her repeated mantra connects her decision to geographical space: 'there is no Kashmira. There was only Kashmir' (218). In voicing this mantra, though, Kashmira becomes even more fully entangled with Kashmir: not only named after the region, she becomes interchangeable with it, embodying that location. In *Midnight's Children* Saleem, too, embodies the location of his history – born at the moment of Indian independence, his face depicts the country: his bullying school teacher sees in his face 'the whole map of *India* . . . the Deccan peninsula hanging down . . . These stains . . . are Pakistan! [the] birthmark on the right ear is the East Wing; and [the] horrible stained left cheek, the West!' (232).

If the protagonists embody the history of Kashmir as it is told, then does this have an impact on what the present moment is? Is the present moment as fleeting as a human life and as fragile as a human body? Does the embodiment of the location historicize what might otherwise have remained intangible and in the 'now'? The body is 'indivisible, a one-piece suit' and on attacking the body, 'God knows what you permit to come tumbling out' (237). The body, then, is a temporary receptacle for history, as unreliable as any textual container; it tries to maintain integrity, but when attacked, may leak 'revolutionary' changes to what was once believed to be real: Saleem's switching at birth is the dramatic equivalent of the flawed historical record that when interrogated is proven false.

The structure of the novel determines the construction of the history that it engenders. Saleem Sinai has 'always been in the grip of a form-crazy destiny which enjoys wreaking its havoc on numinous days' (444). If a narrator's destiny is form-crazy, it is determined by the form that shapes his text. Oral narrative is shaped differently to linear narrative and *Midnight's Children* explicitly aims to replicate oral narrative form:

> the story is told in a manner designed to echo . . . the Indian talent for non-stop regeneration. This is why the narrative constantly throws up new stories, why it "teems". The form – multitudinous, hinting at the infinite possibilities of the country – is the optimistic counterweight to Saleem's personal tragedy.[36]

Shalimar the Clown similarly teems with stories (those of Cinderella, Rumplestiltskin, Alice in Wonderland, Scheherazade and The Arabian Nights, Anarkali, Sita, Romeo and Juliet) that are retold throughout the novel, making a cyclical narrative structure that resembles oral narrative, and signifying the novel's self-conscious concern with narrative form. Ashcroft, Griffiths and Tiffin cite Rushdie on the awareness that his narrative form 'reproduce[s] the traditional techniques of the Indian oral narrative tradition'. They describe this technique as 'circling back from the present to the past, of building tale within tale, and persistently delaying climaxes', suggesting that these 'are all features of traditional narration and orature'.[37] They refer to, as an example of this technique, 'the narrative technique of the traditional clown-narrator (the 'Vidushka') in the ancient Indian performance art of *Kuttiyattam*'.[38] This provides an interesting connection to Shalimar's narrative, suggesting that perhaps Shalimar has greater control over the narrative, if he is linked to the novel's structure by his place in traditional orature. An example of cyclical storytelling, *The Arabian Nights* disrupts notions of linear narrative and desperately avoids an ending, although, perhaps it invokes a greater need for an ending, in Kermode's terms, by doing so. Oral narrative follows a cyclical and not a linear narrative direction or structure, 'circling back from the present to the past, . . . building tale within tale, and persistently delaying climaxes'.[39] Kristeva ascribes a comparable (but less apparent) cyclical structure to all narrative, suggesting that texts are bound by loops beginning with binary oppositions like life-death, beginning-end, good-evil, which are 'connected and mediated by a series of utterances whose relation to the originally posited opposition is neither explicit nor logically necessary'.[40] *Shalimar the Clown*, then, is structured on loops of desire-hatred, feast-fast and the beginning-end opposition which is constantly deferred in order to replace or rewrite missing or flawed histories. The story cannot end until there is both 'completion of one of the loops (resolution of the oppositional dyads)' and an 'appearance, within the novelistic utterance, of the very work that produces it, here, on the actual page. Speech ends when its subject dies and it is the act of the writing (of work) that produces this murder'.[41] The character or concept apparent at the beginning of the loop must return and be completed – or killed – by the act of its being written at this later stage in the text. When Boonyi leaves Shalimar, the desire-revenge loop is instigated, and in order for this loop to be closed with an attempt to 'kill the children' (61) from her affair, Shalimar must reappear at the end of the text. The necessary linear narrative structure or sense of apocalypse is only restored by the closure of this loop by magical means: when Shalimar escapes from prison by doing 'the impossible' and running along a wall, had 'simply taken off', as if he was flying, or, making the ultimate performance of his career and walking a tightrope made of 'gathered air' (394–5). Carrying out the revenge plot provides a satisfaction of the hunger in each narrative strand and a closing of each of the narrative 'loops'.

But echoing oral narrative and counterbalancing the tragic events of narrator Saleem's family history with the multitude of possible histories in a text on the subject of partition of a nation (and embodied in a narrator whose flesh, resembling that nation, is fragmenting as his story is told) isn't the only reason for the structure of these novels. It's possible that literature wants to do something specific with the way in which it tells history. Perhaps history exists to justify a desire for control, and in a wider sense, to assuage guilt for past desires or wrongs. But literature aims to satisfy a desire and not just to justify it. So its engagement with history is of a different kind; even postmodern and postcolonial renderings tell history differently. Oral narrative may do something different from the historical narrative. A traditional tale like a myth or a folk tale can be summarized as 'a metaphor which entertains and instructs: a narrative in the first instance oral, which is the product of no single person, place or time, and which has been retuned and sometimes reclothed by those who have transmitted it'.[42] This is very similar to the purpose of telling a history: we tell histories to both entertain and instruct, but a history is vulnerable to the 'clothing' and 'tuning' of its teller. A translation of a myth or history in the manner of oral narrative looks like this: it still carries that history within the 'clothes' or to the 'tune' of a speaker's ideology and reflects back the other ideologies that have informed it. As a result, it is inadequate to simply translate or retell a history in a new form or for a new audience or with new meaning – the history has to be rendered in question and in flux in order to truly represent a location or consciousness. In this sense, Rushdie's texts have to do more than represent oral narrative: their tellings of history are not oral narrative versions to correct Western versions of the history of Kashmir.

The now

What is gained by presenting Kashmir's history as a present moment – as the now – instead of rewriting the history in a way that retells it and alters the perception of Kashmir in its history, but still fixes that history? Rushdie amends the adage that 'the past is a foreign country' by suggesting that the present is foreign, that the past is home, albeit a lost home in a lost city in the mists of time.[43] So Rushdie is aware that the present is foreign: if we extend this to the narrative, then we could suggest that if the present is foreign, it alienates and confronts the reader in a more productive way than any retelling of history, from any perspective, could do – an uncomfortable history might provoke a dismissal from the reader but the reader can't dismiss the now.

Rushdie claims that Saleem's story 'is not history, but it plays with historical shapes'.[44] *Midnight's Children* was 'born' from the author's wish to 'restore the past to [him]self'[45] but to be able to do this, writing a new history was inadequate. According to Rushdie, the story became no longer a search for lost time but the way in which we remake the past to suit our present purposes, using memory as our tool – because Saleem wants the central role, he is cutting up history to suit himself.[46] So on the literal level, Saleem reproduces history, or retells it, and attempts to do so in a way that retells that history from a particular perspective. That is the only way that any history can be told. But examining the novel's structure and the way that Kashmir represents that past and future that frames Saleem's history, the text does more than retelling a history: it tells the present moment.

Telling the present

The love story of Boonyi and Shalimar begins with a promise, a promise of a future-to-come in Derrida's sense: Shalimar swears: 'don't you leave me now, or I'll never forgive you, and I'll have my revenge, I'll kill you and if you have any children by another man I'll kill the children also' (61). For the reader, this promise is a promise of conclusion, it implies an ending. Shalimar's promise and his ghostly presence in the text offer clues as to how the need for narrative conclusion, for Frank Kermode's sense of an ending (which equates to the need for an accepted version of history) is explored in *Shalimar the Clown*. Kermode suggests that our sense of history and narrative is based on the Bible as a 'familiar model' which begins at the beginning and ends with apocalypse.[47] He claims that:

> Change without potentiality in a novel is impossible, quite simply . . . No novel can avoid being in some sense what Aristotle calls "a completed action." This being so, all novels imitate a world of potentiality, even if this implies a philosophy disclaimed by their authors. They have a fixation on the eidetic imagery of beginning, middle, and end, potency, and cause. Novels, then, have beginnings, ends, and potentiality, even if the world has not.[48]

Perhaps it is too difficult for the reader to engage with the idea that a narrative should not end or cannot end. If we acknowledge that the past is a country from which we've all emigrated,[49] then we must also acknowledge that we cannot return to that past, that there might be no happy ending available, and this awareness brings with it a sense of loss. Derrida suggests why there is, in general, a need for an ending, and that might in turn explain why that need is, I argue, defeated by Rushdie. For Derrida, something like Shalimar, something that haunts, might both force an ending and at the same time, deny an ending: 'haunting is historical . . . but it is not *dated*, it is never docilely given a date in the chain of presents, day after day, according to the instituted order of a calendar'.[50] What haunts (and what haunts a text) is perceived as something historical – in the sense that it has come from the past – but at the same time, can't be tied to a historical moment because it recurs to present its historical self frequently and is also expected to return. Therefore, it exists as an unstable or shifting past and present and future: 'the ghostly would displace itself like the movement of this history'.[51] Shalimar is that ghostly inhabitant of the past, present and future, and his promise haunts the past, present and future of this novel which is denied an ending. Derrida refers to Kojève's concept of a future where 'there is necessarily some promise and therefore some historicity as future-to-come'.[52]

Derrida suggests that in order to avoid the possibility or even the accusation of 'failure' or 'disjunction' or being 'out of joint', we imagine this future '*to come*, not . . . in the future present', but in a less determined *living present*.[53] This 'living present' of Kashmir in *Midnight's Children* and *Shalimar the Clown* is, then, the only way to tell the history of Kashmir without producing a 'failure', without creating a 'disjuncture' between the need to tell or retell a history, and the awareness that to tell a history is always to tell a certain history, an ideologically motivated history, which at some time and for some reader, will always be 'out of joint'. History can't be told because any history is flawed. Rushdie, as a consequence, tells a present moment. History is reformed into a present moment, a 'now' – history becomes now, and similarly l'histoire/the story – narrative – becomes something other than a narrative: it is not a literary history or historical literature, but instead an exercise in defeating the sense of an ending required, in the usual order of things, by narrative form and by the reader.

Derrida's sense of a promise is something that is at once present, past and future: a promise might be spoken at a time in the past, it might hold sway over the present and refer to a time in the future – and of course the verb 'promise' is the performative that produces the act to which it refers as it is spoken. The kind of history or present or past represented in *Shalimar the Clown* is one of a promise of a 'historicity as future-to-come'.[54] The power of the haunting promise is its remarkable historicity: 'Ghosts don't have to live in the real world'[55] and 'only the living dead are . . . free of time' (225). However, the power of haunting carries heavy burdens, as Boonyi's father's stuttering claim that 'the living dead are f-f-f-free of time' suggests: for some, 'the present is already too much' and it would be unthinkable to have to 'cope with the future as well' (53). For Boonyi, an inability to think about the future (in the manner that Saleem could as narrator of his history) means that her notion that 'ghosts don't have to live in the real world' is cruelly rendered a false assumption: returning to Kashmir after a self-imposed exile, Boonyi is rejected by her family and becomes a ghost, 'the living dead' who on her return to the past, to her childhood home, instead of achieving the 'happy ending' (220) that she had anticipated, can only 'haunt' a woodshed on a mountain in Kashmir (223–4).

Defeating the sense of an ending produces a sense of defeated desire: the novel's aim is, then, to leave the reader stranded in the middle. Like narrative, histories try to oppress the reader into following a specific route. That is true for all histories, subaltern or not – if 'the "subaltern" cannot appear without the thought of the "elite"'[56] then the subaltern history is similarly compromised by the existence of dominant or colonial histories, and that is why, according to Spivak, the subaltern cannot speak. Hayden White asserts the similarity between literary and historical narratives, suggesting that 'histories gain part of their explanatory effect by their success in making stories out of mere chronicles; and stories in turn are made out of chronicles by an operation . . . called "emplotment"'.[57] White concurs with the idea that 'the historian was above all a story teller', noting that 'historical sensibility was manifested in the capacity to make a plausible story out of a congeries of "facts"'[58] which made no sense, were fragmentary and incomplete.[59] White notes that historians employed what Collingwood called 'the constructive imagination', but goes further than this to describe a process of telling history that is more akin to creating fiction. He suggests that:

> no given set of casually recorded historical events can in itself constitute a story; the most it might offer to the historian are story *elements*. The events are made into a story by the suppression or subordination of certain of them and the highlighting of others, . . . in short, all of the techniques that we would normally expect to find in the emplotment of a novel or a play.[60]

The historian may produce a narrative as unreliable as fiction, then: and *Midnight's Children* is an oft-cited example of how just unreliable fictional narration can be. However, in *Midnight's Children*, the historian or 'teller-of-tales' (448) has a 'peripheral' role (447) rather than an authoritative one, and perhaps this is why the historian's role can be perverted by this narrative; instead of producing a history in linear fashion which posits a reliable interpretation of events and concludes with a certain ending, this narrative refuses a happy ending, or an ending of any kind.

Narrative uncertainty renders the assumption of an ending impossible. It also calls into question the present moment, asking, what is the now? Can the 'now' best be understood as a kind of rift (or partition) that like an island or border can be seen physically? Is that why timelines exist? Or does the need to locate the present moment on a timeline render it false and impossible, because to mark it on a historical continuum is both to relegate it to the past and to anticipate it in the future? This sense of the impossible timeline or continuum, the historian's tool, when telling the history of Kashmir, is the reason for the constantly disrupted, circumvented, questioned, restarted, rendered impossible family tree in *Midnight's Children*, by all of the adoptions, renamings and namings, false mothers and doubles.

Is postmodern reality or poststructuralist narrative a simple explanation for this rift, and for the way in which the narrative in *Midnight's Children* and *Shalimar the Clown* is constructed? Or does the sense of questioning and uncertainty come from elsewhere or serve a different purpose? Frederic Jameson 'uses the language of psychoanalysis (the breakdown of the signifying chain in psychosis) to provide a genealogy for the subject of postmodern cultural fragmentation'.[61] To put this idea in the context of *Midnight's Children* is to enable a whole new approach to the way that history is presented in the text: Saleem tells a 'family history' as the kind of history that he can engage with – his narrative is a genealogy of a postmodern subject. Homi Bhabha responds to Jameson's approach by suggesting that:

> Psychoanalytic temporality . . . invests the utterance of the "present" – its displaced times, its affective intensities – with cultural and political value. Placed in the scenario of the unconscious, the "present" is neither the mimetic sign of historical contemporaneity (the immediacy of experience), nor is it the visible terminus of the historical past (the teleology of tradition).[62]

Are either of those two imaginings of the 'present moment' – the immediacy of experience, or the perceptible closure of what is understood as 'the past' the way that the present moment occurs in *Midnight's Children* or in *Shalimar the Clown*? Or is something else happening? For Bhabha, the postcolonial text is constructed in 'a new international space of discontinuous historical realities' aware of 'interstitial passages' that are inscribed in the 'in-between' which is perceived as the sudden awareness of historical fault, or a 'sudden disjunction of the present'. This is a necessary process for Bhabha, because 'it is only through a structure of splitting and displacement – "the fragmented and schizophrenic decentring of the self" – that the architecture of the new historical subject emerges at the limits of representation itself'.[63] Bhabha claims that hybrid cultural identifications remake boundaries beyond simple oppositions, and:

> such assignations of social differences – where difference is neither One nor the Other but something else besides, in-between – find their agency in a form of the "future" where the past is not originary, where the present is not simply transitory. It is . . . an interstitial future, that emerges *in-between* the claims of the past and the needs of the present.[64]

Saleem is significant as a migrant individual in contributing towards the postmodern concept of the real. Or, perhaps it is the migrant author or literary historian who is significant in the postmodern conception of the real. Both demonstrate the way that the present must be imagined or constructed. But if this is all they do, they are determining knowledge as much as a retelling of history would. Whereas, to see the text in the place of its narrator or its author is to enable the present moment to exist in full, in the way that it is able to, unrestricted by history. And this is what is at work at the end of the text of *Midnight's Children*:

> The present of the world, that appears through the breakdown of temporality, signifies a historical *intermediacy*, familiar to the psychoanalytic concept of *Nachträglichkeit* (deferred action): "a transferential function, whereby the past dissolves in the present, so that the future becomes (once again) an *open question*, instead of being specified by the fixity of the past." The iterative "time" of the future as a becoming "once again open", makes available to marginalized or minority identities a mode of performative agency.[65]

As the text of *Midnight's Children* is about to come to a physical end, the narrator's subject is the future, and he questions the purpose of writing about the future in what started as a historical narrative, because future events cause discomfort: wet-nurse Durga enters the text in the final few pages, and 'every day a dozen new stories gushed from her lips'. Saleem only admits her into the narrative 'with the greatest reluctance' because 'her name . . . had the smell of new things; she represented novelty, beginnings, the advent of new stories events complexities' at a point when he is 'no longer interested in anything new' (445). Nevertheless, she is included, and similarly, Picture Singh's future narrative is begun at this point. Saleem struggles to conclude his narrative, saying: 'I shall have to write the future as I have written the past, to set it down with the absolute certainty of a prophet. But the future cannot be preserved in a jar; one jar must remain empty . . . I shall reach my birthday . . . and no doubt a marriage will take place . . . and Kashmir will be waiting' (462). The future has not yet happened, but a perceived ending exists only in that future, meaning that for now and until after the end of the text, the narrative rests in the present. What follows this expectation of a future in the waiting Kashmir (a Kashmir that 'will be waiting', that in a future time will exist in a present moment of waiting for something to happen and will have been existing in that state for a time ever since a past moment at which it 'began' to wait, like waiting for the fruition of a promise) is a hurried summary of all the people and events from Saleem's past, present and future, from his grandfather Aadam Aziz to his son Aadam Sinai, and the sudden perception that he 'shall never reach Kashmir' but instead, 'shall die with Kashmir on [his] lips' (462).

This is the way that Kashmir appears throughout the text: 'women have done their best', Saleem says, to shape his life, and to shape the telling of it, as is evidenced by the demanding narratee Padma who cries, three quarters of the way through the text: 'begin all over again' (347). Kashmir as a future 'dream' returns the historical narration of those women to the present moment (406). Like Shalimar's promise of revenge that continues beyond the ending of the narrative of *Shalimar the Clown*, what remains after everything for Saleem Sinai is the haunting promise that his body will be reduced to 'specks of voiceless dust' as will the generations after him, who remain, at the close of the text, 'unable to live or die in peace' (463), ahistoric, ghost-like, unrepresentable in history.

6

Translating Theory: If *Grimus* Fails

Rushdie's *Grimus* was not an especially successful first novel in comparison with his later work. Nor was it particularly well received in Rushdie scholarship. Perhaps one reason for this is the feeling that postcolonial sensibilities were somehow misapplied in the novel to a vague Native American context. Though there are common concerns between postcolonial and Native American contexts, they are not, perhaps, so easily interchangeable. Instead, the novel can be read more fruitfully as an early example of the twenty-first-century meeting between ecocriticism and postcolonial theory. This chapter considers *Grimus* from a postcolonial-ecocritical perspective, and via Said's travelling theory, which offers a methodology for understanding Rushdie's motivation to translate – or 'travel' a postcolonial condition of migrancy to a Native American and science-fiction context, dominated by an emphasis on environmental power.

Edward Said's travelling theory described a process by which theory might travel, or, translate. This chapter begins with a discussion of the text's 'failure', its reception as an awkwardly located precursor to Rushdie's later fiction which deals with ideas of imperialism and postcolonial subjects, often migrant figures. *Grimus* is concerned with a Native American migrant figure, though, who is displaced to a location that is closer to science fiction than to Rushdie's later magic realist environments. The text lacks some of the industrialized landscapes and the tools of science fiction; these are replaced by an emphasis on nature and wildlife. This emphasis on nature in a Native American context and Rushdie's preoccupation with dominating forces and migration invite an ecocritical reading via Edward Said's travelling theory. The postcolonial migrant figure (Flapping Eagle) and the imperial symbol (the eponymous Grimus) travel to a Native American context which is heavily reliant on the natural environment for meaning and power in ways that resemble ecocritical sensibilities, and in this way the postcolonial context of *Grimus* that readers have read back into the text becomes an early example of postcolonial ecocritical writing, or, writing that merits a postcolonial ecocritical reading. The narrative itself invites the idea of travelling theory because it deals with theories that must pass through the new contexts of different individuals and alter when in their new position. Because of this, the idea of travelling theory is doubly applicable to the novel.

Receiving *Grimus*

Compared with most of Rushdie's novels, *Grimus* has been neglected in academic work, and not just because the text preceded *Midnight's Children* so quietly. Some readers have suggested that the novel in some ways circumvents the issue of postcolonial migration; the text does not directly deal with the colonial context that is explored in Rushdie's later works. Andrew Teverson notes that 'Reading Grimus retrospectively, and with a socio-political awareness that the text itself does not encourage the reader to adopt, it is possible to see in the novel a foreshadowing of the historical and cultural interrogations that are characteristic of Rushdie's later fictions'.[1] It is the later texts that have imposed a reading context on to *Grimus*, encouraging readers to see the text as a tentative step towards the issues explored in later novels. There are some compelling arguments which initially seem to legitimize this approach, in comparison with the alternative suggestion that the novel was never intended as a comment on colonialism. Grimus was first written for a science fiction competition necessitating generic conventions, met by the exploration of immortality and multiple dimensions but also by a non-specified population with a future that is conveyed as in flux; this generic need might account for the sense that the novel evades a more materially grounded exploration of concepts pertinent to postcolonial thinking. Published material on *Grimus* tends towards Catherine Cundy's and Philip Engblom's assessments of the novel, as valuable only when read as a precursor to the later works. For Cundy, the text prefigures both styles and themes that will be explored in later works, suggesting that issues of 'personal national identity, the legacy of colonialism, [and] the problems of exile'[2] are presented here, yet handled with more maturity in the later novels. Engblom calls the novel 'competent' but lacking in comedic power and in some way limited by its function as allegory.[3] Gregory Rubinson reads *Grimus* in more direct postcolonial terms with reference to the idea of migration. Rubinson again reads *Grimus* as a precursor to the portrayal of the migrant and their 'adaptability' in later works, especially *The Satanic Verses*, but, in particular, notes that the novel begins a sequence of questions about received information. As Rubinson suggests, while in *Midnight's Children*, Padma questions Saleem's sanity because his version of Indian history does not match dominant representations, and Gibreel in *The Satanic Verses* questions the sanity of prophecy, in *Grimus* Virgil Jones comments that 'a man is sane only to the extent that he prescribes to a previously-agreed construction of reality' (62). This, for Rubinson, is a more general statement which implicitly refers to colonial and postcolonial constructions of historical and religious knowledge and reality.[4]

However, it is unsatisfactory to read *Grimus* simply as a tentative first step towards the real subject of postcolonial migration, not least because this strategy fails to address the particular choices made in the novel, such as: why engage specifically with the Native American figure? Why is there such overt textuality in the novel? What is the function of the intriguingly named Media? As well as the commonly used definition of the term 'media' to refer to means of mass communication, an alternative and older definition from linguistics refers to the voiced stop or unaspirated stop in Ancient Greek, implying that Media occupies a liminal space mid-utterance, the kind of space where, outside the logic of grammar, the other things associated with translation (the temptations explored in the introductory chapter to this book, for instance) might rest. Media might also imply mediation, a role as mediator that translators often fulfil. This chapter will consider these questions with reference to Edward Said's 'Travelling Theory' and 'Travelling Theory Reconsidered' to engage with the way that a literary text can participate in the translation of theory. If a history can be translated, or a story, a character, an image, can't a theory be translated, too?

Grimus: A theory?

My position in this chapter rests on the idea that a novel – a literary rather than an academic or critical text – can present or even produce theory. Postcolonial theory has been constructed as much from its literary texts as its theoretical ones; beginning within departments of literary studies and related disciplines, postcolonial theory has often been supplementary to the literary texts produced in colonial and decolonized locations. A good example to support this idea is Aimé Cesaire's work, and in particular his long poem *Return to my Native Land* (*Cahier d'un retour au pays natal*, 1956), and his revision of Shakespeare's *The Tempest*, *A Tempest* (Une Tempête, 1969). *Return to my Native Land* is at once a presentation of the sense of alienation felt by the colonial migrant after a prolonged period living in the land of the colonizer, and it is a call for a renewed sense of identity and pride for the colonized Antillean. The poem celebrates, bitterly and in the sense of battle, the death of the 'good nigger' who submitted unquestioningly to a sense of 'unworthiness';[5] such sentiments are required to die in order to make way for black people with enough fight to demand an end to the colonial regime. The poem may be read as an early example of writing (or theory) on the subject of migration for the colonized subject. *A Tempest* rewrites Shakespeare's play, a text of fundamental interest for postcolonial studies because of the master-slave relationship between Prospero, a European newly arrived on a tropical island, and Caliban, a brutally dominated figure who is the island's only native inhabitant aside from spirits (also under Prospero's command). Cesaire writes a translation of the play specifically for a black audience, a translation for a colonized audience but also a translation into the language of the colonizer in Martinique, French. Although Shakespeare's Caliban has no specific racial identity (though his mother had blue eyes), in Cesaire's play, Caliban is positioned as a black slave and Ariel, the most powerful spirit, a mulatto slave. The play conveys a theoretical stance in its very specific recontextualization of the Prospero-Caliban relationship, conveying the potential for the black slave to achieve freedom and for the enslaved workers to achieve freedom in general through organization: when Ariel and Caliban work together, the ending (of the play, and metaphorically) is very different: instead of Caliban's penitent obedience and Prospero's authoritative afterword in Shakespeare's play, there is 'freedom' in *A Tempest*. In this way, the literary text of resistance pre-empts theoretical engagements with the same subject.

More recently, Anastasia Valassopoulos has read Ahdaf Soueif's *The Map of Love* as an example of how the postcolonial novel may in fact be read as self-conscious theory. The novel brings together three generations of women: an American finds her ancestor's diaries from her life as a British migrant in Egypt initially as part of a colonial party and later when she is married to an Egyptian. The American travels to Egypt to find another descendent of the same family who can translate the diaries and letters into English for her. The result is a thorough rereading – quite literally – of the colonial project in Egypt and its marginal figures on both sides, as well as a response to the dominant records of the colonial project. Because postcolonial authors are, Valassopoulos argues, already using interdisciplinarity when writing, it is difficult to situate the author as writing from just a literary position, and instead they must be seen to be coming from a critical perspective, too: in this way, in *The Map of Love*, Soueif 'not only integrates post-colonial theory into her writing but also manages to expose the tensions that lie within post-colonial theory by further revealing its unavoidable complicity with differing disciplines'.[6] This specific example establishes a precept for reading the postcolonial literary text as postcolonial theory. Rushdie's position, of challenging the English language with a new English that aims to write back to the colonial centre, inevitably positions him as creating theory rather than existing outside it.

Theory: Travelling or translating?

These examples of postcolonial literary texts with theoretical attitudes share a common feature: in each there is an instance of migration. On the level of plot, each text refers to an act or to several acts of migration. But each text is at the same time an exploration of the impact of colonial and postcolonial migration. *Grimus* too shares the preoccupation with migration; Flapping Eagle is the wandering protagonist with the dubious gift of immortality. Seeking his sister and the figure whose potions sustain immortal life, Sispy (who is later revealed to be Grimus), Flapping Eagle arrives at K (Qâf or Calf Island) and makes a further journey into the centre in order to confront Grimus. This second journey compels Flapping Eagle to develop a tolerance to dimension fever that normally attacks all those embarking on this journey. Dimension fever is a kind of darkness and hallucination, like monsters that 'come from inside you' but can be kept away by daylight (69).Grimus maintains his power at the centre (which can, of course, be read as the colonial or metropolitan centre) by sustaining a gateway which works by overpowering feeble minds with the concept of dimensional coexistence. Clearly this can be read, in simple terms, as colonial mythology; this mythology has hitherto prevented challenges to the imperial Grimus's authority: for Dolores O'Toole, for example, the idea of challenging Grimus instead of tolerating the status quo is so disturbing that she refuses to acknowledge Flapping Eagle, saying 'You're not here' (59), and when Dolores's partner Virgil Jones informs her that he is also leaving with Flapping Eagle, she simply repeats 'Nothing will change, will it, Virgil?' (62), in a refusal to contemplate change that speaks of an inability to admit the impact of migrants and their migrations on the centre, a feeling that the text rejects with its thoroughly mobile characters.

In 'Travelling Theory' Said asks, as the title suggests, whether a theory can travel in space or time, and what happens to it when it does. Said's concept is based on his observation that 'ideas and theories travel – from person to person, from situation to situation, from one period to another'.[7] This travelling can take various forms: 'acknowledged or unconscious influence, creative borrowing, or wholesale appropriation'.[8] All of these forms seem to replicate language used to describe translation where the original exerts its influence, and is adapted to various degrees by the translator, depending on their approach to the debate over faithfulness and freedom in translation. The third term, 'wholesale appropriation', certainly seems to refer to the kind of translation undertaken as part of the colonial project, which involved an intensive translation project, that Said has discussed in *Orientalism*; the first Orientalists were accomplished translators like William Jones and Abraham-Hyacinthe Antequil-Duperron, and their translations furthered the colonial project. Getting even closer to the kinds of questions asked repeatedly of translation, Said asks whether, in the process of movement, the theory 'gains or loses in strength' or 'becomes altogether different'.[9] He also calls this pattern 'discernible and recurrent'[10] implying a uniformity to the process resembling the kind of scientific endeavour that translation has sometimes been thought to possess, particularly in its earliest examples when theories were at their most prescriptive.

There is, he suggests, a three- or four-stage pattern to the movement of a theory, which involves: first an original set of circumstances in which the idea was first conceived (and this might be in either an Eastern or a Western location); secondly a process during which the theory passes through the pressure of various contexts and into its new place or time; next is a set of conditions of acceptance or resistance during which the idea is introduced, and finally a partial transformation of that idea in its new context.[11] Said implies that this fourth circumstance is not always present by referring to a three- *or* four-stage process in the theory's journey, suggesting that this transformation is not always required. The implication of this for translation is perhaps that is it only when the fourth stage is put into practice (for whatever reason) that a translation of the theory itself takes place. Without this partial transformation of the idea to meet the demands of its context, the theory remains stable, and simply operates in a different location. It might be pertinent to ask what circumstances are required for this fourth stage, or indeed, why only some theories are 'transformed' when the process of translation is initiated.

It might be difficult to conceive of exactly what Said identifies as travelling theory; he is describing a more transformative process than would occur when theories are simply seen as applicable to a range of contexts. The difference between using theories in different locations or times, and translating theories when they travel, is to do with what is lost or gained – which is also a fundamental question for translation theory. In 'Travelling Theory Reconsidered', Said specifies that it is power and rebelliousness that might be lost when a theory travels. Alternatively, as he describes in relation to Fanon, a theory may gain a specific kind of power when it travels. He discusses how, in *The Wretched of The Earth*, Fanon has used Lukacs's subject-object dialectic.[12] Said notes that Lukacs and Adorno share European culture and Hegelian tradition, a culture and a tradition that Fanon doesn't share. However, Fanon has moved from the Caribbean with *Black Skin, White Masks* to Algeria, and his response to the progress of the Algerian revolution is that it 'has deepened and widened the gulf between France and its colony'[13] in Fanon's later work, *The Wretched of the Earth*. Said notes that while *The Wretched of the Earth* is firmly dependent on Lukacs, Fanon does not apply Lukacs's dialectic straightforwardly; he has a different focus: 'The issue for Lukacs was the primacy of consciousness in history; for Fanon it is the primacy of geography in history, and then of history over consciousness and subjectivity. That there is subjectivity at all is because of colonialism'.[14] In the colonial situation, Fanon realizes, 'neither the colonist nor the colonized behaves as if subject and object might someday be reconciled'.[15] Said notes that, in his new theoretical and geographical context, and in order to set out the history of a nation and of decolonization, Fanon gives prominence to the 'national element' that was missing in Lukacs's *History and Class Consciousness*.[16]

It is important to be alert to the similarity between the manner in which Said discusses the way that theories should be received once they have travelled and the way that translation is described. Said writes that when others use Lukacs (and his examples include Adorno and Fanon) we don't think of those theorists as 'coming after', as having the second-degree status that had conventionally been applied to translations. Instead, they transform Lukacs by 'pulling him from one sphere or region into another' to suggest 'the possibility of actively different locales, sites, situations for theory, without facile universalism or overgeneral totalizing'.[17] Said notes that in analysing the way a theory might translate:

> theory has to be grasped in the place and the time out of which it emerges as a part of that time, working in and for it, responding to it; then, consequently, that first place can be measured against subsequent places where the theory turns up for use.[18]

If we accept that Grimus's theory (and the theoretical basis of *Grimus*) is imperialist and homogenizing, then it is by applying Said's ideas about travelling theory that it becomes possible to see the relevance of displacing the postcolonial migrant figure of Flapping Eagle and the figure of colonial power in Grimus, to the Native American context. The text offers an opportunity to make connections between different versions of displacement and cultural erosion that are at work in both postcolonial and Native American contexts.

Grimus and postcolonial ecocriticism

Ib Johansen has read *Grimus* as a comment on the possibilities of magic in narrative, of enchantment and disenchantment,[19] and also as a metafictional narrative which, in particular, revises Farid ud-Din 'Attâr's *Conference of the Birds*, a mid-twelfth-century poem about the Grimus (or Simurg in 'Attâr's poem) God-like figure and the relationship between God (Simurg/Grimus) and man (the 30 birds in 'Attâr's poem; the other immortals in *Grimus*). In *Grimus*, Johansen suggests, the relationship is flawed, while 'Attâr's reading conveys it as ideal. The God and Man relationship has been read as relating to colonizer and colonized by Johansen, where the clash in value systems is between the metaphorical third-world (the townspeople) and the metaphorical colonizer (Grimus who remains in control from his palace on the hill), although the minority group represented in this text is the Native American rather than the South Asian under British colonial and decolonized conditions, the subjects of Rushdie's later novels.[20] It is in this way that we can first see the sense of travelling theory in Edward Said's terms, as represented in the movement of a specific theoretical concern from one context to another: from the science-fiction fantasy set in a North American Native American encounter in Grimus (1975), to the colonized and decolonized South Asia in *Midnight's Children* (1981), *Shame* (1983) and *The Moor's Last Sigh* (1995) and also to the South Asian postcolonial diaspora in the UK (*The Satanic Verses,* 1988) and America (*Shalimar the Clown,* 2005). When Flapping Eagle as a postcolonial migrant figure meets Grimus as an imperial symbol, the postcolonial sensibilities underlying the text are located in a natural environment that dominates events. The power of the wildlife and natural imagery invites a reading from a postcolonial-ecocritical position.

It is useful to consider why the text engages specifically with a Native American figure as the receptacle for theory, than with a more straightforwardly postcolonial migrant figure, which might be expected on the basis of Rushdie's later body of work. One response to this question might be to consider the text as an early example of postcolonial ecocritical writing, as a precursor to the very recently established theoretical field of postcolonial ecocriticism. Ecocriticism is, in brief, the study of the relationship between literature and the environment. The concept emerged in the 1970s but the theory only started to be applied in the USA in the late 1980s and in the UK in the early 1990s. Cheryll Glotfelty is one of its founding scholars, who has edited collections of essays on the subject and founded a literary association – Interdisciplinary Studies in Literature and Environment. Recently, analogues between postcolonial and ecocritical perspectives have been identified, and Graham Huggan and Helen Tiffin's *Postcolonial Ecocriticism* (2009) is the founding text in this field. *Grimus* invites an ecocritical reading because time and again, the natural environment, the sea and the landscape, asserts its authority over the actions of human figures.

Grimus is a science-fiction novel: it was initially written for entry into a science fiction competition, and it involves some of the features common to the genre, including the existence of multiple dimensions and an ability to travel through them, and a reliance on telepathy. But it lacks other common science-fiction tropes: the story is set at a time that feels more like the past than an imagined future; there is no technology; and there is no industrialized environment. These factors (technology, industrialization) are replaced in *Grimus* with alternatives that open up possibilities for an ecocritical reading. The object of power that replaces technology is a rose (albeit a stone rose). The rose is a symbol of a certain kind of nature that is both tamed and untamed: roses are tended, pruned, taught to grow around objects imposed on to their environment, they are grafted, genetically altered to produce different colours and varieties, and yet in spite of all this interference they retain their thorns and so they are never fully subject to human will. In this way, the location of power at the centre of the text is not necessarily a human source and nature rather than humanity might emerge at the centre of the story. Likewise, the rose demonstrates the ecocritical preoccupation that the division between nature and culture in the novel is not clear-cut. This idea is also conveyed in the use of Grimus's birds, who are a key to his power, and the division between the natural and the human worlds remains uncertain because of the identities of Flapping Eagle and Bird-Dog, whose animal names connect them with the natural world. More importantly, though, is the omnipresent natural world which remains outside human control or even explanation. Ecocriticism insists that everything cannot be contained in or explained by linguistic or social structures; nature is a real force or entity and not just a concept. Calf Island is 'the most terrible place in all creation' (15), it is unfathomable and uncontrollable, and at its centre is the mountain which exerts its power over humanity: 'The mountain drew its own kind to itself' (16). In the midst of this terrible strength of nature is the frailty of humanity, unable to tackle the natural environment by linguistic means: 'language makes concepts. Concepts make chains. I am bound . . . bound, and I don't know where' (15), says Virgil Jones, who has remained free from the island to an extent, but not because of his application of human linguistic or social structures, which he knows are fallible, nor through resistance: instead, Virgil Jones knows that the island could exert its power if it chose to, and he inhabits a temporary freedom: 'we seem to survive' (15), he says.

Travelling theory in *Grimus*

The narrative invites the idea of travelling theory because it deals with Grimus's theory of immortal singularity, a theory that relies on all of the island inhabitants' consciousnesses combining with Grimus's and ultimately being consumed by him to create one singular, and immortal, consciousness. Grimus's theory, then, must pass through the new context of those other consciousnesses, notably Flapping Eagle's whose consciousness offers the strongest resistance, and in doing so, it will either meet acceptance or resistance, and ultimately it may alter. This plot means that the idea of travelling theory is doubly applicable to the novel: not only does it address the novel's reception in academia, but also it suggests that the novel is itself concerned with the translation of theories.

The first stage in Said's travelling theory involves establishing the original set of circumstances in which the idea was first conceived. In order to apply the idea of travelling theory to the events of the narrative, it is important to consider how the text establishes its original set of circumstances, to refer to Said's formula for the first stage of travelling theory. The original set of circumstances concerns Flapping Eagle, an Axona Indian who acquires this name at his 21st birthday. Flapping Eagle is the medium through which the theory at the centre of the text must travel. The specific theory which must travel through Flapping Eagle belongs to Grimus, the eponymous figure who inhabits a God-like peripheral position in the text. His theory rests on the possibility of amalgamating all of the island's consciousnesses into an immortal singularity; this is a position that implies unity – in that all of the consciousnesses are intended to come together to create a coherent whole – but is in fact hierarchical, because Grimus intends to remain as the only surviving consciousness, constructed or strengthened by all the individuals whose consciousnesses must be sacrificed when they are amalgamated with his own. The theory resembles colonialism to an extent: the desire to take disparate identities and to remould their concepts of self evokes Gayatri Spivak's sense of epistemic violence as explored in 'Can the Subaltern Speak?': Grimus isn't governing by direct force, but his aim is to destroy the sense of identity and structure underlying reality for the inhabitants of Calf Island. Grimus's motivation is to test the limits of his own power, for his own sense of glory. The theory might be summarized as an attempt to control and make uniform through epistemic violence. Flapping Eagle embodies the new set of circumstances through which this theory must pass in order to be translated.

Another question concerns Media, whose peripheral role is nevertheless pivotal because she mediates between Flapping Eagle and Grimus in the guise of translator-mediator. Like Aoi Ue from *The Moor's Last Sigh* who I've also read as a translator, Media is positioned as a female supporter to a male protagonist in a fantastical and restrictive location. And like Aoi, Media is 'a resilient woman . . . but very near breaking point' (227). Also like Aoi, Media occupies a position with limited freedom, under the control of the owner of the house: she is a prostitute subject to the brothel madam, Jocasta. She is more obedient than Aoi, though, obeying her employer 'unquestioningly' (115). Media's role in the text is peripheral, but important: she mediates, as her name implies she should, to persuade Jocasta to grant refuge to Flapping Eagle (186), fulfilling the translator's role of mediator, but also falling victim to the translator's temptation for their material: '*Where he goes, I go*' (187), Media thinks, staring at Flapping Eagle's face. Media is also responsible for reconnecting Flapping Eagle with his sister, Bird-Dog, at a moment where she performs the linguistic definition of her name (the voiced stop in Ancient Greek) by hovering somewhere between speech and silence: 'Media was about to speak, but remained silent' (222). As an obedient and often silent figure, Media's role as translator is far from subversive and corresponds with the silent, invisible translator that Lawrence Venuti has described, a translator who is subordinate to authors, publishers and patrons. Media is a part-formed character, a mediator, lacking personal goals and motivations other than a desire for Flapping-Eagle. Yet she is also the thread that binds translations and originals, that resuscitates old texts with the breath of new languages when, at the end of the text, while trying to assert his identity and to remain distinct from Grimus, Flapping Eagle speaks to Media in order to remain focused and retain control (252).

Stage two involves a process during which the theory passes through the pressure of various contexts and into its new place or time. In the second stage of translation, a theory must pass through contexts which exert pressure. In the example of Grimus, the imperialist theory of immortal singularity must pass through the figure of the Native American as postcolonial migrant and meet all of the pressures of resistance offered therein. There are separate stages to this process. In order to destroy Grimus's power, Flapping Eagle must at first acquire his theory. This is achieved by sitting, just 'listening', because at this early stage 'There was not much else that he could do' (231); he needs to understand the kind of power that he will appropriate when he breaks the mythology that maintains Grimus's power. Grimus's theory has rested on the sense of balanced control which is – despite his own superior status – meant to rest on the well-being of those he governs over, who make up the metaphorical thirty birds within his singular-bird being. This, Flapping Eagle reminds him, is a myth: Flapping Eagle himself had been close to committing suicide using the blue liquid that would ensure his death before he found the island, but worse, in terms of Grimus's plan, the inhabitants of the island had also started to commit suicide even though they had supposedly been chosen for their superior ability to endure. The myth of immortal singularity is exposed as ultimately impossible because of this. The theory, Flapping Eagle tells Grimus, 'has already shattered too many lives' (236). Flapping Eagle's accusation is reminiscent of a postcolonial response to the brutalizing impact of colonialism. Albert Memmi's position in *The Colonizer and the Colonized*, that colonialism does not only have a brutalizing effect on the colonized but that it also brutalizes the colonizer who seeks to find ways to justify his brutality, has an analogue in the response to the bigger impact of Grimus's myth, that 'You can't control it. It controls you' (241). Consumed by the myth, the participants are reduced to the level of symbol, like the oriental and occidental created by Orientalism, in Said's conception, as Flapping Eagle accuses: 'You have reduced all other lives to the same level of unreality as your own. They are fictions now' (237). Like the failure of the so-called civilizing mission of colonialism, the activist Flapping Eagle, performing the role of postcolonial interrogator, asks: 'Don't you consider your Experiment to have been a failure since the Effect has changed its course so completely?' (239). It is also worth noting the violence in response to Grimus's myth which corresponds with the violence that, for Frantz Fanon in *The Wretched of the Earth*, is an inevitable aspect of decolonization.

Stage three involves a set of conditions of acceptance or resistance during which the idea is introduced. Flapping Eagle eventually fuses with Grimus physically and intellectually, having been tricked into taking part in Grimus's discovery of a telepathic device named the *Subsumer*, a name which reveals its unequal intentions, to subsume meaning to bring the new element (in this instance Flapping Eagle, standing in for the third-world or colonized subject) under the control or rule of the existing element (Grimus, who in this relationship is the colonizer). It is telling that this fusion between Flapping Eagle, unequal and based on trickery as it might be, begins with a strong awareness of the Self: Flapping Eagle reasserts his identity rather than having it diminished: 'Self. My self. Myself and he alone' (242). Grimus is conspicuously alone here and can be defeated because he lacks the power of the colonial centre. Alone, Grimus is revealed as at most only equal to Flapping Eagle as their minds '*commingle*', as expressed by the balance in the realization of their connection: '*You into me into you*' (242). Grimus's position is understood to be a theoretical one determining the need for absolute control from the centre no matter how violent the result. Flapping Eagle only gradually learns about Grimus who is protected by The Grimus Effect, or metaphorical 'monsters' which can work 'with devastating effects' upon the 'Inner Dimensions' or the 'universes . . . locked within one's mind' (55). The Grimus Effect is readable as colonial constructions which force the colonized subject to perceive the universe according to colonial mythology and in the process destroying the subject's identity. In the end, Grimus is defeated because Flapping Eagle retains his sense of identity – he is not, in the end, subsumed, as he reveals in a statement reminiscent of an anticolonial call for revolution that 'There is still an *I*. An *I* within me that is not *him*' (243).

Virgil Jones's diaries chart the beginning of Grimus's power and his theory. This theory rests in the power of Simurg, the Great Bird, whose name provided the anagrammatical source of his own, and means 'Thirty Birds. Si, thirty. Murg, birds' (209). This great bird is not simply the king of birds, but it is 'all-powerful and singular . . . the sum of all birds' (209), both a singular force and a multiple one containing all other consciousnesses. The Stone Rose which Virgil Jones, Nicholas Deggle and Grimus find and experiment with replicates this sense of singularity and unity as it is the gateway to interdimensional travel, and it is this gateway that permits Grimus to locate liquids – yellow for eternal life and blue for eternal death. Elsewhere (not fully specified within the text), Grimus locates a crystal which permits him to visualize a type of person who might be an ideal recipient of the gift of eternal life. With these liquids and the power to travel between locations (enabled by eternal life) and dimensions, Grimus intends to create a world populated by deserving, immortalized inhabitants. The element of visualization means that in the end, though, the distinction between concept and reality is somewhat blurred: as Virgil writes, it is 'Impossible to say whether we *found* the island or *made* it' (211). The option that it was already there not waiting to be discovered (in an undisturbed precolonial form, perhaps) is left unsaid, although the island's power undermines the notion of exploration and discovery implied by Virgil's words.

The repeated element of overt textuality in *Grimus* offers a further level of ambiguity: these are Virgil's records of the events and so express his understanding of Grimus's theories. In fact, the only time at which Grimus's theories are revealed is at this point, when Liv rereads Virgil's diaries. Because Grimus's theories are not revealed elsewhere in the text, this implies a need for textual recording of theory, perhaps to imply that the narrative proper is not an adequate place for revealing theory. This is further supported by the footnote in reference to the first mention of the Arabic letter K, or Kâf, the name given to the island. The footnote states that the correct Arabic letter is Qâf, but that Kâf is used here, risking confusion with the different letter Kaf, because the author of the footnote cannot pronounce Qâf properly (209). It might be assumed that Virgil is the author of this footnote as it is attached to his diary entry, yet Virgil reveals later that he pronounces the name 'Calf', as he is unable to pronounce the Arabic letter correctly (211). So whose footnote is it, and why the need to produce such explicit textuality? Well, by textualizing the theory, it has a fixed and specific context. If it had been expressed more gradually or as part of the narrative, it would have permeated the text and its changes and developments would have been far less pronounced. Because the theory is fixed so precisely, it invites a reading in response to Said's Travelling Theory once the context changes and the theory is challenged.

Grimus's theory was first conceived of in response to finding The Stone Rose which enabled him to travel and to acquire objects to increase his power. His theory of a perfectly balanced and united immortal society, which is governed by the ruler who is at once a powerful force but is at the same time constructed from all of the individuals over whom he rules, in part because he created them – perhaps he constructed them, perhaps he found them, but he created their immortal state – is undisturbed until Flapping Eagle challenges his power. This challenge enables a reference to the second part of Said's travelling theory, the process during which the theory passes through the pressure of various contexts and into its new place or time.

The theory passes from Grimus to Flapping Eagle, who at the end of the novel joins with and then becomes Grimus, and destroys the rose which has enabled his existence in his current form. Between these two states, the various contexts that the theory passes through, and which exert pressure, might include the separate stages of Flapping Eagle's journey. This journey is undertaken 'methodically' (33), beginning with a search for his sister Bird-Dog and Sispy/Grimus which lasted years. The key to finding Grimus is in the diaries, in the novel's explicit textuality. At every level, this section of the text screams its overt textuality at such a level that it cannot be ignored: reading from the diary (with its ambiguously authored footnote) takes up 11 pages (207–18), a significant chunk of the short novel, during which time the mediation seems only to enhance the sense of textuality, as the reader is constantly reminded that there is reading of a text going on; with the statement, for instance, that at one point, 'Liv turned several pages, jerkily' (213). In this way, the approach towards Grimus's theory is through a reinscription or a reinvention: Liv rereads the text/theory, Flapping Eagle reimagines it, and in the text there is a sense of reinscription or even reinvention.

Finally, there is a possible fourth stage which involves the partial transformation of the idea in its new context. As the text concludes, the relationship between Grimus and Flapping Eagle can most clearly be read as one of resistance to the colonizer figure of Grimus from the formerly colonized Flapping Eagle, who, 'in the company of the orchestrator of his life, had finally found a voice for himself' (236). Flapping Eagle's complaints directed towards Grimus could find an equal home if directed towards a generalized image of colonialism: Flapping Eagle accuses the dominating figure of playing a game based on 'power-lust', which has 'stunted and deformed the lives of the people you brought here' (236). It is this generalization that feels dissatisfying when the text is read straightforwardly as an attempt to address postcolonial subjectivity, but the resonance between this science-fiction scenario and an abstracted colonialism is visible. The people whose lives have been deformed by Grimus's scheme are now represented by Flapping Eagle who becomes a spokesperson for those displaced by imperialism: 'you have brought me here in the condition you wanted for the lunatic purpose you envisaged', he writes. Grimus's attempt to justify his position is in the language of colonial paternity; he seeks to justify his role as benevolent, as caring for a community that would otherwise destroy itself: 'Who do you think it is that watches over K? Do you not think that those ancient houses would have fallen down by now? Do you not think that much-tilled soil would be exhausted by now?' (237). For Flapping Eagle, the only solution is to destroy that figure of unjust power; like the colonial situation, though, it is not possible to return to a precolonial state even if Grimus is destroyed: effects of colonialism will remain. It is here that Grimus's theory, having met its strongest resistance, alters to suit its new surroundings. When Flapping Eagle takes over, he doesn't exactly 'take [Grimus's] place', as Grimus ordered. To do so would be to continue Grimus's legacy but under a new name. Instead, Flapping Eagle makes a more permanent change to the structure of society (as Ngugi has described is necessary in *Decolonizing the Mind*); he effects 'an adjustment of the Rose' as symbol of power, by 'Re-Conceptualizing' (237). He undermines the binary between dimensions that has persisted – 'There was no Gate now. Calf Island was one place again' (248) – and achieves 'A fascinating new status quo' (250). Flapping Eagle becomes 'I-Eagle' (250) and is transformed by the process of translating or travelling theory in Bill Ashcroft's positive sense as described in *Postcolonial Transformations*: rather than 'flapping' aimlessly, his struggle for identity is over when he welcomes his identity as 'I', 'I-Eagle'.

The postcolonial migrant figure has achieved a sense of positive identity by challenging the basis of imperial power through resistance, but this battle has taken place in the context of a powerful natural environment dominated by birds, roses, an island with magnetic force and the tides that lap the borders of that island. *Grimus* has resonance with postcolonial thinking but can be read as a more successful novel if its postcolonial sensibilities are understood as being translated into an ecocritical framework. Yet, it remains to address the question of why this conflict has been played out in this particular context rather than in the metropolitan centres that Rushdie's later works explore. The focus on the natural world could be read as a retreat from more pressing questions of politics, a way of sidestepping postcolonial materiality. On the other hand, it could point to the ongoing impact of imperialism on landscapes and natural environments in a time of increasing globalization. It could enable a dialogue between indigenous and postcolonial concerns that is otherwise elided by postcolonial theory. It may, too, be an attempt to speak of the translatability of concepts such as hybridity and migration, or an indicator of Rushdie's comments of resistance to academic pigeonholing that have led him to dismiss his categorization as postmodern or postcolonial, a tendency that points to Rushdie's self-conscious position as author and public figure that has recently been explored in his memoir, *Joseph Anton*, which is addressed in Chapter 8 of this book.

7

Paint, Patronage, Power and the Translator's Visibility[1]

The patron is traditionally an important figure in translation, holding a significant level of power over what is translated, for whom and how. The same can be said of art patronage. This chapter explores Rushdie's engagement with painting as an intersemiotic translation process, where stories are translated into their visual form and, as in the case of Dashwanth in *The Enchantress of Florence*, afterwards translated from art into flesh. This chapter also focuses on *The Moor's Last Sigh* where Aoi Uë, like Dashwanth, carries out visual work under a patron's guidance until enabled, by the medium they work with, to transgress. Ultimately, this chapter explores Lawrence Venuti's position on the translator's invisibility and Rushdie's attempt to make the translator visible again. *The Enchantress of Florence* begins with a description of the effect the paintbrush has on its viewer in the decadent style that is typical of Rushdie's works: 'Paint her into the world . . . for there is such magic in your brushes that she may even come to life, spring off your pages and join us for feasting and wine' (120). Paintings evoke extreme reactions, especially in their patrons. This is exemplified by both Dashwanth's paintings of the lost princess Qara Köz in The Enchantress of Florence and Vasco Miranda's painting of a naked, pregnant Aurora in The Moor's La*st Sigh*. Both these artists transform the subject by painting them: Dashwanth's painting literally reawakens the princess who had been lost from memory in the royal family's stories. Aurora's story is conveyed by her son only when Vasco's obsessive desire for her leads him to imprison an art restorer, Aoi Uë, who is ordered to uncover the painting. The original image had been painted over with a more conventional work when it was rejected as obscene by its patron, Aurora's husband. The transformations of Aurora and Qara take place in the visual medium of painting, yet they evoke similar textual transformations, or translations, common to Rushdie's body of work as a whole. This chapter argues that the translator's role is transformed in works that engage with visual culture. This transformation enables the translator's transgressive power to be demonstrated more effectively, as the translator wrests control away from his or her patron. Power in patronage is normally enabled because the painter, writer or translator works within the parameters defined within the patron's worldview. By reading these translations into art through the framework of visual culture, the postcolonial urge to transform through retelling becomes clear: as Ella Shohat and Robert Stam point out, visual culture represents a breaking away from Eurocentrism.[2] The intentions of visual culture as a theoretical framework match Rushdie's, and an analysis of *The Enchantress of Florence* and *The Moor's Last Sigh* demonstrates the power of the translator as a figure for transgressive transformation in its positive, political, postcolonial sense.

Patronage determines the eventual product; the work created must please its patron, as André Lefevere has suggested: 'ideology is often enforced by the patrons, the people or institutions who commission or publish translations' and other works.[3] In Rushdie's novels, art works are commissioned by a patron who ultimately sanctions the work, initially restricting the freedom of the artist or translator. This restriction is figured explicitly in *The Enchantress of Florence*, where the artist Dashwanth who is hired to depict the lost princess Qara Köz becomes trapped in his canvas. It is also made literal in *The Moor's Last Sigh*, where Vasco Miranda, at one time imprisoned by the work that he was commissioned to produce, turns gaoler and forces Moor to translate his life story into textuality from a prison cell, and into a story that is pleasing to the captor who has commissioned the work. He is accompanied by art restorer Aoi Uë who is also held captive and is ordered to restore and uncover Vasco's original painting, destroying the 'translated' image which has been painted on top. In this role, she becomes a translator figure, who is at the same time Moor's narratee and thus the translator of his text too. Appropriate to dominant imaginings of an unobtrusive translator, Aoi is invisible throughout the majority of this text (the reader only becomes aware of her in the last chapter of the novel). Even so, her reception of Moor's text has just as strong an impact on the way that it is written as Vasco's more visible control. Visual culture studies is interested in the culture of gazing or looking; the point at which Aoi enters the text represents Moor's unwillingness to engage with the visual, to look at himself. He sees himself as physically flawed, enters Vasco's fortress shrouded in robes rendering him anonymous and metaphorically, too, he has difficulty looking at the events that form his own life story. He then admits to the reader that he is writing under the direct gaze of someone – of the translator figure, Aoi – and that the text thus far has been contaminated by her gaze and Vasco's. He realizes that in order to correct the effect of this contamination, he must disrupt the Eurocentric assumption of linearity in his verbal text and recreate it in visual form: this is why he disperses the pages of his work across the landscape instead of retaining the conventional verbal cohesion in a linear narrative in a book.

Art as translation

In *The Moor's Last Sigh*, as an art restorer, Aoi's role is to remove the top layer of paint from a canvas in an inversion of a palimpsest, the later work being discarded to reveal what remains protected beneath. Her task means that she becomes a priest-figure, working in the invisible, separate space where the translator is meant to reside, a space resembling purgatory: 'that thin film . . . separated the earlier picture from the later. Two worlds stood on her easel, separated by an invisibility' (426–7). Aoi Uë is 'orderly' and works with 'formality, precision' and 'neatness' (423) to a timetable to which she and Moor 'rigorously adhere'. A translator should, according to Lawrence Venuti, remain invisible leaving the original visible, because 'the more invisible the translator . . . the more visible the writer or meaning of the foreign text', the original.[4] If Aoi is revealing a painting, then that seems to be the opposite of invisible work, because she endeavours to reveal the painting underneath. In fact, revealing the first painting is an act of translating invisibly, because what becomes apparent is the original: the later work – the translation – is effaced. This later work is a translation in every sense: because the original painting was deemed offensive, the second picture was produced as a reinterpretation (or translation); when the first image was censored, a different translation rendered the same message acceptable.

Aoi Uë and narrator Moor are imprisoned and rendered invisible by their containment in a cell: under their gaoler's instructions, Aoi's task is to reveal a painting and Moor's is to write his life story. Aoi Uë is 'a miracle of vowels . . . the five enabling sounds of language' (423). She instructs Moor on how to write and to stay sane in the confines of their cell. She reads Moor's text and perhaps as powerfully as Vasco determines its contents because for Moor to offend such a morally good figure as Aoi with the tales he tells about his life is unthinkable. In this sense, she is the ultimate translator. She is also described as Moor's 'fellow-captive' (419), which equalizes the relationship between writer-figure and translator-figure: author and translator are equally present in the text as opposed to 'the individualistic conception of authorship' as dominant.[5] Art restoration and translation have a corresponding purpose: art restoration is performed to preserve 'history and culture', [6] while similarly, Lefevere claims that translation occurs in order to 'represent a foreign text in one's own culture'.[7] The methodology employed is also comparable: the translator translates a text according to the target language, which is dependent on the historical period and the linguistic characteristics of that time; the art restorer has a similar need to 'find a suitable modern equivalent' to 'the pigments and binder used in a piece of artwork'. [8]

Dashwanth is a painter who, through his patron, is forced to become a translator of others' desires in *The Enchantress of Florence*: 'The emperor's own life-giving powers had been temporarily exhausted by the immense effort of creating and then sustaining his imaginary wife Jodha, and so in this instance he was unable to act directly, and had to rely on art'. It is Dashwanth who mediates, like a translator, to produce the work conceived of by the emperor but that only Dashwanth has the ability to create. Specifically, Dashwanth is instructed to paint the stories told by the wandering messenger Vespucci, stories of a princess who had been lost from the historical records. Obediently, Dashwanth painted canvases so powerful that 'All Ferghana sprang to life' (120). Although this princess had been forgotten or, being absent from all records, was perhaps little more than the work of the storyteller's imagination, the painter's art recreated the princess: 'The painting itself worked a kind of magic, because the moment old Princess Gulbadan looked at it in Akbar's private rooms she remembered the girl's name', Qara Köz (121). In the visual medium of art, despite the lack of textual support from historical records, the translator demonstrates his power: his work creates the historical figure who had been absent before. Yet even though the painter has a power that his patron, without him, could never achieve, he remains trapped by the invisibility required of translators. He conveys this by creating an image of the princess and her relationships with others. Qara Köz was forgotten because her memory had been obliterated by her more powerful and still remembered half-sister, Khanzada. Dashwanth's painting reveals that Khanzada ordered Qara Köz to accompany her into a forced marriage and in turn, Qara Köz compelled The Mirror, a slave girl, to accompany her, too. The three girls are painted in a circle, each one grasping the wrist of the next: 'The slave-girl could sometimes imprison the royal lady. History could claw upwards as well as down. The powerful could be defeated by the cries of the poor' (125). Perhaps the emperor should have interpreted this image as a threat that the translator can demand visibility, in the same way as the lost princess; he didn't, and Dashwanth eventually takes back his art in a dramatic statement when he literally becomes his final painting.

Translation, Lefevere suggests, 'needs to be studied in connection with power and patronage'.[9] The patron determines what work will be created and the form it should take. Often, the result is a sanitized or inoffensive text or painting, and certainly a piece of work that reflects the worldview of the patron. For Susan Bassnett and Harish Trivedi, it is such ideological compulsions that determine the translator's selectiveness during translation: there is a 'temptation to erase much that is culturally specific, to sanitize much that is comparatively odorous'.[10] So Dashwanth is taking a risk with his career as court artist and with his life when he paints a canvas making the dangerous suggestion that a former king may have fallen to his death and to Hell, a crime in artwork 'punishable by death, containing as it did the suggestion that His Majesty might be headed the same way' (123) as his ancestor. Dashwanth is permitted this and other reckless acts of the paintbrush in *The Enchantress of Florence* because of the persuasive power of the stories his canvases tell. Vasco Miranda in *The Moor's Last Sigh* was subject to a more rigid patron who ordered him to destroy his painting of a pregnant Aurora: he follows orders bitterly by painting a second image over the first. Just as inflexibly, Vasco later controls both Moor who is told he must write the story of his life and the art restorer Aoi Uë who is forced to remove this later image to reveal the original. Dashwanth translates his patron's stories into painting, and while Moor translates his stories when he authors a text produced for a controlling patron, Aoi Uë translates a sanitized and sanctioned painting into a censored one. The impact of all three resulting works tells history in a particular way, and tells history for public consumption.

Translate or die

Lefevere mistrusts a translation endowed with power to influence, and this is an especially potent concern if the translation has been created under duress. Members of the 'receptor culture' (those who will read the text or perceive the painting after it has been translated) must be able to trust an individual translator; otherwise, they may not know whether or not 'the imported text is well-represented'.[11] However, the receiving public cannot make this judgement effectively if the translator remains invisible, as Venuti has described. There are, for Venuti, constraints other than ideological ones at work between the translator and their patron. Traditionally, the translator is not fairly compensated for his or her work, either in terms of recognition or in the amount that he or she is paid. According to Venuti's collated figures, translators work under exploitative contracts for 'below-subsistence fees'.[12] Aoi Uë's exploitation is literal; in order to complete this particular contract, Aoi is held in chains and the eventual result of her employment is her death. Dashwanth is also constrained: his position as court painter was only created to protect him from bodily harm after 'he covered the walls of Fatehpur Sikri with . . . caricatures of the grandees of the court so cruelly accurate that they all became determined to hunt him down as soon as possible and cut off these satirical hands' (118). This graffiti is notably (explicitly) visual rather than textual. The emperor 'commanded Dashwanth to join the imperial art studio immediately, and forbade any person in the court to do him harm' (118). This patronage of a hated, radical artist demonstrates both the patron's power and his protection: Emperor Akbar commands Dashwanth to produce art works under threat, but this is also his only way to be protected following the graffiti caricatures he created. Becoming almost imprisoned as a result of his rebellious work, the relationship between patron and artist replicates the prisoner's typical relationship with their captor which is one of dependence, of fear combined with submission. Here the similarity of this partnership to the relationship between Moor and Vasco again comes to mind: Moor's submission to Vasco's rule is as much a result of their previous connection when Vasco was a playful and irreverent guardian as it is due to Moor's physical constraint.

The product of such a relationship will surely be problematic, reflecting the artist's restriction. Indeed, good translations, Ann Dacier wrote, are created in an environment free from 'constraints'.[13] Neither Dashwanth nor Aoi Uë is free from constraints, yet they refuse to conform to the demands of their patron who requires something resembling the safe, bland copy that Dacier suggests the talented translator avoids. Working in the visual medium, artists can find ways to fight back: while Dashwanth takes suicidal risks, Aoi Uë inserts coded messages into her letters home, enabling the translator to circumvent an ideology she distrusts by rebelling against it. Working in the textual medium, Moor is less able to resist and so his text is produced for his patron and reader until he is able to overthrow Vasco, and then in that moment the text becomes visual: it is strewn across the landscape and in this configuration resembles an installation more than a cohesive, linear narrative.

The Emperor Akbar epitomizes the power of patronage: he saw Dashwanth's value – as an imperial tool as well as a talented artist – and proclaimed: 'we do not want such a talent extinguished by an angry nobleman's sword' (118). But Dashwanth's freedom as an artist is limited; not only his position, but also the subject matter of his art, is under the king's instruction:

> Dashwanth quickly became one of the brightest stars of Mir Sayyid Ali's studio and made his name painting bearded giants flying through the air on enchanted urns, and the hairy, spotted goblins known as *devs*, and violent storms at sea, and blue-and-gold dragons, and heavenly sorcerers whose hands reached down from the clouds to save heroes from harm, to satisfy the wild, fantastic imagination – the *khayal* – of the youthful king. (119)

In the relationship between artist and patron, the artist remains simply an employee, literally a hired hand, while the patron retains the glory associated with the vision that inspires the painter's creations, where, 'although his hand held the brush it was the emperor's vision that was appearing on the painted cloths' (119).

Like the later British colonial project which constructed India through its ideologically motivated translations, the Mughal Empire as conceived in *The Enchantress of Florence* was created through patronized art. Dashwanth's unwillingness to be a part of a process that he sees as irreversible resembles Aoi's: Aoi is also forced to complete work which 'had little appeal' (420). Gayatri Spivak endorses this position of powerlessness in the process of translation, suggesting that a translator should 'adopt a procedure of "love" and "surrender" towards the original'.[14] If translators must surrender to their texts, they take on the function assigned by Dryden, the role of a slave, a 'wretched translator' who is 'tied to the thoughts' of the master who invented the original.[15] This position accurately describes the role of Aoi Uë, forced to work in captivity. At the same time, explicitly defining her translator-role as 'slave' is an acknowledgement of the reciprocal nature of her relationship with her master, in Hegel's conception of the master-slave relationship, where 'the consciousness for-the-Master is not an independent but a dependent, consciousness'.[16] Thus, according to Benjamin Graves, 'the slave ironically *shares* in the master's power because the master defines himself only in opposition to the slave; that is, the master *needs* the slave in order to legitimate his comparative privilege'.[17] In Aoi Uë's case, Vasco is both legitimated as master by her slavery, and in addition, he gains power by the work that she produces. The original and the translation are mutually dependent. Empowering the slave in this way, Spivak's instruction can be read anew: by willingly adopting this procedure of love and surrender, a translator can achieve the translation that he or she desires to produce. Aoi's apparent submissiveness is undercut by her subversive messages in letters home. The translator can subvert their patron's instructions in order to achieve a desired translation.

Venuti's well-supported assertion that in general, all translations are 'judged by the same criterion – fluency'[18] suggests that to a degree, all texts possess the status of holy texts, and that any mistranslation which results in an interruption of fluency is treated as if it is a desecration. Norman Shapiro's argument is that invisibility is the ideal for which translators strive: 'A good translation is like a pane of glass. You only notice that it's there when there are little imperfections – scratches, bubbles. Ideally, there shouldn't be any. It should never call attention to itself'.[19] Venuti suggests that in attempting to render the text fluently, 'the more invisible the translator' becomes.[20] This state of invisibility is bound to have an impact on the amount of prestige afforded to the translation: if a translator remains invisible, then their work is seen as something inferior to 'writing', so far subordinate that it sometimes goes entirely unacknowledged. Bassnett and Trivedi perceive 'translation as rewriting . . . or translation as "new writing"'.[21] If translation is rewriting, then translating or rewriting a text renders the translator responsible for the text that he or she produces and in turn the translator must be seen as the author of that work, and the translation becomes an alternative 'original' text. It logically follows that this should be reflected by the translator's rights and responsibilities as understood either in public (in the public response to translated works) or in legal terms (in the working conditions comprising translators' contracts). Venuti suggests that this is not the case, however, and that 'the translator is . . . subordinated to the author'.[21] This subordination is enacted both by readers: 'many newspapers . . . do not even list the translators in headnotes to reviews, [and] reviewers often fail to mention that a book is a translation',[22] and by publishers who often retain the copyright of translated works. Venuti claims that the ideal of 'the translator's invisibility' is based on the 'individualistic conception of authorship' suggesting that the author's work is 'viewed as an original and transparent self-representation, unmediated'. The translation, in opposition to this, is 'derivative, fake, potentially a false copy'.[23] In order to become invisible, though, the translator must perform an act of 'illusion', making the author visible in a text which he or she has not really written, and becoming invisible, in an act which Venuti says is equivalent to self-effacement.[24] This illusion – not the act of translation – is the act of deception, a transgression performed in order to produce a perfect translation.

Dashwanth's level of visibility fluctuates. He had been invisible in society and in the community, 'an apparently ignorant' boy 'whose father was one of the emperor's palanquin bearers' (117–18). Dashwanth was employed in an invisible role as a draughtsman but was determined to become visible by grappling with his invisibility: his 'genius was bursting out of him. At night when he was sure nobody was looking he covered the walls of Fatehpur Sikri with graffiti' (118). Dashwanth's act represents a demand to become visible: during this period of invisibility (when 'nobody was looking'), he created the work that made him visible and indeed from this point onwards, he would be 'recognised as the finest of the Indian painters' (120). Yet even after his talent has been acknowledged, his patron ensures that he remains largely invisible, and instead of becoming a public figure, Dashwanth's existence conveys the kind of postmodern alienation and invisibility associated with contemporary office workers: in later years, Dashwanth 'sat in his little cubicle at the art studio staring for hours at an empty corner, as if it contained one of the monsters he had depicted' (119–20).

Translator as transgressor

The artist, the translator, is a transgressive figure by nature, who has within reach the power of translation, which can be 'potentially subversive' because of its ability to influence, as Victor Hugo suggests.[25] When a readership rejects the translation, they do so by casting the translator as a 'traitor', a 'robber', a 'seducer', a 'betrayer'.[26] In such a context, according to Lefevere, 'translation nears the edge of the impossible'.[27] Translators do translate, though, and to do this, they must employ transgressive methods. Rather than translation being impossible, then, instead, translation without transgression is impossible. Translators have admitted to significant alterations of texts in order to produce an 'elegant translation'[28] or to suppress 'customs where they may appear shocking'.[29] The original is transformed by these editorial decisions in order to render it acceptable to the cultural or historical expectations of the target readership.

This kind of editing practice resembles the way that Frank Kermode describes the Jewish tradition of rewriting religious material, known as midrash. Midrash is 'an interpretive tradition'[30] like translation, and according to Kermode is a practice whereby 'ancient texts were revised and adapted to eliminate or make acceptable what has come to be unintelligible or to give offence'. This involves 'sometimes very free' alterations employed when 'updating texts' or 'translating them into another language'. Kermode suggests that 'an unfamiliar foreign expression, or the interpretation of a difficult part of the law, or a story which, in the course of time, had come to seem ambiguous or even indecent . . . might prompt midrash'.[31] Kermode's response to midrash in effect presents it as a surreptitious method of altering a text in accordance with the interests of those who wield power. This interpretation aligns midrash with colonial translation, suggesting that in both colonial and midrashic revisions the translator gains extraordinary power to alter the text, motivated by ideological justifications or in an apparent attempt to render a more commonsensical version of a text to a contemporary readership. As Kermode suggests, 'to rewrite the old in terms of a later state of affairs is an ancient Jewish practice',[32] and this is exactly what Moor does when he writes his life story from within a prison cell, under the patronage of Vasco (and his pistol), the withdrawal of whose support may not mean only the abrupt end of the text, but also the end of Moor's life. Negotiating his Catholic and Jewish heritages informs the revisionary process by which he rewrites and re-presents the story of his life.

The imprisonment scene in *The Moor's Last Sigh* is rich with Judaeo-Christian images, from the 'sackcloth' of martyrdom to requests for 'absolution' (428) and the reference to Jehovah, whose name, the Tetragrammaton, like the name of God, is ineffable, unsayable, in the Jewish faith. Tetragrammaton translates to mean 'the four-letter word', something too offensive to speak. This is a four-letter word transcribed as 'YHWH', unpronounceable without the vowels to insert between the consonants, which are provided by the 'miracle of vowels', Aoi Uë. This image is entirely textual (or linguistic) instead of visual: this textual bias is then opposed by an apparently incongruous cartoon image which functions to reaffirm the presence of visual culture in the prison-cum-art studio location. Moor performs this obscenity, the unsayable, with light-hearted abandon: 'Popeye the sailor-man – along with Jehovah – had it just about right. *I yam what I yam an' that's what I yam*'. Here Rushdie translates Jehovah as 'I am' which is a common interpretation, and Moor confirms the reference by repeating Jehovah's communication to Moses in the form of the Burning Bush: 'Tell them, I AM hath sent me to you'. Thus Moor, mixing Biblical and cartoon figures with his 'nutty cathjew confusions', deliberately and mischievously taunts language and the unsayable, having been enabled by Aoi Uë (who provides the necessary vowels as well as the visual medium by her association with art) to do so. Moor longs for linguistic change in order to rewrite his family story with Aoi's help: 'we were consonants without vowels: jagged, lacking shape. Perhaps if we'd had her to orchestrate us, our lady of the vowels' (427–8). Visual and textual practices require each other.

Aoi is also transgressive, but she unwillingly transgresses against her own professional principles: she is forced into an act of 'destruction, rather than the preservation of art' which has 'little appeal' (420). Her transgression causes the successful creation of the text, however; during the destruction of one painting (or text) to reveal another, she creates a new text, written by Moor under her enabling influence. In this way, the translator's ability to create a brand new original is sustained. The text created by Moor fills the gap left by the missing child in the painting which Aoi uncovers. The text replaces the Madonna's missing child, standing in for the figure of Christ; the text which is born is a rewriting of Christ's nativity. In addition, the Nativity scene is evoked by the primitive environment reminiscent of the biblical barn, where the 'sleeping-place was a straw palliase covered with sackcloth' (426). Moor's words recall the agony of labour, and at the same time, conjure other figures popularly depicted at the Nativity scene: 'my breaths hee-hawed donkey-fashion as I wept' (426). This Christian birth scene is an unsayable event for Moor's Jewish half. In acknowledgement of his transgression, in place of words, Moor, evoking the image of a woman in labour, 'stamp[s], flail[s], weep[s]' (426). The 'practical' Aoi Uë plays the part of the father, comforting Moor as he 'shook in her arms' (426). In imprisonment Moor is made inarticulate and can only overcome his inarticulacy because of Aoi Uë's 'enabling' presence.

Even a faithful translation 'takes the greatest liberties'.[33] Whatever kind of translation is undertaken – faithful or free – the very act of translation can be undertaken only because of the translator's transgression. Transgression may be a form of textual self-defence, performed in order to permit the production of a translation. As George Steiner argues, there is often a connection between textual alteration and self-preservation: 'in the creative function of language, non-truth or less-than-truth is, we have seen, a primary device. The relevant framework is not one of morality but of survival'.[34] When Dashwanth is called 'the miscreant' (118) he is immediately deemed transgressive. Dashwanth becomes trapped in his art due to the forced act of translation, and in this way, his story too conveys the combination of visual and textual cultures. And the translator's sudden visibility in their work enables a reimagining of the translator's role. In both texts a forced act of translation enables visual and textual cultures to combine.

Though the translator is instinctively transgressive, he or she is restricted by their patron to produce work to order. Ultimately, in both *The Enchantress of Florence* and *The Moor's Last Sigh*, this results in the physical conjunction of the artist and their work. Moor narrates and writes down his complete life story from inside the prison cell which he enters in the last chapter of the novel. The body of this narrative is the text of *The Moor's Last Sigh* and the lifespan of Moor's body is only as long as his text. The whole of his text (which is also his body) is read, a page per day, by Aoi Uë, who becomes (along with the reader) a voyeur, in the manner described by Ross Chambers, who suggests that 'the narrator, in producing himself as eavesdropper/voyeur and sharing his knowledge of others' business with the narratee, simultaneously implicates the latter in this invasive act'.[35] For Dashwanth, too, the creative work dictates his physical being: 'He became even scrawnier than usual and his eyes began to bulge. His fellow painters feared for his health. "He looks so *drawn*," Abdus Samad murmured to Mir Sayyid Ali. "It's as if he wants to give up the third dimension of real life and flatten himself into a picture"' (126). Eventually, the other artists 'saw him succumb to the final madness of the artist, heard him pick up his pictures and embrace them, whispering *Breathe*' (126). In the end, 'he had somehow managed to vanish. . . . He had simply disappeared as if he had never been, and almost all the pictures of the *Qara-Köz-Nama* had vanished with him, except for this last picture' (127). Inevitably, the invisible translator is consumed by the work that they have produced: a 'hidden section of the painting was revealed [and] . . . there, crouching down like a little toad, with a great bundle of paper scrolls under his arm, was Dashwanth the great painter' (127).

Contra-diction

The work produced in both *The Enchantress of Florence* and *The Moor's Last Sigh* is primarily in the visual medium: Akbar is clearly keen to create a visual documentation of history with the help of his workshop of artists, but even Moor's written text was only ordered as an afterthought when Moor turned up searching for Vasco; the recovery of the painting was Vasco's first priority. In spite of this, the patrons are preoccupied with language and textuality, and in addition, the novels are both self-consciously concerned with textual structure.

In *The Enchantress of Florence*, this is played out in linguistic uncertainty, in questioned, halted or repeated language. The novel is constructed to convey an underlying sense of repetition and the sense of linguistic uncertainty by the pause that begins each new chapter: each chapter is named, but the name is only partial, because it corresponds with the first few words of the chapter that is about to begin. The reader is forced to read the same words twice as each new chapter begins and in this way the textual structure is made explicit, and the pause between each chapter is tangible while it is also a repetition. There is a need for the novel to be explicitly textual and self-consciously about uncertainty in textual and linguistic matters because of the visual subject matter, which cannot necessarily be contained or described adequately by the text. Names and terms of address are also problematized:

> Abul-Fath Jalaluddin Muhammad, king of kings, known since his childhood as Akbar, meaning "the great", and latterly, in spite of the tautology of it, as Akbar the Great, the great great one, great in his greatness, doubly great, so great that the repetition in his title was not only appropriate but necessary in order to express the gloriousness of his glory. (30)

This tautological naming was a potential catastrophe for an emperor, because 'names were things of power, and when they did not fit the thing named they acquired a malign force' (96). If his public designation was confused, his private one was even more complex: 'He, Akbar, never referred to himself as "I", not even in private, not even in anger or dreams. He was – what else could he be? – "we". He was the definition, the incarnation of the We. He had been born into plurality' (31). Almost as if challenging the combined linguistic rules and the empire's customs – a process resonating with the powers of postcolonial translation – Akbar began to play with his linguistic identity: '"I," he practised under his breath. *Here "I" am. "I" love you. Come to "me"*' (32). Akbar is a contradiction, 'huge and strong' with 'girlish' features, a 'philosopher-king: a contradiction in terms' (33) who inevitably sets forth policies of contra-diction or anti-language: in the spirit of his uncomfortable linguistic identity, he patronizes art in order to replace a similarly flawed textual history – flawed because it is missing Qara Köz, of course – with a more complete visual representation.

The products created in both texts are at once textual and visual, ultimately. Qara Köz was invisible because she did not have a verbal identity: 'all records of her birth had been obliterated' and she was a 'princess without a name' (117). Until she is given a name in the novel (as a result of Dashwanth's painting) she remains somewhat insubstantial. Visual culture is employed and this renders her verbal; it corrects a prior lack of text. In *The Moor's Last Sigh*, the palimpsest being both restored and destroyed by Aoi Uë, and the fragmentary text recounting Moor's life which is eventually strewn across the landscape, are created together. Moor's text becomes visual when it is scattered outside for others to find, and Aoi's work is made visible and verbal because it is contained in Moor's written text. Aoi has a 'heroic role' (419) within the text, implying that the translator's role in the creation of a text is heroic, that the translator becomes somehow similar to a main character. If this is the case, the translator loses her invisibility. The translator becomes visible in order to perform her heroic role and is assigned characteristics and motivations like any other character in the text. Aoi's are the typically heroic attributes of 'courage, inventiveness and serenity' (419). Her 'inventiveness', resembling the translator's craft, 'glow[s]', 'like a beacon' illuminating the text from 'darkness' (of incomprehension, perhaps) and providing something for Moor to 'cling to' so that he does 'not sink' under his despair in captivity (419). Aoi is 'a beacon' because this allows her to fulfil another translator's task, of preventing the text from being lost.

Body/Text

In both texts, visual and verbal cultures collide because of a need to question Eurocentric storytelling forms and structures. Unlike the western tradition of the *bildungsroman*, where the self is in continual development, Moor tears through layers of his identity, questioning every act and influence on the pages of his life story, acknowledging 'the burning spice-fields, Epifania dying in the chapel while Aurora watched . . . crookery, murder' (427). Meanwhile, Aoi Uë tears away strips of the paint which cover the picture of Moor's mother and his origin. Moor understands that his life is 'horror' only through the gaze of the translator, Aoi Uë, who because of her position as translator is 'so unfairly trapped' in his story (427). In *The Moor's Last Sigh*, textual and bodily shredding becomes a midrashic exercise. Moor rewrites the text of his life story for a specific audience, namely his captor, Vasco and Aoi Uë whose shock at the events of his life renders her gaze an editorial one, leaving him asking, 'has it been such a bad life, then?' (427). Aoi Uë's translation from one visible painting to another is also a midrashic revision, providing the audience with a version of the (visual) text it finds pleasing. The painting which is discarded was itself a revision in midrashic terms, because it was painted in order to hide (but also to revise and re-present) what was offensive. The prison cell hosts a continual re-staging and re-translation of the same text to omit what offends. The prison cell also heightens the emotional connection between translator and text: unable to separate the text from life because those two states are becoming interdependent (and may only be 'separated by an invisibility'), 'at the worst moments of the tale [Aoi Uë] would bury her face in her hands and shake her head' (427).

In the final section of *The Moor's Last Sigh*, Moor's life and the text of his life story have become difficult to separate; the final section is presented as an italicized afterword, disassociating it from the character Moor. In this final section, Moor's is the narrative voice, but what he narrates is no longer his own life, but the life of the text. Moor's 'breaths are numbered' (432) like the pages of his manuscript, or like the verses, chapters and books of the Bible. As with the organization of the Bible, which as Kermode describes, begins with Genesis and ends with apocalypse,[36] Moor is conscious of a predetermined ending, which is 'numbered . . . in reverse' and towards which 'the countdown to zero is well advanced'. Numbered in reverse, the text remains unconventional. Moor has 'finished' his writing, and is 'freed' of his 'shackles', both the iron chains around his feet and those less visible ones which controlled the laboured production of his text (433). Once the text has been completed, Moor is compelled to leave it in the care of humanity, so that they can 'know everything there is to know' (433). His desire for the text echoes religious devotion; it is constructed from 'the love that endures beyond defeat', and 'that most profound of our needs' (433), a profound need which can be imagined as a kind of faith. Embodying his text, Moor echoes Christ's destiny as 'the defeated love that is greater than what defeats it'. His journey is a 'pilgrimage', and the objective is to nail the story to the landscape in an act reminiscent of Martin Luther nailing his reformation tract to the church door, and also of the crucifixion: he was 'happy to shed th[e] load' that is his flesh in order to 'give the knowledge' to those who would read his text (433).

Moor dies in order to create a text which tests his faith, and if he does not symbolize Jesus precisely, then his conversion experience involves heavy Judeo-Christian symbolism suggesting that the transgressive act of conversion involves a communication with those objects of faith: the 'thorns' that tear at his skin and the 'wounds' that he ignores in search of his higher purpose, which is the distribution of his text. Moor dies hoping to 'awaken' after taking some ritual 'wine' in an act of communion or redemption, 'into a better time' (434). The result of this text's creation is a transgression of the boundary between the body and the text occurring at 'the end' of 'frontiers' and the end of 'the boundaries of the self' (433). Moor and his text become fused, and while Moor's body dies in this afterword to the text, his life is contained in the papers which remain distributed across the landscape. The boundary between man and God is also questioned by Moor's act of communion where, after replicating Christ's wounds, he takes an informal holy communion at the gravestone without the mediation of a priest figure whose presence (as well the location of the church altar) enables the transubstantiation ritual to be conducted according to tradition.

Moor is one in a tradition of imprisoned writers (fictional or not) whose writing materials take on an elevated significance in the prison cell. Imprisoned, Wole Soyinka became his writing materials: he renames his ink 'Soy-ink',[37] and therefore, the text is written using the substance of his body. Once it exists, that body of text is also the body of the writer. Moor becomes his text, just as Dashwanth becomes his painting, and this is where the textual and visual media at work in both novels become distinct: while Moor preserves the memory of visual art through recording it in his text, Dashwanth creates what will become a textual history after its portrayal in visual art: the lost princess in the end 'was actually entering the book, moving out of the world of earth, air and water and entering a universe of paper and ink' (334). Her storyteller had the power to leave the text, though: 'Vespucci's story was concluded. He had crossed over into the empty page after the last page' (343). And this explicit engagement with the textual is again appropriate because Dashwanth is in the end a very textual or linguistic painter; not only did his paintings dictate what would come to be the written histories, but he also wrote verse into paintings that were based on verse in the first place, Qara Köz was inspired by a poem, and Dashwanth 'painted a part of the last verse into the pattern of the fabric of Qara Köz's garment' (125). Under his patron's power, Dashwanth was forced to make such decisions surreptitiously, to retain the prized translator's invisibility. Only when his work was completed could he make himself visible in that work when he became a part of it, and by doing this he retains power over the painting to equalize the roles of patron and painter, translator of the patron's ideas, to redress the notion that a translation is inferior to the original. Where the translator remains invisible, the translation is not valued. In the face of over-zealous patronage, the translator becomes visible within the text and takes possession of that visual-linguistic text.

At the end of the text, Moor leaves his story 'nailed to the landscape' (433). In the opening lines of the novel, Moor says, 'I have lost count of the days that have passed since I fled the horrors of Vasco Miranda's mad fortress . . . and left a message nailed to the door' (3). The first chapter acts as both epilogue – because it provides information not supplied at the end of the novel – and prologue, because it cannot be part of the main text, which we know began at Vasco's command in the prison cell. Moor says at the end of this chapter that 'there are no secrets any more' (6), but Aoi Uë is kept secret. Aoi is not introduced or referred to at all throughout the majority of the text, meaning that she remains an invisible editor, translator and reader of the text until the very last chapter, at which point the sense of the novel is recast by her presence. In this sense, *The Moor's Last Sigh* conforms to Kermode's claim that, 'in much the same way as the end of the Bible transforms all its contents, our sense of, or need for, an ending transforms our lives "between the *tick* of birth and the *tock* of death" and stories simulate this transformation'.[38] The awareness of and need for the ending visible in the final chapter of *The Moor's Last Sigh* transforms the contents of the novel. The text is always being written from that end point and with that known ending in mind, just as Kermode describes the Bible as a 'familiar model of history' because when 'Christians took over the Jewish Bible' their 'account of the ending' recast the text so that the Bible ends with Apocalypse.[39] Because of this, like the narration of *The Moor's Last Sigh*, the way that we read what comes in the middle is transformed.

The reason provided for Aoi's very late introduction to the text is that she and Moor 'met so near the end' of their stories, so there was 'neither time nor space' for her story to be told 'in full' (422). However, she has been present throughout the story; Moor began narrating (and the text of *The Moor's Last Sigh* began) when he was given pencils and paper in this prison cell. Until this point, Aoi has performed the role of the perfect, 'invisible' translator. Aoi Uë becomes visible where she was previously invisible because she has transgressed. Like Dashwanth's rejection of three dimensions for two, Aoi's presence in the text renders the boundary between verbal and visual cultures imprecise, but in both novels, the boundary is breached when the patron loses control over those in his dictatorial employ: the visual and the verbal combine at the loss or rejection of the patron, because only at this point is the formerly hidden translator or artist rendered visible and made powerful.

8

Salman Rushdie: A Split Subject

This final, short chapter considers Rushdie's presence as a literary figure and as a public personality, in the context of the fatwa. This chapter considers the ways in which Rushdie has represented the fatwa and its effect on his writing in two forms: first, Rushdie has described the effect of censorship using his most direct metaphors in his writing for children, *Haroun and the Sea of Stories* (1990) and *Luka and the Fire of Life* (2010). Secondly, he has addressed the impact of the fatwa in *Joseph Anton*, a 2012 memoir of his experience of the fatwa. The restriction on Rushdie's personal freedom as a result of the fatwa is not an issue consigned to the past; the ongoing effects were made plain in January 2012 when Rushdie's appearance at the Jaipur Literary Festival was cancelled in the light of protests about his presence in India, and in February 2013 Rushdie was denied entry to Kolkata, where he was due to promote the new film of *Midnight's Children*.

One thousand and one nights: Telling stories as survival

In *Shalimar the Clown*, when India/Kashmira sleeptalks she is connected with The Thousand and One Nights (or, Arabian Nights) tales that Rushdie recalls frequently: 'According to one report she sounded guttural, glottal-sloppy, as if she were speaking Arabic. Night-Arabian, she thought, the dreamtongue of Scheherazade' (3). Scheherazade tells stories to save her life and the life of other young women who would otherwise be sacrificed to assuage King Shahryar's need for vengeance for his wife's infidelity. *Haroun and the Sea of Stories* (1990) is indebted to The Thousand and One Nights for the names of its main protagonist, Haroun and his father Rashid, whose names are taken from the Haroun al-Rashid who takes part in many Arabian Nights stories. More than this, though, the story structure and the text's key concern with the importance of unrestricted imagination and storytelling is a direct response to The Thousand and One Nights. Andrew Teverson notes that the context of *Haroun and the Sea of Stories* was the impact of the fatwa: the stories were based on those that Rushdie had invented for his son at bathtimes, but they were 'formalized during the time that Rushdie spent being shuttled from safe house to safe house by Special Branch police'. Teverson suggests that 'on a practical level, *Haroun* became a means for Rushdie to connect to his son at a time when they had been forcibly separated from one another' while:

> On a more allegorical level, Rushdie also uses the fantasy of *Haroun* as a way of responding to his detractors by indirect means – celebrating storytelling and its freedoms, and condemning censorious persecutors (Khattam Shud) who unleash the forces of oppression against the creative artist.[1]

In *Haroun and the Sea of Stories*, the storyteller, like King Shahryar, is heart-broken by his wife's infidelity. She leaves him for their neighbour, telling him that she can no longer tolerate a husband with a mind 'full of make-believe', and that instead, Mr Sengupta, her lover, 'has no imagination at all. This is okay by me' (22). The storyteller's heartbreak does not incite a desire for revenge or violence, though: instead, it leaves him bereft of stories to tell. The text insists that restricting the imagination in any way results in the loss of storytelling altogether, and this was Rushdie's fear for literature after the fatwa was issued: Rushdie lamented that many stories will now never be written (never mind published), as a result of the fatwa. *Haroun and the Sea of Stories* speaks of this loss for new generations of readers, a role played by the storyteller's son, Haroun.

While it recalls The Thousand and One Nights, *Haroun and the Sea of Stories* is a novel which makes use of the short story form. The title suggests a collection of short stories as does the structure of chapters and their full titles, which read like the titles of short stories: for example, 'The Spy's Story', 'The Shah of Blah' and 'Haroun's Wish'. Why should this text choose to use the form of a collection of short stories, when the stories are connected by character, theme and are presented chronologically? Perhaps this structure was used to more easily convey the anti-censorship message. The peril of storytelling and imagination is restated in each story, and instead of allowing the villains to develop complex personalities leaving the reader more free to empathize with their fiction-destroying motivations, the short story form allows the villains to remain symbols of destruction and the stories to retain an element of fable: as in all fairy tales, the reader is taught a moral message, which in this case is the value of imagination, and the threat from censorship. *Haroun and the Sea of Stories* also described the inherently political nature of stories and the political battles that storytellers are forced to referee. Wooed by 'politicos' (20) requesting his storytelling services to win over the crowds at political rallies, Rashid the storyteller finds himself silent at the head of a political rally: 'he had run out of stories to tell' (22). It is Haroun's challenge to combat the forces that wish to misuse or prevent storytelling (those forces, in the story, are led by the evil Khattam-Shud) and to permit freedom of the imagination so that his father can tell stories again: 'There were so many Streams of Story, of so many different colours, all pouring out of the Source at once . . . . Haroun understood that if he could prevent the Source from being Plugged, everything would eventually be all right again' (168).

Both *Haroun and the Sea of Stories* and *Luka and the Fire of Life* are directly concerned with the perils of restricting or preventing storytelling. *Luka and the Fire of Life* engages with the same essential story, the halting of storytelling. The protagonist of *Luka and the Fire of Life*, Luka, is Haroun's younger brother, and his task is to rescue their father Rashid's storytelling power, although this time the threat to storytelling seems to come from old age: Rashid was 'slowing down' at a rate so alarming that soon, Luka feared, he might 'completely grind to a halt' (15). Rashid at first falls asleep and will not be woken, and then starts to disappear. He is under threat from the 'Mists of Time' (102) and 'The Great Stagnation' (103) this time, rather than from censorship, and once again the text relies upon the connection and disconnection between generations: the threat to the storyteller is his age, his speed and the speed of the literary text in comparison with the pace and movement of alternatives like computer games. *Luka and the Fire of Life* employs the terminology of computer gaming once Luka takes narrative control and tries to find his father: 'Luka had the strangest feeling: as if they had crossed an invisible boundary; as if a secret level had been unlocked and they had passed through the gateway that allowed them to explore it' (25). The language of boundaries, levels and unlocked gateways allows the narrative to create a bridge between computer gaming and literary texts which speaks of the need to reinvigorate writing with all that is new. The reference to The Thousand and One Nights remains, though this time it is through the constant presence of the author-figure whose life can only be saved by storytelling (like Scheherazade's). *Haroun and the Sea of Stories* is a celebration of rewriting or translating. As Andrew Teverson notes, the text draws freely 'upon a range of narrative pre-texts, including European, Middle Eastern and Indian fairy tale, pop music lyrics, English children's classics, Indian cinema, Persian poetry, political allegory and science fiction'.[2] When he writes for younger readers, the possibilities offered by translation in Rushdie's stories are wholly positive: translating stories, structures and themes from The Thousand and One Nights and the vast Kathasaritsagara, the Ocean of the Streams of Stories, the outcome is that storytelling is vital and that freedom in telling those stories is equally essential.

The shift in emphasis between the two children's texts – from censorship in *Haroun and the Sea of Stories* to age and generational disconnections in *Luka and the Fire of Life* – implies that the influence of the fatwa has dwindled significantly over the 20 years between the publication of the two books. And Rushdie's public presence might also suggest that this is the case: in addition to his appearance in mainstream films like *Bridget Jones's Diary*, Rushdie's movements have, in general, become far less restricted. Laura M. Holson writes: 'Mr. Rushdie has emerged as an indefatigable presence on the New York night-life scene', in an article that describes his regular appearances at high-profile public events.[3] Significantly, though, Rushdie's visibility is only newsworthy because of its contrast with his former situation, and Holson's article is titled 'From Exile to Everywhere'. The continued impact of the fatwa has been made clear in 2012 by two things: the first is Rushdie's prevention from making an appearance at a literary festival, and the second is the publication of *Joseph Anton*, Rushdie's memoir of the fatwa years, which makes clear the significance of the fatwa for writing and freedom more generally.

Authorship and autobiography

Rushdie was scheduled to appear twice at the Jaipur Literary Festival in 2012, which ran from January 20 to 24. He was advised not to attend because of the strength of protest from groups in South Asia who remain hostile to the writer as a result of the fatwa following *The Satanic Verses*. In support of Rushdie and as a gesture of solidarity against censorship, authors Hari Kunzru and Amitava Kumar read extracts from *The Satanic Verses* at the festival. Rushdie has always had strong support from other writers, but at the same time, there have been a small number of organizations and individuals who have disassociated with him, and the Jaipur Literary Festival was one of those organizations that felt it needed to maintain distance; following the reading by Kunzru and Kumar, the festival organizers issue a press release stating:

> It has come to their attention that certain delegates acted in a manner during their sessions today which were without the prior knowledge or consent of the organizers. Any views expressed or actions taken by these delegates are in no manner endorsed by the Jaipur Literature Festival. . . . The Festival organizers are fully committed to ensuring compliance of all prevailing laws.[4]

In this context, Rushdie's autobiography seems to offer a particularly appropriate response. Reviewers have commented on the length of *Joseph Anton* which, at 633 pages, is vast. Pankaj Mishra, for instance, complains that the text is 'unquickened by hindsight', that its tone is 'peevish' and that the use of 'third-person narration frequently makes for awkward self-regard'.[5] Although it might be considered somewhat arrogant to write such a long life-story, it should be expected for an author of Rushdie's verbosity, and it could be argued that the length is justified in response both to the fatwa and to the years afterwards when Rushdie spoke so dismissively and defensively about the situation and seemed unwilling to acknowledge its impact in his texts – the novels published during this intermediate period, *Fury* and *The Ground Beneath Her Feet*, are remarkable for their lack of political motivation.

Pankaj Mishra's review of *Joseph Anton*, though it is somewhat dismissive, points to some of the important features of the text that speak to the uncertain boundary between auto/biography and fiction: the third-person narration immediately lends the text a fictionality, and with the fictional narrator established, it is little wonder that his narration is 'unquickened by hindsight'. Such features make this text something more than a recollection of events; they enable an analysis of postcolonial subjectivity from an author whose role as Distinguished Writer in Residence at Emory University brought him closer to literary academia. More and more frequently in recent years, Rushdie's texts offer an academic kind of response to postcolonial or other contexts. In *Shalimar the Clown*, India/Kashmira thinks about her own name: '"India" still felt wrong to her, it felt exoticist, colonial, suggesting the appropriation of a reality that was not hers to own' (5). The use of the terms 'exoticist' and 'colonial' conveys a more direct engagement with theoretical or academic language, and the same can be said of *Joseph Anton*: soon after the announcement of the fatwa, Rushdie wonders whether he will be able to keep his promise to his son, Zafar, to write a story that he can read and also whether 'the death of the author' (7) is a reasonable excuse for breaking his promise.

The text attaches a level of fiction to events and to the people involved. As well as fictionalizing his own voice with the use of third-person narration and the use of 'this author' (11) to identify himself, Rushdie fictionalizes his ex-wife Clarissa by forging a connection between her and Samuel Richardson's famous heroine Clarissa Harlowe – Clarissa attended 'Harlow Tech' for a short time, and this 'strange echo' (13) is made much of in order to establish the sense of duality that persists throughout the text, a duality that divides the author's name into two: 'the *Salman* his friends knew' and 'the *Rushdie* who was the author of *The Satanic Verses*' (5). The title of the memoir is, of course, another marker of the literariness of the author's condition: Joseph Anton is the name Rushdie chose when asked to create a pseudonym that the police could use without arousing suspicion, and it is constructed from the first names of Rushdie's two favourite authors: Joseph Conrad and Anton Chekhov. Even here, the author evades the position of sovereign, unified self that characterizes the traditional autobiographical subject, as his name is constructed from the names of two (two very literary) people, and it further divides Rushdie from his cultural or racial heritage – a police requirement to prevent his detection.

Ever since Paul de Man's influential essay, 'Autobiography as De-facement', auto/biography as a genre has occupied an uneasy position between fiction and an assumption of factual, reliable self-representation. De Man asks whether sometimes, it might be impossible to discern fact from fiction: this becomes undecidable in the autobiographical text which is a way of reading rather than a genre of writing.[6] This is an effect of our inability to know ourselves: as Phillipe Lejeune has suggested, the name on the cover of an autobiography is just a kind of legal contract and isn't in any way the name of a subject capable of self-knowledge and understanding.[7] In his recently published *Postcolonial Life-writing*, Bart Moore-Gilbert observes that men's autobiographical writing in the postcolonial context is usually decentred through the narrative subject's diffusion of self into society, while the subject is decentred in women's postcolonial autobiography through an intimate relationship between the narrative subject and their mother.[8] Aside from the fact that this makes some problematic assumptions about women's life-writing, when applied to Rushdie's text the idea of diffusion of self into society is turned upon its head. For Rushdie, the problem with self-representation is that he has been forcibly diffused into society to the extent that he has lost all sense of a coherent selfhood: 'He had begun to lead two lives: the public life of the controversy, and what remained of his old private life' (132). This doubleness results in assigning his life an odd textuality; he regularly finds 'plot-holes' in his life, 'something wrong' with the narrative – Marianne's explanation for her shifting moods (106), his parents' religious explanation for their move from Bombay to Karachi (54). And in the midst of the fatwa problems, when friends asked what they could do to help, Rushdie's answer was: 'defend the text' (115) as if, by defending the text, his own life might be saved.

Paul De Man is wary of autobiography, saying 'autobiography veils a defacement of the mind of which it is itself the cause'.[9] Defacement can be understood as losing the sense of self, so de Man is suggesting that autobiography tries to hide the incoherence and uncertainty of the narrative persona through a false certainty and sureness of self as represented by the text, but it's the act of writing an autobiography that in fact causes the narrating self or the writer to endure this defacement. For Rushdie, this kind of defacement is adopted as a strategy: he uses the autobiography to address the multiplicity forced on him by the fatwa and emerges stronger: he is aware that to face this fiction is to evade defacement: 'People pretended that there was such a thing as *ordinary*, such a thing as *normal*, and that was the public fantasy, far more escapist than the most escapist fiction, inside which they cocooned themselves' (104). And his sense of doubleness is not all down to the fatwa; Rushdie describes how the condition of migrancy remained a formidable force in his life throughout:

> "He was a migrant. . . . Migration tore up all the traditional roots of the self" (53), he writes, so that "the migrated self became, inevitably, heterogeneous instead of homogeneous, belonging to more than one place, multiple rather than singular, responding to more than one way of being." (54)

In the end, the fatwa does not divide the writer utterly: instead, he would later 'find the strength to go on, and to be more fully himself' (57). And crucially, the memoir ends with an assertion of stability accompanied by the downgrading of his threat status, or, the reassurance that his life is no longer considered to be in imminent danger:

> Mr Joseph Anton, international publisher of American origin, passed away unmourned on the day that Salman Rushdie, novelist of Indian origin, surfaced from his long underground years and took up part-time residence in Pembridge Mews, Notting Hill. (610)

The autobiography does not mention the threats faced (and the bodily harm suffered) by Rushdie's translators, though it does discuss the shooting of his

Danish publisher William Nygaard. Nygaard made a full recovery, and perhaps the translators' stories, with their much more permanent and violent outcomes, would not have performed as satisfactorily in the narrative that conveys a memoir while constructing a narrative about endurance and recovery, recovery from all the assaults that the self faces when the author becomes public property because of a text, and his life is rendered textual.

Conclusion

This concluding chapter summarizes the importance and the impact of considering Rushdie's work alongside translation theories, and the importance of translation in contemporary scholarship in relation to postcolonial literary studies. Maria Tymoczko, referring to the same etymological connection between metaphor and translation used by Rushdie, suggests that 'postcolonial writing might be imagined as a form of translation'.[1] Rushdie has, of course, discussed the etymological connection between translation and metaphor through the words' origins meaning to 'carry across'. Rushdie says: 'I formed the idea that the act of migration was to turn people somehow into things, into people who had been translated, who had, so to speak, entered the condition of metaphor'.[2]

This process may have the undesired effect of turning migrants into metaphors in the gaze of their host location, or, as is the case in *The Satanic Verses*, turning people into 'things' like manticores and glass-skinned women and mutating horned and cloven-hoofed devils.[3] Translation, then, is a metaphorical way to think about writing which Rushdie suggests is a particularly appropriate way to represent the postcolonial subject. In this sense, metaphorical applications of the term 'translation' are the most appropriate for postcolonial writing, where language is a contested terrain, and the boundary between the language of the colonizer and the colonized is unclear. It is by broadening the definition of translation to include Rushdie's metaphorical sense of the word that we can challenge the idea that such polyglot readers identified by Lefevere, who can read both the language of the original and of the translation, and who are able to read the original and the translation together to 'appreciate the difference between the two language games',[4] no longer exist: rather than those readers taking the form of linguists and multilingual scholars whose interest is in the grammars of different languages and the associated cultural influences upon those grammars, comparable contemporary readers are postcolonial and migrant readers or those readers with an awareness of postcolonial studies, who are in this way able to read a text from multiple perspectives and observe the cultural and metaphorical conjunctions used to create a text in which the 'foreign' shines through on the page. Walter Benjamin claims that translation 'ultimately serves the purpose of expressing the central reciprocal relationship between languages'.[5] This is also the concern of postcolonial fiction, the subjects of which express themselves in that central, reciprocal space between the languages that they speak. Lefevere goes further, asking whether in fact, 'translations have been made with the intention of influencing the development of a culture' and even considering whether 'translations have been made with the intention of influencing the development of a literature'.[6] These joint aims are characteristics of postcolonial literature.

I have argued that in Rushdie's work, translation is sometimes more possible than at other times, and that the short story might be a narrative form which offers a platform for successful translation, not least because of the tradition of storytelling to which the majority of short story forms have adhered, and still adhere, which involves a close relationship between the narrator and the reader. This strategy, along with the short story's penchant for defamiliarization, enables what George Steiner suggests is the function of translation: 'to bring different world-pictures back into perfect congruence' and, at the same time, 'to find and justify an alternate statement'.[7] Taking Rushdie's short stories in *East, West* as an example, what is achieved by this process is a sense of balance, harmony between Eastern and Western stories and Eastern and Western literary traditions, exemplified by the 'unsaxogrammatical' retelling of *Hamlet*, in 'Yorick'.[8] However, this chapter concluded by suggesting that a successful and harmonious translation might not produce as fertile a text for discussion as the postmodern postcolonial novel, where the effort to translate is fraught with transgressions and temptations.

The idea of the untranslatable is approached in *Shame* and *The Satanic Verses*, driven by images of the harem and the veil. The harem prevents translation by veiling women; thus, it may be argued, 'veils and masks are . . . codes of disguise'.[9] It is only through unveiling (or leaving the harem) that even a flawed translation may be obtained. David Robey's discussion of Fredric Jameson's 'prison-house' of language provides a bridge between translation and the depiction of the harem as a prison:

> Our everyday perception of the world is enclosed within the conventional sign-systems that we use, what Fredric Jameson (1972) has called the "prison-house" of language. Art helps us to break out of this prison-house by subverting conventional sign-systems and forcing us to focus our attention on signs themselves rather than taking them for granted. It is through this process that

> art leads, as Mukařovský puts it, to a "renewed awareness of the manifold and multivalent nature of reality".[10]

A multivalent reality is perhaps one that, like Farah Zoroaster's in *Shame*, is multilingual: this makes translation much more complex. The linguistic space allotted to Farah is one that attempts to 'break out of this prison-house by subverting conventional sign-systems'. This may be a space, where, opposed to the '"prison-house" of language' controlled by *takallouf* and located in marital homes, art may be free to subvert social as well as linguistic conventions. Farah embodies the multivalent, in a postcolonial sense, too: she is difficult to pin down, and invites the kind of interpretation that Benita Parry suggests can occur in contemporary reassessments of the postcolonial – Parry suggests that the task of the postcolonial theorist is no longer simply to find the voice of the recovering 'disenfranchised'. Instead, contemporary postcolonials can 'disregard the importance to once or still dominated populations of recognizing the continuities and persistence of indigenous temporalities within transformed and plural cultural formations, or of recovering the evidence and traces of resistance to colonialism'.[11] Farah, who has no concern for continuity, attempts to construct her own future, but perhaps her explicit connection to the border complicates this process – her border-life attracts others, less able to become dislodged from their histories which were constructed through 'resistance to colonialism', like Omar. Parry's suggestion that 'borders' are not necessarily 'negotiatory or interstitial' but rather constitute 'ground that is policed as well as transgressed'[12] imparts a kind of warning to Farah. Farah's opportunity for translatability is thwarted when Omar distorts that space and, without her knowledge, during hypnotism, has sex with her and makes her pregnant: this situation is literally unspeakable and she is afterwards omitted from the narrative. Nevertheless, a fragmentary location has been used as a basis for art to subvert and translate. This pattern of fragmentation is continued in *The Moor's Last Sigh* with the figure of art-restorer Aoi Uë, whose name is constructed from the five vowels, 'the five enabling sounds of language'[13] and who, therefore, represents the figure of the translator. This translator figure is imprisoned and ordered to recover the original layer of a palimpsest painting by chipping away flakes of the work on top. Inhibited by the physical boundaries of the cell rather than the linguistic control from *takallouf*, the translation performed by Aoi Uë and her narrator engages with Babel and the result is a form of religious conversion involving the successful production of a text. The communication with God implicit in the concept of Babel, though, is difficult for Gibreel Farishta to contemplate, and when he becomes an unwilling messenger in *The Satanic Verses*, translating the words of God into those of humankind, he approaches madness. An unwilling translator is a flawed translator, whose transgressions into 'bad' language and whose temptations to satisfy desires of romance or hunger result in the continuation of that ambiguous linguistic space between languages which, according to Rushdie, offers more opportunity to 'play'.[14]

The concept of translation offers a sense of possibility, of unexplored interstices within and between languages which are not governed by rules and grammars. Steiner defines the translator's role as both 'deeply ambivalent' and inventive, words that could equally apply to the postcolonial writer. Steiner suggests that 'the translator re-experiences the evolution of language itself, the ambivalence of the relationships between language and world, between "languages" and "worlds"'. For Steiner, 'in every translation the creative, possibly fictive nature of these relationships is tested'.[15] The hunger and desire of the translator is satisfied by the short story, but where that hunger remains, in longer narratives, the text is permitted to do more interesting things.

If imperfect translation is more interesting to translation theory than perfect translation, then the unilingual ideal future promised by Pentecost may not be so ideal, after all. It is the imperfections of translation and the efforts to produce the translation – rather than its flawless completion – which make the theory so rich and fascinating. As Derrida writes, it is the translator who complicates the text: in his analysis of Plato's *Phaedrus*, Derrida draws attention to the translation of the Greek word *pharmakon*, which in Greek, stands for both 'remedy' and 'poison'. As Barbara Johnson explains,

> In the original language, it is as though the *pharmakon* is the medium that exists prior to division. Only the translators have to decide between "poison" and "remedy". . . . Derrida's reading of Plato's text recaptures the lack of division between the antithetical senses of the word *pharmakon*.[16]

It is only in translation that the divergences and separations occur. Translation, performed in that in-between space, may offer the most potential to the writer and to the reader, who is positioned in a more powerful place because of this linguistic ambiguity – as Catherine Cundy suggests, Rushdie's reader is always part of the process of creating the text: 'the reader of a Rushdie text is characterised as being drawn into a symbiotic relationship with the writer, where the reader is involved in the text and colludes in the very act of creativity'.[17] This situation is caused by the ambiguity of reference which the space between-languages can provide.

Rushdie's work offers a fluid linguistic texture which is meant to work harder, to shape-shift, to transgress linguistic boundaries and to tempt the reader into an unconventional translating relationship with the narrative – as Rushdie says, he has 'always tried to find a very fluid language, which can, among other things, make very quick transition from comedy to tragedy, from danger to comfort, so that the reader is kept a little off balance as to whether . . . [to] laugh or cry'.[18] Thus, in Rushdie's texts, translations are always, tantalizingly, at play.

Notes

Introduction

1 Bassnett, Susan and Harish Trivedi, eds, *Post-colonial Translation: Theory and Practice* (London: Routledge, 1999), p. 2.
2 Bassnett and Trivedi, *Post-colonial Translation*, pp. 2, 4.
3 Ibid., p. 5.
4 Fitzgerald, Edward, translator's introduction and notes, *Rubaiyat of Omar Khayyam*, 1879, available online via http://www.gutenberg.org/2/4/246/, accessed 22.06.09.
5 Fitzgerald, online.
6 Ibid.
7 Bassnett and Trivedi, *Post-colonial Translation*, p. 13.
8 Said, Edward, *Orientalism* (London: Penguin, 2003 [1978]), p. 38.
9 Said, *Orientalism*, p. 40.
10 Tymoczko, Maria, 'Post-colonial writing and literary translation', in Bassnett and Trivedi, eds, *Post-colonial Translation* (London: Routledge, 1999), p. 19.
11 Jakobson, Roman, 'On Linguistic Aspects of Translation', in Lawrence Venuti, ed., *The Translation Studies Reade*r (London: Routledge, 2000), p. 139.
12 Monier-Williams, Sir Monier, *A Sanskrit-English Dictionary Etymologically and Philologically Arranged* (Delhi: Motilal Banarsidass, 1997 [1899]), p. 38.
13 Chinua Achebe, 'The African Writer and the English Language', in Patrick Williams and Laura Chrisman eds, *Colonial Discourse and Post-Colonial Theory: A Reader* (Hemel Hempstead: Harvester Wheatsheaf, 1993).
14 Tymoczko, Maria, 'Post-colonial Writing and Literary Translation', in Bassnett and Trivedi, eds, *Post-colonial Translation* (London: Routledge, 1999), p. 20.
15 Ashcroft, Griffiths and Tiffin, *The Empire Writes Back: Theory and Practice in Post-Colonial Literatures* (London: Routledge, 2002), pp. 204–5.
16 Jakobson, Roman, 'On Linguistic Aspects of Translation', in Lawrence Venuti, ed., *The Translation Studies Reader* (London: Routledge, 2004), p. 139.
17 Lefevere, André, *Translation, History, Culture: A Sourcebook* (London: Routledge, 1992), p. 14.
18 Eco, Umberto, *Mouse or Rat? Translation as Negotiation* (London: Weidenfeld & Nicolson, 2003), p. 174.

19 Eco, *Mouse or Rat?*, p. 174.
20 Spivak, cited in Bassnett and Trivedi, *Post-colonial Translation*, p. 9.
21 McWhorter, John, *The Power of Babel* (Arrow: London, 2003), p. 2.
22 McWhorter, *The Power of Babel*, pp. 1–2.
23 Ibid., p. 2.
24 Eco, *Mouse or Rat?*, p. 109.
25 Ibid.
26 Eco, *Mouse or Rat?*, p. 110.
27 Ibid.
28 Arrojo, Rosemary, 'Interpretation as Possessive Love – Hélène Cixous, Clarice Lispector and the ambivalence of fidelity', in Bassnett, Susan and Trivedi, Harish, eds, *Post-colonial Translation: Theory and Practice* (London: Routledge, 1999), p. 144.
29 Arrojo, 'Interpretation as Possessive Love', p. 148.
30 Ibid., p. 154.
31 Ibid., p. 160.
32 Rushdie interviewed in Reder, Michael, ed., *Conversations with Salman Rushdie* (Jackson: University of Mississippi Press, 2000), p. 77.
33 Bhabha, Homi, *The Location of Culture* (London: Routledge, 1994), p. 224.
34 Steiner, George, *After Babel* (Oxford: Oxford University Press, 1992), p. 49.
35 Manto, Saadat Hasan, 'Toba Tek Singh', in *Kingdom's End and Other Stories* (London: Penguin, 1989), p. 11.
36 Manto, 'Toba Tek Singh', p. 14. (The Urdu words spoken by Toba Tek Singh roughly translate to the English or evoke similar meanings due to the similar sounds of words as follows: uper = [Upaar: Vesication]; gur = Jaggery [sugar], Skill; dhayana = [Daayamii: Perpetual, Routine; Daanaa'i: Wisdom; Dąah: Envy, Jealousy, Malice; Daa'i: Midwife] mung = mung bean [Munh: Kisser, Mouth, Orifice]; dal = meal [Dhaal: Manner, Mode, Mould, Taunt]).
37 Said, Edward, *Culture and Imperialism* (London: Vintage, 1993), p. 397.
38 Gonzales, Madelena, *Fiction after the Fatwa – Salman Rushdie and the Charm of Catastrophe* (Amsterdam: Rodopi, 2005), p. 5.
39 Rollason, Christopher, 'Rushdie's Un-Indian Music: The Ground Beneath Her Feet', in Rajeshwar Mittapalli and Pier Paolo Piciucco, eds, *Studies in Indian Writing in English*, vol. II (New Delhi: Atlantic, 2001), p. 122.
40 See the following works: Lisa Appignanesi and Sara Maitland, eds, *The Rushdie File* (London: Fourth Estate, 1989); Catherine Cundy, *Salman Rushdie* (Manchester: Manchester University Press, 1996); D. C. R. A. Goonetilleke, *Salman Rushdie* (London: Macmillan, 1998); Malise Ruthven, *A Satanic Affair* (London: Chatto & Windus, 1990); Daniel Pipes, *The Rushdie Affair – The Novel, the Ayatollah, and the West*, second edition (London: Transaction, 2003).

41 Dayal, Samir, 'Splitting Images: *The Satanic Verses* and the Incomplete Man', in Kain, Geoffrey, ed., *Ideas of Home – Literature of Asian Migration* (East Lansing: Michigan State University Press, 1997), p. 87.
42 Chrisman, Laura, *Postcolonial Contraventions: Cultural Readings of Race, Imperialism and Transnationalism* (Manchester: Manchester University Press, 2003), p. 9.
43 Rushdie, Salman, *Shame* (London: Vintage, 1995 [1983]), p. 104.

Chapter 1

1 Jean Baudrillard, 'After the Orgy', in *The Transparency of Evil – Essays on Extreme Phenomena* (London: Verso, 1993), pp. 12–13.
2 'It's true that some passages in *The Satanic Verses* have now acquired a prophetic quality that alarms even me'. Salman Rushdie, *Imaginary Homelands* (London: Granta, 1992), p. 407.
3 'Book of Acts 2:1:

1. And when the day of Pentecost was fully come, they were all with one accord in one place. 2. And suddenly there came a sound from heaven as of a rushing mighty wind, and it filled all the house where they were sitting. 3. And there appeared unto them cloven tongues like as of fire, and it sat upon each of them. 4. And they were all filled with the Holy Ghost, and began to speak with other tongues, as the Spirit gave them utterance.'

4 Book of Acts 2:1.4.
5 I Corinthians 13.1 New King James Version, available online at: http://www.biblegateway.com/passage/?search=1%20Corinthians%2013;&version=50;.
6 I Corinthians 13.2.
7 I Corinthians 13.8-10.
8 Perrot d'Ablancourt cited in André Lefevere, ed., *Translation/History/Culture: A Sourcebook* (London: Routledge, 1992), p. 9.
9 Steiner, *After Babel*, p. 35.
10 Porter, ed., *The Faber Book of Madness*, p. 155.
11 Ibid., p. 280.
12 William Sargant, excerpt from *The Unquiet Mind: The Autobiography of a Physician in Psychological Medicine,* in Porter, ed., *The Faber Book of Madness*, p. 309. Earlier treatments for madness, particularly in women patients, also focused on the removal of parts of the body, but these were usually genitalia, as in the case of a 'hysteroepileptic' patient in 1884 whose treatment involved the cutting of her genitalia: 'a surgical dilation of the external cervical os is

performed via a cross-like incision. Several wedge-shaped sections of the cervical canal are extirpated'. This was despite the fact that, aside from her epileptic fits, 'from the psychological point of view, the only thing out of the ordinary is her somewhat erotic facial expression'. This statement suggests a preconceived notion that sex and madness are somehow connected, that sexual emotions or behaviour could be suggestive of, or interchangeable with, insanity. Writing about contemporary Islamic societies, Geraldine Brooks describes similar treatments used to control women, whether or not they demonstrate any symptoms of what would be classified as insanity in their communities: 'one in five Muslim girls lives today in a community that sanctions some sort of interference with her genitals'. Suicidal behaviour, contemporarily viewed as often being a result of mental illness, is also discussed by Brooks in relation to women in Islamic society, and with reference to sex: an 11-year-old girl in Saudi Arabia committed suicide, 'climbed to the roof of her house and threw herself off' because her teachers repeatedly accused her of promiscuous behaviour because her *magneh*, a cowl-like hood, 'was pulled too far back, letting her hair spill out provocatively' and because of this, her mother was told that she would, 'in all probability, grow up to be a whore'. Geraldine Brooks, *Nine Parts of Desire – The Hidden World of Islamic Women* (London: Hamish Hamilton, 1995), pp. 36, 100, 101.

13 Porter, ed., *The Faber Book of Madness*, p. 154.

14 Ibid.

15 Susan Sontag, *Illness as Metaphor* (London: Penguin, 1991), p. 8.

16 Morton Schatzman, *The Story of Ruth: One Woman's Haunting Psychiatric Odyssey*, in Porter, ed., *The Faber Book of Madness*, p. 111.

17 Diana Gittins, *Madness in its Place – Narratives of Severalls Hospital 19131997* (London: Routledge, 1998), p. 5.

18 From the Urdu. D. C. R. A. Goonetilleke, *Salman Rushdie* (London: Macmillan, 1998), p. 78.

19 Steiner, *After Babel*, p. 30.

20 Cundy, *Salman Rushdie*, p. 36.

21 Definitions provided at websites: Salahuddin: http://www.babynology.com/arabic_name-meaning_Salahuddin_m.html (last updated 01.10.06), accessed 04 July 2005, Chamchawala: Paul Brians, 'Notes for Salman Rushdie: *The Satanic Verses*', first published online 1996 via http://www.wsu.edu/~brians/anglophone/satanic_verses/intro.html (last updated 04.10.06), accessed 04 July 2005.

22 Goonetilleke, *Salman Rushdie*, p. 76.

23 Jean Baudrillard, *Simulacra and Simulation*, translated by Sheila Faria Glazer (Ann Arbor: University of Michigan Press, 1994), p. 3.

24 Baudrillard, *Simulacra and Simulation*, p. 4.

25 Ibid.
26 D. C. R. A. Goonetilleke, *Salman Rushdie* (London: Macmillan, 1998), p. 78.
27 Walter Benjamin, 'Theses on the Philosophy of History', in *Illuminations*, translated by Harry Zohn (London: Pimlico, 1999 [1955, 1968]), Theses I, II, pp. 245, 246.
28 Peter Lamborn Wilson, *Angels* (London: Thames & Hudson, 1980), p. 37.
29 Benedict Anderson, *Imagined Communities*, revised edition (London: Verso, 1991), p. 93.
30 Michel Serres, *Angels – A Modern Myth*, translated by Francis Cowper (New York: Flammarion, 1993), pp. 22–3.
31 OED.
32 Malise Ruthven, *A Satanic Affair* (London: Chatto & Windus, 1990), p. 16.
33 Lamborn Wilson, *Angels*, p. 36.
34 Ibid., p. 28.
35 Benjamin, 'Theses on the Philosophy of History', in *Illuminations*, p. 249.
36 Ibid.
37 Susan Bassnett and Harish Trivedi, eds, *Post-Colonial Translation* (London: Routledge, 1999), p. 5.
38 Fanon, *Black Skin, White Masks*, p. 170.
39 Frank Kermode, *The Sense of an Ending* (Oxford: Oxford University Press, 2000 [1966]), p. 194.
40 Kermode, *The Sense of an Ending*, p. 190.
41 Jean Baudrillard, 'After the Orgy', in *The Transparency of Evil – Essays on Extreme Phenomena*, translated by James Benedict (New York: Verso, 1993), p. 4.
42 This translates to the first line of the passage following, 'it was so it was not in a time long forgot' (p. 544). Translation source: John T. Platts, A Dictionary of Urdu, Classical Hindi and English online: http://dsal.uchicago.edu/dictionaries/platts/index.html (last updated 20.10.06), accessed 02 July 2005 11:00am. 'Kan' = since that; 'ma' = which/that which/as much as/as far as/wherefore, suggesting 'kan ma kan' is idiomatic for 'it was so it was not'; 'fi' = in/of/concerning; 'qadim' = ancient/old/immemorial/archaic; 'az' = of; 'zaman' = season/time/period/duration/a long time.
43 Steven Connor, *Dumbstruck – A Cultural History of Ventriloquism* (Oxford: Oxford University Press, 2000), p. 3.
44 Connor, *Dumbstruck*, p. 3.
45 Salman Rushdie, in Gűnter Grass, 'Fictions Are Lies That Tell the Truth: Salman Rushdie and Gunter Grass: In Conversation', in Michael Reder, ed., *Conversations with Salman Rushdie* (Jackson: University of Mississippi Press, 2000), p. 77.

46 Benjamin, 'The Task of the Translator', in *Illuminations*, p. 74.
47 Ibid., p. 75.
48 Madhu Jain, review from *India Today*, 15 September 1988, in Lisa Appignanesi and Sara Maitland, eds, *The Rushdie File* (London: Fourth Estate, 1989), p. 36.
49 Ruthven, *A Satanic Affair*, p. 28.
50 Jacques Derrida, *Writing and Difference*, translated by Alan Bass (London: Routledge & Kegan Paul, 1978), p. 210.
51 The idea of 'phonetic' writing is relevant to the ending of *The Satanic Verses* where Gibreel's verses, recited in his native tongue, are reproduced using something similar to phonetic spelling in order to render them readable to an English-speaking reader.
52 Derrida, *Writing and Difference*, p. 217.
53 Simon Gottschalk, 'Escape from Insanity: "Mental Disorder" in the Postmodern Moment', in Dwight Fee, ed., *Pathology & the Postmodern – Mental Illness as Discourse and Experience* (London: Sage, 2000), p. 23.
54 Gonzales, Madelena, *Fiction after the Fatwa – Salman Rushdie and the Charm of Catastrophe* (Amsterdam: Rodopi, 2005), pp. 24–5.
55 Salman Rushdie, interviewed by Jean W. Ross, in Reder, ed., *Conversations with Salman Rushdie*, p. 7, and cited in Gonzales, *Fiction after the Fatwa*, p. 11.
56 Julian Wolfreys, *Writing London – The Trace of the Urban text from Blake to Dickens* (London: Macmillan, 1998), p. 146.
57 Wolfreys, *Writing London*, p. 146.
58 Gottschalk, 'Escape from Insanity: "Mental Disorder"', p. 38.
59 Jean Baudrillard, *Simulacra and Simulation*, translated by Sheila Faria Glazer (Ann Arbor: University of Michigan Press, 1994), p. 21.
60 Baudrillard, *Simulacra and Simulation*, p. 43.
61 Ibid.
62 Genesis 32: 22-32.
63 Lamborn Wilson, *Angels*, pp. 104–5.
64 Iser, 'On Translatability', pp. 8–9.
65 Kathleen Higgins, 'Reading *Zarathustra*', in Robert C. Solomon and Kathleen M. Higgins, eds, *Reading Nietzsche* (Oxford: Oxford University Press, 1988), p. 134.
66 Higgins, 'Reading *Zarathustra*', p. 136.
67 Ibid., p. 142.
68 Jacques Lacan, *Écrits: A Selection*, translated by Alan Sheridan (London: Tavistock, 1977), p. 2.
69 Lacan, *Écrits: A Selection*, p. 2.
70 Julia Kristeva, *Revolution in Poetic Language*, translated by Margaret Waller (New York: Columbia University Press, 1984), p. 25.

71 David Fisher, 'Kristeva's Chora and the Subject of Postmodern Ethics', in David Crownfield, ed., *Body/Text in Julia Kristeva* (Albany: State University of New York Press, 1992), p. 96.
72 Fisher, 'Kristeva's Chora and the Subject of Postmodern Ethics', p. 98.
73 Ibid.
74 Kristeva, Julia, *Desire in Language – A Semiotic Approach to Literature and Art* (Oxford: Basil Blackwell, 1980), p. 74.
75 Kristeva, *Desire in Language*, p. 74.
76 Ibid.
77 Venuti, Lawrence, *The Translator's Invisibility* (London: Routledge, 1995), p. 2.
78 Venuti, *The Translator's Invisibility*, pp. 8–9, 17.
79 Ibid., p. 7.
80 Ibid., p. 17.
81 Stewart, Susan, *On Longing – Narratives of the Miniature, the Gigantic, the Souvenir, the Collection* (London: Duke University Press, 1993), p. x.
82 Harper, Graeme, ed., *Comedy, Fantasy and Colonialism* (London: Continuum, 2002), p. 7.

Chapter 2

1 Dupatta: 'a doubled or two-layered length of cloth worn by women as a scarf, veil, or shoulder wrap' (OED).
2 Leslie P. Peirce, *The Imperial Harem – Women and Sovereignty in the Ottoman Empire* (Oxford: Oxford University Press, 1993), pp. 6–7.
3 N. M. Penzer, *The Harem* (London: Spring Books, 1936), pp. 177, 174.
4 Frithjof Schuon, *Understanding Islam* (London: Unwin, 1986 [1963]), p. 44.
5 Wolfgang Iser, 'On Translatability', in Jean-Claude Guédon, ed., *Surfaces* electronic journal, vol. 4 (Montreal: University of Montreal Press, 1994), pp. 3–4.
6 Iser, 'On Translatability', pp. 3–4.
7 Ibid.
8 Susan Bassnett and Harish Trivedi, eds, *Post-Colonial Translation: Theory and Practice* (London: Routledge, 1999), p. 2.
9 Bassnett and Trivedi, eds, p. 7.
10 Ibid., p. 8.
11 Ibid., p. 7.
12 Iser, 'On Translatability', pp. 8–9.
13 'The Pakistan Flag was designed by Ameer-ud-din Khidwai. The national flag of Pakistan is dark green in colour with a white bar, a white crescent in the

centre and a five-pointed star. The significance of the colour and symbols used in the Pakistan Flag is as follows: The white and dark green field represents minorities & Muslim majority, respectively. The crescent on the flag represents progress. The five-rayed star represents light and knowledge.' *Dov Gutterman*, Flag of Pakistan on http://flagspot.net/flags/pk.html (last updated 14.06.03), accessed 21.02.06.

14 Lama Abu Odeh, 'Post-Colonial Feminism and the Veil: Thinking the Difference', in *Feminist Review*, No. 43, Issues for Feminism (Spring 1993), p. 27.

15 Lama Abu Odeh, 'Post-Colonial Feminism and the Veil: Thinking the Difference', p. 27.

16 Fadwa El Guindi, *Veil: Modesty, Privacy and Resistance* (Oxford: Berg, 2000), p. xi.

17 El Guindi, *Veil: Modesty, Privacy and Resistance*, p. xii.

18 Sitara Khan, *A Glimpse Through Purdah – Asian Women – The Myth and the Reality* (London: Trentham Books, 1999), p. 12.

19 Malek Alloula, *The Colonial Harem* (Manchester: Manchester University Press, 1986), p. 4.

20 El Guindi, *Veil: Modesty, Privacy and Resistance*, p. xi.

21 Ibid.

22 Ibid.

23 Ibid.

24 Anna Smith, *Julia Kristeva: Readings of Exile and Estrangement* (London: Macmillan, 1996), pp. 130–1.

25 M. A. Doane, cited in Daphne Grace, *The Woman in the Muslin Mask – Veiling and Identity in Postcolonial Literature* (London: Pluto, 2004), p. 34.

26 'Philomela and Procne were the daughters of King Pandion of Athens. Procne was married to King Tereus of Thrace (one of the sons of Ares), and had a son by him, Itys. Tereus conceived an illicit passion for Philomela and contrived to get her sent to Thrace; he raped her, and then cut her tongue out and imprisoned her so that she could tell no one of his crime. However, Philomela wove a tapestry which revealed the facts of the matter to Procne. In order to get revenge, Procne killed Itys and cooked him, so that Tereus ate his own son for dinner. When Tereus discovered the ghastly trick, he pursued the two women, trying to kill them. Before the chase could end, all three were turned into birds—Tereus into a hoopoe, Procne into a swallow, and Philomela into a nightingale. (Hence the nightingale is often called a 'Philomel' in poetry)'. James Hunter, 'Philomela' in *Encyclopedia Mythica* from Encyclopedia Mythica Online, http://www.pantheon.org/articles/p/philomela.html (last updated 15.12.99), accessed 11.02.06.

27 Deszcz, Justyna, 'Salman Rushdie's attempt at a feminist fairytale reconfiguration in Shame'. *Folklore (UK)* 115(1), (2004), 27–44.

28 Ziauddin Sardar and Merryl Wyn Davies, *Distorted Imagination: Lessons from the Rushdie Affair* (London: Greyseal, 1990), p. 119.
29 Penzer, *The Harem*, p. 174.
30 Schuon, *Understanding Islam*, p. 44.
31 Ibid.
32 Schuon, *Understanding Islam*, p. 59.
33 Ibid.
34 Bassnett and Trivedi, eds, p. 6.
35 Wilhelm von Humboldt, from the preface to his translation of Aeschlus' Agamemnon (1816), reproduced in Andre Lefevere, *Translation/History/Culture* (London: Routledge, 1992), p. 138.
36 Cecilia Wadensjö, *Interpreting as Interaction* (London: Longman, 1998), p. 28.
37 Kristeva declared that 'every text is from the outset under the jurisdiction of other discourses which impose a universe on it'. She argued that rather than confining our attention to the structure of a text we should study its 'structuration' (how the structure came into being). This involved siting it 'within the totality of previous or synchronic texts' of which it was a 'transformation'. Cited in Daniel Chandler, 'Intertextuality' in *Semiotics for Beginners*, 2003, http://www.aber.ac.uk/media/Documents/S4B/sem09.html (last updated 04.10.03), accessed 23.02.06.
38 Wadensjö, *Interpreting as Interaction*, p. 27. In postcolonial literature written and read in English, rather than a traditional translation of a text, instead there is a metaphorical text which has to be transferred, and this is the postcolonial subject.
39 Wadensjö, *Interpreting as Interaction*, p. 27.
40 Stanley Fish, 'Interpreting the Valorium', in Dennis Walder, ed., *Literature in the Modern World* (Oxford: Oxford University Press, 1990), p. 58. Fish's argument is presented at pp. 55–62, passim.
41 Wadensjö, *Interpreting as Interaction*, p. 6.
42 Wadensjö, *Interpreting as Interaction*, p. 6. For Wadensjö, this process is emotional because of the context in which interpreters frequently operate: in courtrooms, in police interviews and during mediation between families, where the emotional content of the conversation is high.
43 Fish, 'Interpreting the Valorium', p. 59.
44 Sitara Khan, *A Glimpse Through Purdah – Asian Women – The Myth and the Reality* (London: Trentham Books, 1999), p. 27.
45 Khan, *A Glimpse Through Purdah*, p. 27.
46 Leslie P. Peirce, *The Imperial Harem – Women and Sovereignty in the Ottoman Empire* (Oxford: Oxford University Press, 1993), p. 7.
47 Catherine Cundy, *Salman Rushdie* (Manchester: Manchester University Press, 1996), p. 52.

48 Peirce, *The Imperial Harem*, pp. 6–7.
49 Ibid.
50 Goonetilleke, p. 56.
51 Alloula, *The Colonial Harem*, p. xiv.
52 Ibid., pp. 122, 118.
53 Ibid., pp. 62, 74.
54 Shirley Foster, 'Colonialism and Gender in the East: Representations of the Harem in the Writings of Women Travellers', in Nicola Bradbury, ed., *The Yearbook of English Studies: Nineteenth Century Travel Writing*, vol. 34 (Leeds: MHRA, 2004) p. 7.
55 Foster, 'Colonialism and Gender in the East: Representations of the Harem in the Writings of Women Travellers', p. 8.
56 Ibid., p. 9.
57 Ibid., pp. 11.15.
58 Ibid., p. 15
59 Penzer, *The Harem*, p. 13.
60 J. Hillis Miller, cited in John Lye, 'Synopsis of J. Hillis Miller's "The Critic as Host"', 1998, http://www.brocku.ca/english/courses/4F70/host.html (last updated 24.02.98), accessed 08.09.06.
61 J. Hillis Miller, cited in John Lye, 'Synopsis of J. Hillis Miller's "The Critic as Host"'.
62 Penzer, *The Harem*, p. 15.
63 Ibid., pp. 13–15.
64 J. Hillis Miller, cited in John Lye, 'Synopsis of J. Hillis Miller's "The Critic as Host"'.
65 Penzer, *The Harem*, p. 13.
66 Anthony Julius, *Transgressions – The Offences of Art* (London: Thames & Hudson, 2002), p. 8.
67 Salman Rushdie, *Step Across This Line* (London: Vintage, 2003), pp. 440–1.
68 Penzer, *The Harem*, p. 154.
69 Ibid., p. 152.
70 Ibid., pp. 174–5.
71 Qur'an 4:3, cited in Jamal Badawi, 'Polygamy in Islamic Law', 1998, (last updated 05.04.03), accessed 09.02.2006 via http://www.islamfortoday.com/polygamy5.htm.
72 Penzer, *The Harem*, p. 163.
73 Ibid.
74 Penzer, *The Harem*, pp. 174, 177, 185.
75 Bernard Lewis, *The Political Language of Islam*, cited in Peirce, *The Imperial Harem*, p. 9.

76 Peirce, *The Imperial Harem,* p. 9.
77 Ibid., p. 7.
78 Ibid., pp. 267–8.
79 Ibid., p. 272.
80 Ibid., p. 267.
81 Ibid., p. 280.
82 Bart Moore-Gilbert, introduction to Bart Moore-Gilbert, ed., *Writing India, 1757–1900* (Manchester: Manchester University Press, 1996), p. 23.
83 Khan, *A Glimpse Through Purdah*, p. 25.
84 Ibid., p. 14.
85 Salman Rushdie interviewed by David Sheff in 1995, reproduced in Michael R. Reder, *Conversations With Salman Rushdie* (Jackson: University of Mississippi Press, 2000), p. 192.
86 Salman Rushdie, *Midnight's Children* (London: Vintage, 1981), p. 318.
87 The correct meaning of the first usage of the word 'gospel' is good news or good tidings. However, incorrect interpretations (or mistranslations) of this word have interesting implications for Rushdie's use of the name. The common misinterpretation of gospel or 'gód spel' was its compound form, meaning discourse or story, a mistake which the OED claims 'was very natural, as the resulting sense was much more obviously appropriate than that of "good tidings" for a word which was chiefly known as the name of a sacred book or of a portion of the liturgy'. OED.
88 Peirce, *The Imperial Harem*, p. 272.
89 These references are to be found on the following pages of Rushdie, *Shame*, pp. 146, 154–5, 158–9, 162–5, 166–702, 206–7, 228.
90 El Guindi, Veil, p. 3.
91 Khan, *A Glimpse Through Purdah,* p. 27.
92 Purdah is defined by Khan as 'female veiling and seclusion'. Khan, *A Glimpse Through Purdah*, p. 25.
93 Khan, *A Glimpse Through Purdah*, p. 38.
94 Ibid., p. 26.
95 The Confederates 33:53, cited in Thomas Ballentine Irving, Khrshid Ahmad and Muhammad Manazir Ahsah, *The Qur'an – Basic Teachings* (Leicester: Islamic Foundation, 1992), p. 210.
96 B. Aisha Lemu, in Lemu, B. Aisha, and Fatima Heeren, *Woman in Islam* (Leicester: Islamic Foundation, 1998), p. 24.
97 Daphne Grace, *The Woman in the Muslin Mask*, p. 2.
98 Sense 1 of the word 'bikini' in the OED is the obscure sense of the word, 'a large explosion' , presumably used in reference to the nuclear testing carried out at Bikini Atoll in the 1940s and 1950s.

99 Daphne Grace, *The Woman in the Muslin Mask*, pp. 5, 6.

100 Kristeva discussed by Mary Grey in 'The Ordination of Women – Seeking a New Approach', a lecture to the Annual General Assembly of Catholic Women's Ordination, London 7 May 2002, accessed 24.07.06 via http://www.womenpriests.org/theology/grey5.asp.

101 Brad Dijkstra, cited in Elisabeth Bronfen, *Over Her Dead Body – Death, Femininity and the Aesthetic* (Manchester: Manchester University Press, 1992), p. 59.

102 Elisabeth Bronfen, *Over Her Dead Body*, p. 69.

103 Walter Benjamin, 'Goethe's Elective Affinities', in Michael W. Jennings, ed., *Walter Benjamin: Selected Writings Volume 1, 1913–1926* (London: Harvard University Press, 1996), p. 351.

104 Walter Benjamin, 'Goethe's Elective Affinities', p. 351.

105 Bassnett and Trivedi, eds, *Post-Colonial Translation*, p. 4.

106 Sara Suleri, *The Rhetoric of English India* (London: The University of Chicago Press, 1992), pp. 15–16.

107 The Anonymous History of the Trial of Warren Hastings, 1796, discussed in Suleri, *The Rhetoric of English India*, pp. 60–1.

108 Urvashi Butalia, *The Other Side of Silence – Voices from the Partition of India* (London: Hurst, 2000), p. 105.

109 Butalia, *The Other Side of Silence*, p. 105.

110 Khan, *A Glimpse Through Purdah*, p. 27.

111 Salman Rushdie, *The Satanic Verses* (London: Vintage, 1998), p. 376. All subsequent references to this text appear parenthetically immediately following the quotation.

112 Illustration caption to 'A London Courtesan', Antonia Fraser, *The Weaker Vessel* (London: Mandarin, 1984), illustrations preceding p. 477.

113 Bassnett and Trivedi, eds, p. 7. The translator's power to alter the text is demonstrated by Nabokov's explicit statement on his translation of Lermontov's *A Hero of Our Time*: 'I have gladly sacrificed to the requirements of exactness a number of important things – good taste, neat diction, and even grammar' in order to expel all trace of 'Lermontov's prose style in Russian', which is 'inelegant', 'dry and drab', 'crude', 'commonplace', 'hackneyed'. Perhaps this is an argument against writers performing the role of translator. Vladimir Nabokov, translator's foreword (1958) in Mikhail Lermontov, *A Hero of Our Time* (New York: Knopf, 1992), p. 7.

114 Bassnett and Trivedi, eds, p. 2.

115 (Sugata Bose and Ayesha Jalal, *Modern South Asia: History, Culture, Political Economy* (London: Routledge, 1998), p. 136). The rationale for Harappa's comparison is not made explicit: perhaps the harem is meant to refer to the

political yet insular space of the house, and the 'transvestite whores' a subversion of the usual inhabitants, which at the same time plays on Western assumptions of what usually takes place in the harem.

Chapter 3

1 Jakobson, Roman, 'On Linguistic Aspects of Translation', in Lawrence Venuti, ed., *The Translation Studies Reade*r (London: Routledge, 2000), p. 139.
2 Cundy, Catherine, *Salman Rushdie* (Manchester: Manchester University Press, 1996), p. 40.
3 Dharwadker, Aparna, 'Diaspora, Nation, and the Failure of Home: Two Contemporary Indian Plays'. *Theatre Journal* 50.1, (1998), 89–90.
4 Islam, Syed Manzurul, 'Writing the postcolonial event: Salman Rushdie's August 15th, 1947', *Textual Practice* 13(1), (1999), 119.
5 Islam, 'Writing the postcolonial event', p. 134.
6 Ibid., p. 131.
7 Ibid., p. 130.
8 Ibid., p. 125.
9 Ibid., p. 134.
10 Andersson, Lars and Peter Trudgill, *Bad Language* (Oxford: Basil Blackwell, 1990), p. 53.
11 Derrida, Jacques, *Margins of Philosophy*, translated by Alan Bass (Brighton: Harvester, 1982), p. 321.
12 Derrida, *Margins of Philosophy*, p. 321.
13 Ibid., p. 326.
14 For a synopsis of the film, see Mark Westmoreland, 'Cinematic Dreaming: On Phantom Poetics and the Longing for a Lebanese National Cinema'. *Text, Practice, Performance* IV (2002): 33–50, 8–41. See also Bert Cardullo, *In Search of Cinema: Writings on International Film Art* (Kingston: McGill-Queen's University Press, 2004), pp. 202–14.
15 Doueiri, Ziad, director, *West Beirut* (Lebanon: Summit/Spring, ASIN: B00005ALOX 1998).
16 Doueiri, *West Beirut*.
17 Andersson and Trudgill, *Bad Language*, p. 191.
18 Ibid., p. 8.
19 Adams, Robert M., *Bad Mouth* (Berkeley: University of California Press, 1977), pp. 71–2.
20 Andersson and Trudgill, *Bad Language*, pp. 10–11.
21 Leach, in Andersson and Trudgill, *Bad Language*, p. 15.

22 Julius, Anthony, *Transgressions – The Offences of Art* (London: Thames & Hudson, 2002), p. 19.
23 Bhabha, Homi, *The Location of Culture* (London: Routledge, 1994), p. 225.
24 Trivedi, Harish, 'Translating Culture vs. Cultural Translation'. *91st Meridian* 4(1), (2005), available via: http://iwp.uiowa.edu/91st/vol4_n1/trivedi/trivedi.html (accessed 15/12/08).
25 Rushdie interviewed in Reder, Michael, ed., *Conversations with Salman Rushdie* (Jackson: University of Mississippi Press, 2000), p. 178.
26 Samadi, Alyssa, 'Neither Prophets Jesus nor Moses (peace be upon them) ate pork', (last updated 14.08.04), accessed 17.08.06 via http://www.muslimworld.co.uk/porkeater.htm.
27 Islamic Invitation Centre, Frequently Asked Question, (last updated 10.02.04), accessed 17.08.06 via: http://www.islamicinvitationcentre.com/FAQ/diet/FAQ_diet.html.
28 Ruthven, Malise, *A Satanic Affair* (London: Chatto & Windus, 1990), p. 14.
29 Cundy, Catherine, *Salman Rushdie* (Manchester: Manchester University Press, 1996), p. 50.
30 Quayson, Ato, 'Protocols of Representation and the Problems of Constituting an African "Gnosis"', in *The Yearbook of English Studies*, vol. 27, 1997, 'The Politics of Postcolonial Criticism Special Number' (Leeds: W. S. Maney & Son for the MHRA, 1997), p. 140.
31 Goonetilleke, D. C. R. A., *Salman Rushdie* (London: Macmillan, 1998), p. 56.
32 Eteraz, Ali, 'Shooting A Shaykh In The Mouth', 2006, in *Eteraz* accessed 05.09.06, last updated 26.08.06, via: http://eteraz.wordpress.com/2006/08/25/shooting-a-shaykh-in-the-mouth/.
33 Voltaire, *Candide*, translated by John Butt (Middlesex: Penguin, 1947), p. 56.
34 Wieseltier in Appignanesi, Lisa and Sara Maitland, *The Rushdie File* (Syracuse: Syracuse University Press, 1990), p. 166.
35 Rushdie, Salman, *Imaginary Homelands: Essays in Criticism, 1981–1991* (London, 1991), p. 407.
36 Blanchot cited in Parkin-Gounelas, Ruth, *Literature and Psychoanalysis – Intertextual Readings* (Basingstoke: Palgrave, 2001), p. 198.
37 Lacan, Jacques, *Ecrits*, translated from the French by Alan Sheridan (London: Tavistock, 1980), p. 104.
38 Barthes, Roland, 'The Death of the Author', in *Image-Music-Text* (London: Fontana, 1977), p. 148.
39 Parkin-Gounelas, *Literature and Psychoanalysis*, p. 198.
40 Ruthven, *A Satanic Affair*, p. 10.
41 Rushdie, Salman, *Step Across This Line* (London: Vintage, 2002), p. 239.
42 Barthes, 'The Death of the Author', p. 142.

43 Ibid., p. 146.
44 Rushdie, *Step Across This Line*, p. 250.
45 Ruthven, *A Satanic Affair*, p. 51.
46 Akhtar, Shabbir, *Be Careful with Muhammad! – The Salman Rushdie Affair* (London: Bellew, 1989), pp. 71–4.
47 Bhabha, *The Location of Culture*, p. 225.
48 Ibid.
49 Smith, Anna, *Julia Kristeva – Readings of Exile and Estrangement* (London: Macmillan, 1996), p. 130.
50 Ebbatson, Roger, *Imaginary England* (Aldershot: Ashgate, 2005), p. 3.
51 Hunter cited in Parkin-Gounelas, *Literature and Psychoanalysis*, p. 137.
52 Clément, Catherine and Julia Kristeva, *The Feminine and the Sacred*, translated by Jane Marie Todd (Basingstoke: Palgrave, 2001), p. 31.
53 Stendhal cited in Adams, *Bad Mouth*, preface.
54 Adams, *Bad Mouth*, p. 7.
55 Harrison, Nicholas, *Postcolonial Criticism* (Cambridge: Polity, 2003), pp. 121–2.
56 Harrison, *Postcolonial Criticism*, p. 122.
57 Benjamin, Walter, 'Goethe's Elective Affinities', in Michael W. Jennings, ed., *Walter Benjamin: Selected Writings Volume 1, 1913–1926* (London: Harvard University Press, 1996), p. 351.
58 Appignanesi and Maitland, *The Rushdie File*, p. 135.
59 Samad cited in Bhabha, *The Location of Culture*, p. 226.
60 Bhabha cited in Appignanesi and Maitland, *The Rushdie File*, p. 114.
61 Andersson and Trudgill, *Bad Language*, pp. 38–9.
62 Crystal, David, *The Stories of English* (London: Penguin, 2004), p. 10.
63 Sardar, Ziauddin and Merryl Wyn Davies, *Distorted Imagination – Lessons from the Rushdie Affair* (London: Greyseal, 1990), p. 163.
64 Ruthven, *A Satanic Affair*, p. 31.
65 Andersson and Trudgill, *Bad Language*, p. 16.
66 Goonetilleke, *Salman Rushdie*, p. 102.
67 Ruthven, *A Satanic Affair*, p. 19.
68 Rushdie, *Imaginary Homelands*, p. 393.
69 Bhabha, Homi, *Nation and Narration* (London: Routledge, 1990), p. 1.
70 Bhabha, *Nation and Narration*, p. 3.
71 Bhabha, *The Location of Culture*, p. 88.
72 Adams, *Bad Mouth*, p. 6.
73 Bhabha, *The Location of Culture*, p. 5.
74 Chrisman, Laura and Benita Parry, eds, *Postcolonial Theory and Criticism* (Cambridge: Brewer, 2000), p. x.
75 Leach, cited in Andersson and Trudgill, *Bad Language*, p. 16.

76 Bhabha, *The Location of Culture*, p. 5.

77 Young, Robert J. C., *Colonial Desire: Hybridity in Theory, Culture and Race* (London: Routledge, 1995), p. 20.

78 Young, *Colonial Desire*, p. 5.

79 Rushdie, *Step Across This Line*, p. 163.

80 Ibid., pp. 163, 165.

81 Ibid., p. 173.

Chapter 4

1 D'Alembert, cited in André Lefevere, ed., *Translation/History/Culture: A Sourcebook* (London: Routledge, 1992), p. 10.

2 Lefevere, ed., *Translation/History/Culture*, p. 1.

3 Ibid.

4 Susan Bassnett and Harish Trivedi, eds, *Post-Colonial Translation: Theory and Practice* (London: Routledge, 1999), pp. 7–8.

5 Johann Wolfgang von Goethe, cited in André Lefevere, ed., *Translation/History/Culture*, p. 75.

6 Goethe, cited in André Lefevere, ed., *Translation/History/Culture*, p. 75.

7 Ibid., p. 76.

8 Edward Lane, cited in Susan Bassnett and Harish Trivedi, eds, p. 6.

9 Goethe, cited in André Lefevere, ed., *Translation/History/Culture*, p. 75.

10 Ibid., p. 76.

11 Lawrence Venuti, *The Translator's Invisibility – A History of Translation* (London: Routledge, 1995), p. 2.

12 Roger Berger claims that short stories do not represent locations in the 'cartographic' method of describing landscape that Edward Said described (1990:79). Roger Berger, 'The Place of (and Place in) the Anglophone African Short Story', in Barbara Lounsberry, Susan Lohafer, Mary Rohrberger, Stephen Pett, R. C. Feddersen, eds, *The Tales We Tell – Perspectives on the Short Story* (London: Greenwood, 1998), p. 75.

13 Edward Said, cited by Roger Berger, in 'The Place of (and Place in) the Anglophone African Short Story', p. 75.

14 Goethe, cited in André Lefevere, ed., *Translation/History/Culture*, p. 75.

15 The forced sterilization programme has been historically documented. One example is in Syed Ubaidur Rahman, 'Saddest days of Indian democracy', in Milli Gazette (15 July 2000, Vol. 1, No. 13), accessed 05.05.2006 via http://www.dalitstan.org/journal/brahman/bra001/brah0136.html.

16 Bill Ashcroft, Gareth Griffiths and Helen Tiffin, eds, *The Empire Writes Back* (London: Routledge, 2002), p. 19.

17 Lefevere, ed., *Translation/History/Culture*, p. 5.
18 Ibid.
19 Ashcroft, Griffiths and Tiffin, eds, *The Empire Writes Back*, p. 19.
20 Salman Rushdie, cited in Ashcroft, Griffiths and Tiffin, eds, *The Empire Writes Back*, p. 32.
21 Chinua Achebe, cited in Berger, 'The Place of (and Place in) the Anglophone African Short Story', p. 73.
22 Paul Brians, 'Chinua Achebe: *Things Fall Apart* Study Guide', 2005, accessed 12.09.06 via: https://www.wsu.edu/~brians/anglophone/achebe.html.
23 Ian Reid, 'Generic Variations on a Colonial Topos', in Lounsberry et al., eds, p. 89.
24 Goethe, cited in Lefevere, ed., *Translation/History/Culture*, p. 76.
25 Salman Rushdie, in conversation with Gunter Grass (1985), in Reder, ed., *Conversations with Salman Rushdie*, p. 73.
26 Goethe, cited in André Lefevere, ed., *Translation/History/Culture*, p. 76.
27 Lefevere, ed., *Translation/History/Culture*, p. 2.
28 Rocio G. Davis, 'Salman Rushdie's East, West: Palimpsests of Fiction and Reality'. *Passages* 2(1), (2000), 81–92, 86.
29 Graeme Harper, ed., *Comedy, Fantasy and Colonialism* (London: Continuum, 2002), p. 7.
30 Salman Rushdie, 'Out of Kansas', in *Step Across This Line* (London: Vintage, 2003), p. 25.
31 Lefevere, ed., *Translation/History/Culture*, p. 2.
32 Steiner, *After Babel*, p. 28.
33 Goethe, cited in Lefevere, ed., *Translation/History/Culture*, p. 76.
34 Ibid.
35 Lefevere, ed., *Translation/History/Culture*, p. 70.
36 Goethe, cited in André Lefevere, ed., *Translation/History/Culture*, p. 76.
37 Ibid., p. 77.
38 Lefevere, ed., *Translation/History/Culture*, p. 70.
39 Ibid.
40 Goethe, cited in André Lefevere, ed., *Translation/History/Culture*, p. 76.
41 Lefevere, ed., *Translation/History/Culture*, p. 7.
42 Ibid., p. 10.
43 Berger, 'The Place of (and Place in) the Anglophone African Short Story', p. 76.
44 Sitara Khan, *A Glimpse Through Purdah – Asian Women – The Myth and the Reality* (London: Trentham Books, 1999), p. 14.
45 'The "brown sahib" is a recognisable sociological type on the Subcontinent: an uncritical Anglophile', Ziauddin Sardar, 'Extremely wrong about British Muslims', review of From Rushdie to 7/7, by Anthony McRoy, 28 April 2006, in the Independent Online, accessed 10 July 2006 via http://enjoyment.independent.co.uk/books/reviews/article360562.ece.

46 Dipesh Chakrabarty, *Provincializing Europe – Postcolonial Thought and Historical Difference* (Princeton: Princeton University Press, 2000), p. 97. The first use of the term *subaltern* appears in Antonio Gramsci's cultural, Marxist writings, much earlier than its use in postcolonial studies, in his texts *The Prison Notebooks* and *The Modern Prince*.
47 Chakrabarty, *Provincializing Europe*, p. 97.
48 Neil Lazarus, 'Representation and Terror in VY Mudimbe'. *Journal of African Cultural Studies* 17(1), (June 2005), 84.
49 Lefevere, ed., *Translation/History/Culture*, p. 2.
50 Ashcroft, Griffiths and Tiffin, eds, *The Empire Writes Back*, p. 179.
51 Susan Lohafer, introduction to Lounsberry et al., eds, *The Tales We Tell*, p. x.
52 Ashcroft, Griffiths and Tiffin, eds, *The Empire Writes Back*, p. 179.
53 Salman Rushdie, in 'Home is Where the Art Is' with an anonymous interviewer (1994), in Reder, ed., *Conversations with Salman Rushdie*, p. 163.
54 German-English dictionary online, accessed 03 May 2006 via http://www.iee.et.tu-dresden.de/cgi-bin/cgiwrap/wernerr/search.sh?string=oestlich&nocase=on&no_umlauts=on&hits=50.
55 OED 'divan'.
56 Ibid.
57 Ibid.
58 Benjamin, 'The Storyteller', in *Illuminations*, p. 97.
59 Ibid., p. 87.
60 Ibid., p. 88.
61 Ibid., p. 86.
62 Berger, 'The Place of (and Place in) the Anglophone African Short Story', p. 78.
63 Ibid.
64 Roopal Monar, 'Bahadur', in Shyam Selvadurai, ed., *Story-Wallah – Short Fiction from South Asian Writers* (New York: Houghton Mifflin, 2005), p. 171.
65 Ben Okri, 'What the Tapster Saw', in *Stars of the New Curfew* (London: Vintage, 1999), p. 183.
66 Steiner, *After Babel*, p. 246.
67 Ibid.

Chapter 5

1 Victor Hugo cited in Lefevere, André, *Translation, History, Culture: A Sourcebook* (London: Routledge, 1992), p. 14.
2 Gandhi, Leela, *Postcolonial Theory: A Critical Introduction* (New York: Columbia University Press, 1998), p. 170.
3 Rushdie, Salman, *Imaginary Homelands: Essays in Criticism, 1981–1991* (London, 1991), p. 25.

4 Rushdie, Salman, *Step Across This Line* (London: Vintage, 2002), p. 305.
5 Brown, Judith M., *Modern India* (Oxford: Oxford University Press, 1994), p. 9.
6 Rushdie, *Step Across This Line*, p. 305.
7 Ibid.
8 Stewart, Susan, *On Longing – Narratives of the Miniature, the Gigantic, the Souvenir, the Collection* (London: Duke University Press, 1993), p. x.
9 Philips, C. H. and Wainwright, Mary Doreen, eds, 'The Role of Lord Mountbatten', in *The Partition of India* (London: Allen and Unwin, 1970), p. 125.
10 Rushdie, *Step Across This Line*, p. 435.
11 Foucault, Michel, *The Order of Things – An Archaeology of the Human Sciences* (London: Routledge, 1974 [French 1966]), p. 3.
12 Foucault, *The Order of Things*, p. 4.
13 Ibid., p. 6.
14 Gandhi, *Postcolonial Theory*, p. 170.
15 Jakobson, Roman, 'On Linguistic Aspects of Translation', in Lawrence Venuti, ed., *The Translation Studies Reade*r (London: Routledge, 2000), p. 139.
16 Lefevere, *Translation, History, Culture*, p. 1.
17 Niranjana, Tejaswini, *Siting Translation: History, Post-Structuralism, and the Colonial Context* (Berkeley: University of Berkeley Press, 1992), p. 159.
18 Niranjana, *Siting Translation*, pp. 150–1.
19 Ibid.
20 Benjamin, cited in Buck-Morrs, Susan, *Walter Benjamin and the Arcades Project* (Cambridge, MA: MIT Press, 1991), p. 461. 225
21 Niranjana, *Siting Translation*, p. 161.
22 Foucault, *The Order of Things*, p. 11.
23 Ibid., p. 50.
24 Sarup, Madan, *An Introductory Guide to Post-structuralism and Postmodernism*, second edition (New York: Harvester Wheatsheaf, 1993), p. 58.
25 Sarup, *An Introductory Guide to Post-structuralism*, p. 58.
26 Ibid., p. 59.
27 Sarup, *An Introductory Guide to Post-structuralism*, p. 59.
28 Ibid.
29 Kristeva, Julia, *New Maladies of the Soul*, translated by Ross Guberman (New York: Columbia University Press, 1995), pp. 15–16.
30 Kristeva, *New Maladies of the Soul*, p. 10.
31 Talbot, Ian, *India and Pakistan* (London: Arnold, 2000), p. 168.
32 Talbot, *India and Pakistan*, p. 168.
33 Irving, Thomas Ballantyne, Khurshid Ahmad and Muhammad Manazir Ahsah, *The Qur'an: Basic Teachings* (Leicester: Islamic Foundation, 1992), p. 63.

34 Kristeva, Julia, *Desire in Language – A Semiotic Approach to Literature and Art* (Oxford: Basil Blackwell, 1980), p. 48, my emphasis.
35 Ellman, Maud, *The Hunger Artists* (London: Virago, 1993), p. 32.
36 Rushdie, *Imaginary Homelands*, p. 16.
37 Ashcroft, Bill, Gareth Griffiths and Helen Tiffin, *The Empire Writes Back: Theory and Practice in Post-Colonial Literatures* (London: Routledge, 2002), pp. 180–2.
38 Ashcroft, Griffiths and Tiffin, *The Empire Writes Back*, pp. 180–2.
39 Ashcroft, Bill, Griffiths, Gareth and Tiffin, Helen, 'Post-Colonial Reconstructions: Literature, Meaning, Value', in Walder, Dennis, ed., *Literature in the Modern World* (Oxford: Oxford University Press, 1990), p. 300.
40 Kristeva, *Desire in Language*, p. 52.
41 Ibid., pp. 55–6.
42 Crossley-Holland, Kevin, *Axe-age, Wolf-age: Selection from the Norse Myths* (London: Scholastic, 1985), p. 15.
43 Rushdie, *Imaginary Homelands*, p. 9.
44 Ibid., p. 25.
45 Ibid., pp. 9–10.
46 Ibid., p. 24.
47 Kermode, Frank, *The Sense of an Ending* (Oxford: Oxford University Press, 2000), p. 6.
48 Kermode, *The Sense of an Ending*, p. 138.
49 Rushdie, *Imaginary Homelands*, p. 12.
50 Derrida, Jacques, *Specters of Marx*, translated from the French by Peggy Kamuf (New York: Routledge Classics, 2006), p. 5.
51 Derrida, *Specters of Marx*, p. 5.
52 Ibid., p. 92.
53 Ibid., p. 81.
54 Ibid., p. 92.
55 Rushdie, Salman, *Shalimar the Clown* (London: Jonathan Cape, 2005), p. 53.
56 Spivak, Gayatri Chakravorty, 'Subaltern Studies – Deconstructing Historiograhy', in Donna Landry and Gerald Maclean, eds, *The Spivak Reader* (London: Routledge, 1996), p. 212.
57 White, Hayden, 'The Historical Text as Literary Artifact', in Brian Fay, Philip Pomper and Richard T. Vann eds, *History and Theory – Contemporary Readings* (Oxford Blackwell 1998), p. 17.
58 White, 'The Historical Text', p. 17.
59 Ibid.
60 White, 'The Historical Text', p. 19.
61 Bhabha, Homi, *The Location of Culture* (London: Routledge, 1994), pp. 214–15.
62 Bhabha, *The Location of Culture*, pp. 214–15.

63 Ibid., pp. 216–17.
64 Ibid., p. 219.
65 Ibid.

Chapter 6

1 Teverson, Andrew *Salman Rushdie* (Manchester: Manchester University Press, 2007), p. 112.
2 Cundy, Catherine, *Salman Rushdie* (Manchester: Manchester University Press, 1996), p. 128.
3 Engblom, Philip, 'A Multitude of Voices: Carnivalisation and Dialogicality in the Novels of Salman Rushdie', in Fletcher, M. D. ed., *Reading Rushdie: Perspectives on the Fiction of Salman Rushdie* (Amsterdam: Rodopi, 1994), pp. 293–304, 298.
4 Rubinson, Gregory J., *The fiction of Rushdie, Barnes, Winterson, and Carter: Breaking Cultural and Literary Boundaries in the Work of Four Postmodernists* (Jefferson, NC: McFarland, 2005), p. 203.
5 Césaire, Aimé, *Return to My Native Land*, translated John Berger and Anna Bostock (Harmondsworth: Penguin, 1969 [French 1956]), pp. 86–7.
6 Valassopoulos, Anastasia, 'Fictionalising Post-colonial Theory: The Creative Native Informant?' *Critical Survey* 162 (2004), 28–44, 29.
7 Said, Edward, 'Travelling Theory', in Bayoumi, Moustafa and Rubin, Andrew, eds, *The Edward Said Reader* (New York: Vintage, 2000), p. 195.
8 Said, 'Travelling Theory', p. 196.
9 Ibid.
10 Ibid.
11 Ibid.
12 Said, Edward, 'Travelling Theory Reconsidered', in Nigel C Gibson, ed., *Rethinking Fanon: The Continuing Dialogue* (Amherst: Prometheus Books, 1999), pp. 197–214, p. 206.
13 Said, Edward, 'Travelling Theory Reconsidered', pp. 206–7.
14 Ibid., p. 208.
15 Ibid., p. 209.
16 Ibid., p. 210.
17 Ibid., p. 214.
18 Said, 'Travelling Theory', p. 211.
19 Johansen, Ib, 'The Flight from the Enchanter: Reflections on Salman Rushdie's Grimus', in Fletcher, M. D. ed., *Reading Rushdie: Perspectives on the Fiction of Salman Rushdie* (Amsterdam: Rodopi, 1994), pp. 23–33, 24.
20 Johansen, 'The Flight', p. 33.

Chapter 7

1 This chapter was originally published in Mendes, Ana Cristina, ed., *Salman Rushdie and Visual Culture* (London: Routledge, 2011), pp. 87–105.
2 Ella Shohat and Robert Stam, 'Narrativizing Visual Culture: Towards a Polycentric Aesthetics', in Nicholas Mirzoeff ed., *The Visual Culture Reader* (London: Routledge, 1998), p. 27.
3 André Lefevere, ed. *Translation/History/Culture* (London: Routledge, 1992), p. 14.
4 Lawrence Venuti, *The Translator's Invisibility: A History of Translation* (London: Routledge, 2008), p. 1.
5 Venuti, *Translator's Invisibility*, p. 6.
6 Sharp, Emma, 'Art Restoration: a Chemical Perspective', accessed 11 March 2006, http://www.chemsoc.org/ExemplarChem/entries/2001/esharp/default.htm.
7 Lefevere, *Translation/History/Culture*, p. 1.
8 Sharp, 'Art Restoration'.
9 Lefevere, *Translation/History/Culture*, p. 10.
10 Susan Bassnett and Harish Trivedi, eds, *Post-Colonial Translation* (London: Routledge, 1999), p. 7.
11 Lefevere, *Translation/History/Culture*, p. 1.
12 Venuti, *Translator's Invisibility*, p. 10.
13 Cited in Lefevere, *Translation/History/Culture*, p. 13.
14 Cited in Bassnett and Trivedi, *Post-colonial*, p. 9.
15 Cited in Lefevere, *Translation/History/Culture*, p. 24.
16 Benjamin Graves, 'The Master-Slave Dialectic: Hegel and Fanon', accessed 13 September 2008, http://www.postcolonialweb.org/sa/gordimer/july6.html.
17 Graves, 'Master-Slave'.
18 Venuti, *Translator's Invisibility*, p. 2.
19 Cited in Venuti, *Translator's Invisibility*, p. 1.
20 Venuti, *Translator's Invisibility*, p. 1.
21 Bassnett and Trivedi, *Post-colonial*, p. 8.
22 Venuti, *Translator's Invisibility*, p. 8.
23 Ibid., p. 7.
24 Ibid., p. 6.
25 Ibid., p. 5.
26 Cited in Lefevere, *Translation/History/Culture*, p. 18.
27 Bellay cited in Lefevere, *Translation/History/Culture*, p. 22.
28 Lefevere, *Translation/History/Culture*, p. 5.
29 D'Albancourt cited in Lefevere, *Translation/History/Culture*, p. 9.

30 Prevost cited in Lefevere, *Translation/History/Culture*, p. 14.
31 Frank Kermode, *Poetry, Narrative, History* (Oxford: Basil Blackwell, 1990), p. 10.
32 Frank Kermode, *The Genesis of Secrecy: On the Interpretation of Narrative* (Cambridge, MA: Harvard University Press, 1979), pp. 81–2.
33 Kermode, *Poetry, Narrative, History*, p. 47.
34 Dacier cited in Lefevere, *Translation/History/Culture*, p. 12.
35 George Steiner, *After Babel* (Oxford: Oxford University Press, 1992), p. 239.
36 Ross Chambers, *Room for Maneuver* (Chicago: University of Chicago Press, 1991), p. 26.
37 Frank Kermode, *The Sense of an Ending* (Oxford: Oxford University Press, 2000), p. 6.
38 Wole Soyinka, *The Man Died* (London: Arrow, 1972), p. 277.
39 Kermode, *Sense of an Ending*, p. 196.
40 Ibid., p. 193.

Chapter 8

1 Teverson, Andrew, *Salman Rushdie* (Manchester: Manchester University Press, 2007), p. 97.
2 Teverson, *Salman Rushdie*, p. 169.
3 Holson, Laura M., 'From Exile to Everywhere', *New York Times*, http://www.nytimes.com/2012/03/25/fashion/salman-rushdie-out-of-exile-is-a-fixture-on-the-social-scene.html, 23 March 2012 (accessed 25.09.2012).
4 Press Release cited by Shuddhabrata Sengupta, 'Jaipur Literature Festival – Requiescat in Pacem', *Kafila*, http://kafila.org/2012/01/21/jaipur-literature-festival-requiescat-in-pacem/#more-11294, 21 January 2012 (accessed 25.09.2012).
5 Mishra, Pankaj, *Joseph Anton* by Salman Rushdie – review, *The Guardian*, http://www.guardian.co.uk/books/2012/sep/18/joseph-anton-salman-rushdie-review, Tuesday 18 September 2012 (accessed 25.09.2012).
6 de Man, Paul, 'Autobiography as De-facement'. *MLN* 94(5), Comparative Literature (December 1979), 919–30.
7 Phillipe Lejeune cited in de Man, Paul, 'Autobiography as De-facement', p. 922.
8 Moore-Gilbert, Bart, *Postcolonial Life-writing* (London: Routledge, 2009), p. 31.
9 de Man, Paul, 'Autobiography as De-facement', p. 930.

Conclusion

1 Maria Tymoczko, 'Post-colonial writing and literary translation', in Bassnett and Trivedi, eds, *Post-colonial Translation: Theory and Practice* (London: Routledge, 1999), p. 20.

2 Salman Rushdie, in conversation with Gunter Grass (1985), in Michael Reder, ed., *Conversations with Salman Rushdie* (Jackson: University Press of Mississippi, 2000), p. 77.

3 Salman Rushdie, *The Satanic Verses* (London: Vintage, 1998). The sanatorium in London houses the 'manticore' and the woman with 'skin turned to glass', pp. 168–9. Saladin Chamcha is described as 'a fully developed devil, a horned goat-man', p. 251.

4 André Lefevere, ed., *Translation/History/Culture: A Sourcebook* (London: Routledge, 1992), p. 5.

5 Walter Benjamin, 'The Task of the Translator', in *Illuminations*, translated by Harry Zohn, (London: Pimlico, 1999 [1955, 1968]), p. 73.

6 Lefevere, ed., *Translation/History/Culture,* p. 8.

7 George Steiner, *After Babel,* second edition (Oxford: Oxford University Press, 1992), p. 246.

8 'Yorick' in Salman Rushdie, *East, West* (London: Vintage, 1994), p. 65.

9 Daphne Grace, *The Woman in the Muslin Mask – Veiling and Identity in Postcolonial Literature* (London: Pluto, 2004), p. 215.

10 Roy Porter, ed., *The Faber Book of Madness* (London: Faber, 1967), p. 155.

11 Benita Parry, 'The Postcolonial: Conceptual Category or Chimera?', in *The Yearbook of English Studies*, Vol. 27, The Politics of Postcolonial Criticism (1997), p. 11.

12 Benita Parry, 'The Postcolonial: Conceptual Category or Chimera?', p. 13.

13 Salman Rushdie, *The Moor's Last Sigh* (London: Vintage, 1996), p. 423.

14 Salman Rushdie, *Step Across This Line* (London: Vintage, 2002), p. 434.

15 Steiner, *After Babel*, p. 246.

16 Barbara Johnson, *Mother Tongues: Sexuality, Trials, Motherhood, Translation* (London: Harvard University Press, 2003), pp. 13–14.

17 Catherine Cundy, *Salman Rushdie* (Manchester: Manchester University Press, 1996), p. 31.

18 Salman Rushdie interviewed by Charlie Rose, in Reder, Michael, ed., *Conversations with Salman Rushdie* (Jackson: University of Mississippi Press, 2000), p. 207.

Appendix: Annotated Bibliography

This select annotated bibliography is intended to acknowledge the texts on translation and on Salman Rushdie that stand out as essential for readers who would like to pursue questions raised in this book.

Bassnett, Susan and Trivedi, Harish, eds, *Post-colonial Translation: Theory and Practice* (London: Routledge, 1999).

This remains the only book to bring the theoretical fields of translation and postcolonial studies together in an effort to demonstrate the interconnected nature of the ways of thinking. Chapters written by theorists, translators and those who both practice and theorize about translation address the nature of translation, the emotion of translation and the politics of translation in a postcolonial context.

Goonetilleke, D. C. R. A., *Salman Rushdie*, second edition (London: Palgrave Macmillan, 2009).

Goonetilleke's original book on Rushdie has been updated to include responses to his most recent works, including *Shalimar the Clown* and *The Enchantress of Florence*. The book offers a detailed response to the texts, each chapter dealing with a separate text, to provide insight into the literary, historical and cultural references that characterize Rushdie's work, but which can be obscure to many readers.

Lefevere, André, *Translation, History, Culture: A Sourcebook* (London: Routledge, 1992).

Lefevere's fascinating text collects translators' notes, forewords and essays on the practice of translation. The book offers a historical overview of the journey that translators have taken, from the earliest attempts at word-for-word translations of the Bible, and the perils of translating sacred texts, to more recent discussions of the potential for translation to enrich a culture or a national literature.

Mendes, Ana Cristina, ed., *Salman Rushdie and Visual Culture* (London: Routledge, 2011).

Mendes has brought together a number of leading Rushdie scholars to address one of the most fascinating aspects of Rushdie's work: its attention to visual culture: painting, film, the image or icon. Chapters consider the ways in which Rushdie's texts represent visual culture and address all of Rushdie's major literary works.

Niranjana, Tejaswini, *Siting Translation: History, Post-Structuralism, and the Colonial Context* (Berkeley: University of Berkeley Press, 1992).

Niranjana posits that translation is a political act and considers the ways in which translation has been used to exercise power, yet acknowledges too its positive, transformative potential for those in postcolonial contexts.

Teverson, Andrew, *Salman Rushdie* (Manchester: Manchester University Press, 2007).

Andrew Teverson's recent study of Rushdie's major literary texts is another excellent resource for readers keen to explore the ways in which Rushdie has been read through literary theories.

Venuti, Lawrence, *The Translator's Invisibility* (London: Routledge, 1995).

Venuti's work was among the first to address the position of the translator in the modern world of publishing. Venuti explores in both practical and theoretical terms the role and position of translation and argues for an acknowledgement of translation as a practice both by the publishing industry and in the way that translations are produced: by writing a translation that looks like a translation, its translator is acknowledged as a part of that text.

Venuti, Lawrence, ed., *The Translation Studies Reader* (London: Routledge, 2000).

Venuti's extensive edited collection brings together essays by key translators and thinkers who address niche aspects of translation studies. Essays consider subjects as diverse as gender and sexuality in translation, to political motivations for translating works such as *The Thousand and One Nights*.

Bibliography

Abu Odeh, Lama, 'Post-Colonial Feminism and the Veil: Thinking the Difference', in *Feminist Review*, No. 43, Issues for Feminism (Spring 1993).

Achebe, Chinua, 'The African Writer and the English Language', in Patrick Williams and Laura Chrisman, eds, *Colonial Discourse and Post-Colonial Theory: A Reader* (Hemel Hempstead: Harvester Wheatsheaf, 1993).

Adams, Robert M., *Bad Mouth* (Berkeley: University of California Press, 1977).

Afzal-Khan, Fawzia, *Cultural Imperialism and the Indo-English Novel* (Pennsylvania: Pennsylvania State University Press, 1993).

Akhtar, Shabbir, *Be Careful with Muhammad! – The Salman Rushdie Affair* (London: Bellew, 1989).

Alloula, Malek, *The Colonial Harem*, translated by Myrna Godzich and Wlad Godzich (Manchester: Manchester University Press, 1986).

Anderson, Benedict, *Imagined Communities* (London: Verso, 1991).

Andersson, Lars and Peter Trudgill, *Bad Language* (Oxford: Basil Blackwell, 1990).

Appignanesi, Lisa and Sara Maitland, *The Rushdie File* (Syracuse: Syracuse University Press, 1990).

Arnold, David, *Colonizing the Body: State Medicine and Epidemic Disease in Nineteenth Century India* (California: University of California Press, 1997).

Arrojo, Rosemary, 'Interpretation as Possessive Love – Hélène Cixous, Clarice Lispector and the ambivalence of fidelity', in Bassnett, Susan and Trivedi, Harish, eds, *Post-colonial Translation: Theory and Practice* (London: Routledge, 1999).

Ashcroft, Griffiths and Helen Tiffin, 'Post-Colonial Reconstructions: Literature, Meaning, Value', in Walder, Dennis, ed., *Literature in the Modern World* (Oxford: Oxford University Press, 1990).

Ashcroft, Bill, Gareth Griffiths and Helen Tiffin, *The Empire Writes Back: Theory and Practice in Post-Colonial Literatures* (London: Routledge, 2002).

Badawi, Jamal, 'Polygamy in Islamic Law', 1998, accessed 09.02.06, last updated 05.04.03, via http://www.islamfortoday.com/polygamy5.htm.

Baldick, Robert, *The Duel – A History of Duelling* (London: Spring, 1965).

Ballentine Irving, Thomas, Khurshid Ahmad, M. M. Ahsan, *The Qur'an – Basic Teachings* (Leicester: Islamic Foundation, 1992).

Barthes, Roland, *The Death of the Author* (London: Fontana, 1977).

Bassnett, Susan and Harish Trivedi, eds, *Post-colonial Translation: Theory and Practice* (London: Routledge, 1999).

Baudrillard, Jean, *Cool Memories II*, translated by Chris Turner (Cambridge: Polity, 1996).

—, *Simulacra and Simulation*, translated by Sheila Faria Glazer (Ann Arbor: University of Michigan Press, 1994).

—, *The Transparency of Evil – Essays on Extreme Phenomena*, translated by James Benedict (London: Verso, 1993).

Bell, David and Gill Valentine, *Consuming Geographies – We Are Where We Eat* (London: Routledge, 1997).

—, eds, *Mapping Desire: Geographies of Sexualities* (London: Routledge, 1995).

Benjamin, Walter, 'Goethe's Elective Affinities', in Michael W. Jennings, ed., *Walter Benjamin: Selected Writings Volume 1, 1913–1926* (London: Harvard University Press, 1996).

—, *Illuminations*, translated by Harry Zohn (London: Pimlico, 1999 [1955, 1968]).

—, *Reflections* (New York: Schocken, 1978).

—, *Selected Writings Volume 1, 1913–1926* (London: Harvard University Press, 2004).

Bhabha, Homi, *The Location of Culture* (London: Routledge, 1994).

—, *Nation and Narration* (London: Routledge, 1990).

—, 'Of Mimicry and Man'. from *October*, 28 (spring 1984), 125–33.

—, cited in 'Beyond U.S. Multiculturalism?: Asian Diasporas and New Transnational Cultures' proceedings from a symposium held at MIT, 2003 (last updated 30.11.03), accessed 31.08.06 via: http://web.mit.edu/cbbs/events/Asian_diaspora_symposium.pdf.

Bhattacharya, Nandini, '"Behind the Veil": The Many Masks of Subaltern Sexuality'. *Women's Studies International Forum* 19 (May/June 1996), 277–92.

Billig, Michael, *Freudian Repression: Conversation Creating the Unconscious* (Cambridge: Cambridge University Press, 1999).

Biriotti, Maurice and Nicola Miller, eds, *What is an Author?* (Manchester: Manchester University Press, 1993).

Bose, Sugata and Ayesha Jalal, *Modern South Asia – History, Culture, Political Economy* (London: Routledge, 1998).

Brians, Paul, 'Chinua Achebe: *Things Fall Apart* Study Guide', 2005, accessed 12.09.06, last updated 13.12.05, via: https://www.wsu.edu/~brians/anglophone/achebe.html.

Brigg, Peter, 'Salman Rushdie's Novels: The Disorder in Fantastic Order'. *World Literature Written in English* 27 (1987), 119–30.

Bronfen, Elisabeth, *Over Her Dead Body* (Manchester: Manchester University Press, 1992).

Brooks, Geraldine, *Nine Parts of Desire – The Hidden world of Islamic Women* (London: Hamish Hamilton, 1995).

Brown, Judith M., *Modern India* (Oxford: Oxford University Press, 1994).

Buber, Martin and Franz Rosenzweig, *Scripture and Translation*, translated by Lawrence Rosenwald with Everett Fox (Bloomington: Indiana University Press, 1994).

Buck-Morss, Susan, 'Benjamin's Passagen-Werk.' *New German Critique* 29 (1983), 21140.

Burton, Richard, translator, *The Arabian Nights* (London: Penguin, 1997).

Butalia, Urvashi, *The Other Side of Silence – Voices from the Partition of India* (London: Hurst, 2000).

Campbell, Mike, 'Behind the Name: the etymology and history of first names', 1996–2006, accessed 05.08.06, last updated 09.04.06, via http://www.behindthename.com.

Cardullo, Bert, *In Search of Cinema: Writings on International Film Art* (Kingston: McGill-Queen's University Press, 2004).

Carroll, Robert and Stephen Prickett, eds, *The Bible – The Authorized King James Version* (Oxford: Oxford University Press, 1997).

Cesaire, Aime, *Return to my Native Land*, translated from the French *Cahier d'un retour au pays natal* by John Berger and Anna Bostock (Harmondsworth: Penguin, 1969 [1956]).

Chakrabarty, Dipesh, *Provincializing Europe – Postcolonial Thought and Historical Difference* (Princeton: Princeton University Press, 2000).

Chambers, Ross, *Room for Maneuver: Reading (the) Oppositional (in) Narrative* (Chicago: University of Chicago Press, 1991).

Chatterjee, Shampa, review of Malavika Karlekar, *Voices from Within: Early Personal Narratives of Bengali Women* (Oxford: Oxford University Press, 1993), accessed 05.08.06, last updated 19.05.06, at http://www.sawnet.org/books/reviews.php?Voices + from + Within.

Chaturvedi, Vinayak, *Mapping Subaltern Studies and the Postcolonial* (London: Verso, 2000).

Chow, Rey, 'Film as Ethnography; Or, Translation Between Cultures in the Postcolonial World', in Julian Wolfreys, ed., *Literary Theories – A Reader & Guide* (Edinburgh: Edinburgh University Press, 1999).

Chrisman, Laura, *Postcolonial Contraventions: Cultural Readings of Race, Imperialism and Transnationalism* (Manchester: Manchester University Press, 2003).

Chrisman, Laura and Benita Parry, eds, *Postcolonial Theory and Criticism* (Cambridge: Brewer, 2000).

Clément, Catherine and Julia Kristeva, *The Feminine and the Sacred*, translated by Jane Marie Todd (Basingstoke: Palgrave, 2001).

Connor, Steven, *Dumbstruck: A Cultural History of Ventriloquism* (Oxford: Oxford University Press, 2000).

Creed, Barbara and Jeanette Hoorn, *Body Trade: Captivity, Cannibalism And Colonialism in the Pacific* (New York: Routledge, 2001).

Crownfield, David, ed., *Body/Text in Julia Kristeva – Religion, Women, and Psychoanalysis* (Albany: State University of New York Press, 1992).

Crystal, David, *The Stories of English* (London: Penguin, 2004).

Cundy, Catherine, *Salman Rushdie* (Manchester: Manchester University Press, 1996).

—, '"Rehearsing Voices": Salman Rushdie's *Grimus*'. *Journal of Commonwealth Literature* 27(1), (1992), 128–38.

Davis, Rocío G., 'Salman Rushdie's *East, West*: Palimpsests of Fiction and Reality'. *Passages* 2(1), (2000), 81–92.

Dayal, Samir, 'Splitting Images: *The Satanic Verses* and the Incomplete Man', in Kain, Geoffrey, ed., *Ideas of Home – Literature of Asian Migration* (East Lansing: Michigan State University Press, 1997).

de Man, Paul, 'Autobiography as De-facement'. *MLN* 94(5), Comparative Literature (December 1979), 919–30.

Derrida, Jacques, *Acts of Literature*, edited by Derek Attridge (London: Routledge, 1992).

—, *Dissemination*, translated by Barbara Johnson (Chicago: University of Chicago Press, 1981).

—, *Margins of Philosophy*, translated by Alan Bass (Brighton: Harvester, 1982).

—, *On the Name* (Stanford: Stanford University Press, 1995).

—, *Specters of Marx*, translated from the French by Peggy Kamuf (New York: Routledge Classics, 2006).

—, *Writing and Difference*, translated by Alan Bass (London: Routledge & Kegan Paul, 1978).

Desai, Kiran, *Hullabaloo in the Guava Orchard* (London: Faber, 1998).

Desani, G. V., *All About H. Hatterr* (London: Penguin, 1972 [1948]).

Deszcz, Justyna, 'Salman Rushdie's Attempt at a Feminist Fairytale Reconfiguration in *Shame*'. *Folklore (UK)* 115(1), (2004), 27–44.

Dharwadker, Aparna, 'Diaspora, Nation, and the Failure of Home: Two Contemporary Indian Plays'. *Theatre Journal* 50.1. (1998), 71–94.

Di Giacomo, Susan, 'Metaphor as Illness: Postmodern Dilemmas in the Representation of Body, Mind and Disorder'. *Medical Anthropology* 14 (1992), 109–37.

Doueiri, Ziad, director, *West Beirut* (Lebanon: Summit/Spring, ASIN: B00005ALOX 1998).

Eagleton, Terry, *Walter Benjamin or Towards a Revolutionary Criticism* (London: Verso, 1981).

Eco, Umberto, *Mouse or Rat? Translation as Negotiation* (London: Weidenfeld & Nicolson, 2003).

Ebbatson, Roger, *Imaginary England* (Aldershot: Ashgate, 2005).

Engblom, Philip, 'A Multitude of Voices: Carnivalisation and Dialogicality in the Novels of Salman Rushdie', in Fletcher, M. D. ed., *Reading Rushdie: Perspectives on the Fiction of Salman Rushdie* (Amsterdam: Rodopi, 1994), pp. 293–304.

El Guindi, Fadwa, *Veil: Modesty, Privacy and Resistance* (Oxford: Berg, 2000).

Ellman, Maud, *The Hunger Artists* (London: Virago, 1993).

Ephron, Nora, director, *Michael* (USA: New Line Cinema, ASIN: 0780618068, 1996).

Eteraz, Ali, 'Shooting A Shaykh In The Mouth' 2006, in *Eteraz* accessed 05.09.06, last updated 26.08.06, via: http://eteraz.wordpress.com/2006/08/25/shooting-a-shaykh-in-the-mouth/.

Fairclough, Norman, *Language and Power* (London: Longman, 1989).

Fanon, Frantz, *Black Skin, White Masks* (New York: Grove, 1967).

Fee, Dwight, ed., *Pathology and the Postmodern – Mental Illness as Discourse and Experience* (London: Sage, 2000).

Fine, Gary Allan, *Kitchens – The Culture of Restaurant Work* (London: University of California Press, 1996).

Fish, Stanley, 'Interpreting the Valorium', in Dennis Walder, ed., *Literature in the Modern World* (Oxford: Oxford University Press, 1990), 55–62.

Fitzgerald, Edward, translator's introduction and notes, *Rubaiyat of Omar Khayyam*, 1879, available online via http://www.gutenberg.org/2/4/246/, accessed 22.06.09.

Foster, Shirley, 'Colonialism and Gender in the East: Representations of the Harem in the writings of Women Travellers', in Bradbury, Nicola, ed., *Yearbook of English Studies vol. 34 (2004) – Nineteenth Century Travel Writing* (Leeds: W. S. Maney, 2004).

Foucault, Michel, *Discipline and Punish – the Birth of the Prison*, translated by Alan Sheridan (New York: Vintage, 1995).

—, *Language, Counter-Memory, Practice*, translated by Donald F Bouchard and Sherry Simon (New York: Cornell University Press, 1977).

—, *Religion and Culture*, selected and edited by Jeremy R. Carrette (Manchester: Manchester University Press, 1999).

—, *The Order of Things – An Archaeology of the Human Sciences* (London: Routledge, 1974 [French 1966]).

Fraser, Antonia, *The Weaker Vessel* (London: Mandarin, 1984).

Freud, Sigmund, *The Psychopathology of Everyday Life* (London: Penguin, 2002).

Fürst, Elisabeth L., Ritva Prättälä, Marianne Ekström, Lotte Holm and Unni Kjaernes, eds, *Palatable Worlds – Sociocultural Food Studies* (Oslo: Solum Forlag, 1991).

Gentzler, Edwin, *Contemporary Translation Theories* (London: Routledge, 1993).

Girard, Rene, *Deceit, Desire, & the Novel – Self and Other in Literary Structure*, translated by Yvonne Freccero (London: Johns Hopkins University Press, 1976).

Gittins, Diana, *Madness in its Place – Narratives of Severalls Hospital, 1913–1997* (London: Routledge, 1998).

Gonzales, Madelena, *Fiction after the Fatwa – Salman Rushdie and the Charm of Catastrophe* (Amsterdam: Rodopi, 2005).

Goonetilleke, D. C. R. A., *Salman Rushdie* (London: Macmillan, 1998).

Gorra, Michael, *After Empire: Scott, Naipaul, Rushdie* (London: The University of Chicago Press, 1997).

Grace, Daphne, *The Woman in the Muslin Mask – Veiling and Identity in Postcolonial Literature* (London: Pluto, 2004).

Gramsci, Antonio, *Selections from the Prison Notebooks of Antonio Gramsci*, Quintin Hoare and Geoffrey Nowell Smith, eds (London: Lawrence & Wishart, 1971).

—, *Letters from Prison*, translated by Lynne Lawner (London: Jonathan Cape, 1975 [1946]).

Graves, Benjamin, 'The Master-Slave Dialectic: Hegel and Fanon', (1997), accessed 13.09.06, last updated 14.07.06 via: http://www.postcolonialweb.org/sa/gordimer/july6.html.

Grewal, Inderpal, *Home and Harem: Nation, Gender, Empire and the Cultures of Travel* (London: Leicester University Press, 1996).

Grey, Mary, 'The Ordination of Women - Seeking a New Approach', a lecture to the Annual General Assembly of Catholic Women's Ordination, London 7 May 2002, accessed 24.07.06, last updated 01.06.03, via http://www.womenpriests.org/theology/grey5.asp.

Gutterman, Dov, Flag of Pakistan, http://flagspot.net/flags/pk.html.

Harper, Graeme, ed., *Comedy, Fantasy and Colonialism* (London: Continuum, 2002).

Harrison, Nicholas, *Postcolonial Criticism* (Cambridge: Polity, 2003).

Hatim, Basil and Ian Mason, *Discourse and the Translator* (London: Longman, 1990).

Hegel, Georg Wilhelm Friedrich, *Phenomenology of Spirit* (Oxford: Clarendon Press, 1979).

Hoare, Quintin, ed., *Selections from the Prison Notebooks of Antonio Gramsci* (London: Lawrence & Wishart, 1971).

Hodges, Cliff, Mary Jane Drummond and Morag Styles, eds, *Tales, Tellers and Texts* (London: Cassell, 2000).

Holub, Renate, *Antonio Gramsci – Beyond Marxism and Postmodernism* (London: Routledge, 1992).

Holson, Laura M., 'From Exile to Everywhere', *New York Times*, http://www.nytimes.com/2012/03/25/fashion/salman-rushdie-out-of-exile-is-a-fixture-on-the-social-scene.html, 23 March 2012 (accessed 25.09.2012).

Hunter, James, 'Philomela', in *Encyclopedia Mythica* from Encyclopedia Mythica Online, last updated 15.12.99, accessed 11.02.06 via http://www.pantheon.org/articles/p/philomela.html.

Irving, Thomas Ballantyne, Khurshid Ahmad and Muhammad Manazir Ahsah, *The Qur'an: Basic Teachings* (Leicester: Islamic Foundation, 1992).

Iser, Wolfgang, 'On Translatability', in Jean-Claude Guédon, ed., *Surfaces* electronic journal, volume 4 (Montreal: University of Montreal Press, 1994).

Islam, Syed Manzurul, *The Ethics of Travel – From Marco Polo to Kafka* (Manchester: Manchester University Press, 1996).

—, *The Mapmakers of Spitalfields* (London: Peepal Tree, 1997).

—, 'Nomads and Minorities'. *Rhizomes* 03 fall 2001. http://www.rhizomes.net/issue3/islam.htm (accessed 10.08.06).

—, 'Writing the postcolonial event: Salman Rushdie's August 15th, 1947'. *Textual Practice* 13(1), (1999), 119–35.

Islamic Invitation Centre, Frequently Asked Question, (last updated 10.02.04), accessed 17.08.06 via: http://www.islamicinvitationcentre.com/FAQ/diet/FAQ_diet.html.

Ivekovic, Rada, 'Transborder translating', available online via *Eurozine*, http://www.eurozine.com/articles/2005-01-14-ivekovic-en.html (2005) (accessed 17.02.06).

Jakobson, Roman, 'On Linguistic Aspects of Translation', in Lawrence Venuti, ed., *The Translation Studies Reader* (London: Routledge, 2000).

Jefferson, Ann and David Robey, eds, *Modern Literary Theory* (London: BT Batsford, 1986).

Jobling, David, Tina Pippin, Ronald Schleifer, eds, *The Postmodern Bible Reader* (Oxford: Blackwell, 2001).

Jodelet, Denise, *Madness and Social Representations*, translated by Tim Pownall (Hemel Hempstead: Harvester Wheatsheaf, 1991[1989]).

Johansen, Ib, 'The Flight from the Enchanter: Reflections on Salman Rushdie's *Grimus*', in Fletcher, M. D. ed., *Reading Rushdie: Perspectives on the Fiction of Salman Rushdie* (Amsterdam: Rodopi, 1994), pp. 23–33.

Johnson, Barbara, *Mother Tongues: Sexuality, Trials, Motherhood, Translation* (London: Harvard University Press, 2003).

Johnson, Caroline, *Angels* (London: Fount, 1993).

Joshi, Manoj, *The Lost Rebellion* (New Delhi: Penguin Books, 1999).

Julius, Anthony, *Transgressions – The Offences of Art* (London: Thames & Hudson, 2002).

—, *Idolizing Pictures – Idolatry, Iconoclasm, and Jewish Art* (New York: Thames & Hudson, 2000).

Kabbani, Shaykh Hisham Muhammad, 'Salman al-Farisi' last updated 01.02.06, accessed 11.03.06 via http://www.naqshbandi.org/chain/3.htm.

Kain, Geoffrey, ed., *Ideas of Home – Literature of Asian Migration* (East Lansing: Michigan State University Press).

Kalliney, Peter, 'Globalization, Postcoloniality, and the Problem of Literary Studies in *The Satanic Verses*'. *Modern Fiction Studies* 48(1), (2002), 50–82.

Kalvesmaki, Joel, 'The History of the Septuagint, and its Terminology', 2005, available online via http://www.kalvesmaki.com/LXX/, last updated 14.10.05, accessed 01.11.06.

Kasem, Abul, 'Who Authored the Qur'an?an Enquiry', 2004, available online via http://www.mukto-mona.com/Articles/kasem/quran_origin3.htm, last updated 30.11.04, accessed 01.11.06.

Kermode, Frank, *The Genesis of Secrecy – On the Interpretation of Narrative* (London: Harvard University Press, 1979).

—, *Poetry, Narrative, History* (Oxford: Basil Blackwell, 1990).

—, *The Sense of an Ending* (Oxford: Oxford University Press, 2000).

Kershaw, Ian, *The 'Hitler Myth' – Image and Reality in the Third Reich* (Oxford: Oxford University Press, 1989).

Khan, Sitara, *A Glimpse Through Purdah – Asian Women – The Myth and the Reality* (London: Trentham Books, 1999).

Kristeva, Julia, *Desire in Language – A Semiotic Approach to Literature and Art* (Oxford: Basil Blackwell, 1980).

—, *New Maladies of the Soul*, translated by Ross Guberman (New York: Columbia University Press, 1995).

—, *Nations without Nationalism*, translated by Leon S. Roudiez (New York: Columbia University Press, 1993).

—, *Revolution in Poetic Language* (New York: Columbia University Press, 1984).

Kulke, Hermann and Dietmar Rothermund, *A History of India* (London: Routledge, Third Edition, 1998).

Lacan, Jacques, *Ecrits*, translated from the French by Alan Sheridan (London: Tavistock, 1980).

Lazarus, Neil, 'Representation and Terror in VY Mudimbe'. *Journal of African Cultural Studies* 17(1), (June 2005), 81101.

Lefevere, André, *Translation, History, Culture: A Sourcebook* (London: Routledge, 1992).

Lemu, B. Aisha and Fatima Heeren, *Woman in Islam* (Leicester: Islamic Foundation, 1978).

Lounsberry, Barbara, Susan Lohafer, Mary Rohrberger, Stephen Pett, R. C. Feddersen, eds, *The Tales We Tell – Perspectives on the Short Story* (London: Greenwood, 1998).

Lye, John, 'Synopsis of J. Hillis Miller's "The Critic as Host"', 1998, http://www.brocku.ca/english/courses/4F70/host.html, last updated 24.02.98, accessed 08.09.06.

Lyotard, Jean-François, *Libidinal Economy*, translated by Iain Hamilton-Grant (Bloomington: Indiana University Press, 1993).

—, *Phenomenology*, translated by Brian Beakley (Albany: State University of New York Press, 1991).

Malladi, Amulya, *Serving Crazy with Curry* (London: Piatkus, 2004).

Manto, Saadat Hasan, 'Toba Tek Singh', in *Kingdom's End and Other Stories* (London: Penguin, 1989).

Masqood, Ruqaiyyah Waris, *What Every Christian Should Know About Islam* (Leicester: Islamic Foundation, 2000).

McWhorter, John, *The Power of Babel* (Arrow: London, 2003).

Mernissi, Fatima, *Beyond the Veil: Male-Female Dynamics in Modern Muslim Society* (London: Al Saqi, 1985).

Mishra, Pankaj, *Joseph Anton* by Salman Rushdie – review, *The Guardian*, http://www.guardian.co.uk/books/2012/sep/18/joseph-anton-salman-rushdie-review, Tuesday 18 September 2012 (accessed 25.09.2012).

Monier-Williams, Sir Monier, *A Sanskrit-English Dictionary Etymologically and Philologically Arranged.* (Delhi: Motilal Banarsidass, 1997[1899]).

Moore-Gilbert, Bart, ed., *Writing India, 1757–1990* (Manchester: Manchester University Press, 1996)

Moore-Gilbert, Bart, *Postcolonial Life-writing* (London: Routledge, 2009).

Morey, Peter, *Fictions of India: Narrative and Power* (Edinburgh: Edinburgh University Press, 2000).

Nietzsche, Friedrich, *The Antichrist* (New York: Arno Press, 1972 [1888]).

—, *Nietzsche Reader* (Harmondsworth: Penguin, 1977).

Niranjana, Tejaswini, *Siting Translation: History, Post-Structuralism, and the Colonial Context* (Berkeley: University of Berkeley Press, 1992).

O'Brien, Paul, 'Interactive Fiction and Reader-Response Criticism' from http://ucsu.colorado.edu/~obrian/ifrrc.txt, last updated 25.01.06, accessed 11.02.06.

Okri, Ben, *Stars of the New Curfew* (London: Vintage, 1999).

Orlando, Francisco, *Toward a Freudian Theory of Literature, with an Analysis of Racine's 'Phèdre'*, translated by Charmaine Lee (London: Johns Hopkins University Press, 1978 [1971]).

Parkin-Gounelas, Ruth, *Literature and Psychoanalysis – Intertextual Readings* (Basingstoke: Palgrave, 2001).

Parry, Benita, 'The Postcolonial: Conceptual Category or Chimera?', in *The Yearbook of English Studies*, Vol. 27, The Politics of Postcolonial Criticism (1997).

Peirce, Leslie P., *The Imperial Harem – Women and Sovereignty in the Ottoman Empire* (Oxford: Oxford University Press, 1993).

Penzer, N. M., *The Harem* (London: Spring Books, 1965 [1936]).

Philips, C. H. and Wainwright, Mary Doreen, eds, 'The Role of Lord Mountbatten', in *The Partition of India* (London: Allen and Unwin, 1970).

Pickthall, Mohammed Marmaduke, ed., *The Meaning of the Holy Quran* (London: Madras House, 1990).

Pipes, Daniel, The *Rushdie Affair – The Novel, The Ayatollah, and the West* (London: Transaction, 2003).

Porter, Roy, *The Faber Book of Madness* (London: Faber, 1991).

Poster, Mark, ed., *Baudrillard – Selected Writings* (Stanford: University of Stanford Press, 1988).

Prickett, Stephen, *Words and the Word* (Cambridge: Cambridge University Press, 986).

Punter, David, *Postcolonial Imaginings – Fictions of a New World Order* (Edinburgh: Edinburgh University Press, 2000).

Quayson, Ato, 'Protocols of Representation and the Problems of Constituting an African "Gnosis"', in *The Yearbook of English Studies*, vol. 27, 1997, 'The Politics of Postcolonial Criticism Special Number' (Leeds: W. S. Maney & Son for the MHRA, 1997).

Rahman, Syed Ubaidur, 'Saddest days of Indian democracy', in Milli Gazette (15 July 2000, Vol. 1, No. 13).

Reder, Michael, ed., *Conversations with Salman Rushdie* (Jackson: University of Mississippi Press, 2000).

Rollason, Christopher, 'Rushdie's Un-Indian Music: The Ground Beneath Her Feet', in Rajeshwar Mittapalli and Pier Paolo Piciucco, eds, *Studies in Indian Writing in English*, vol. II (New Delhi: Atlantic, 2001).

Rubinson, Gregory J., *The Fiction of Rushdie, Barnes, Winterson, and Carter: Breaking Cultural and Literary Boundaries in the Work of Four Postmodernists* (Jefferson, NC: McFarland, 2005).

Rushdie, Salman, *East, West* (London: Vintage, 1994).

—, *The Enchantress of Florence* (London: Jonathan Cape, 2008).

—, 'The Firebird's Nest', in Nadine Gordimer, ed., *Telling Tales* (London: Bloomsbury, 2004).

—, *Fury* (London: Vintage, 2001).

—, *Grimus* (London: Vintage, 1975).

—, *The Ground Beneath Her Feet* (London: Vintage, 1999).

—, *Haroun and the Sea of Stories* (London: Vintage, 1990).

—, *Imaginary Homelands: Essays in Criticism, 1981–1991* (London: Granta, 1991).

—, *The Jaguar Smile; A Nicaraguan Journey* (London: Vintage, 1987).

—, *Joseph Anton: A Memoir* (London: Jonathan Cape, 2012).

—, *Luka and the Fire of Life* (London: Jonathan Cape, 2010).
—, *Midnight's Children* (London: Vintage, 1995 [1981]).
—, *The Moor's Last Sigh* (London: Vintage, 1996).
—, *The Satanic Verses* (London: Vintage, 1998 [1988]).
—, *Shalimar the Clown* (London: Jonathan Cape, 2005).
—, *Shame* (London: Vintage, 1995 [1983]).
—, *Step Across This Line* (London: Vintage, 2002).
Ruthven, Malise, *A Satanic Affair* (London: Chatto & Windus, 1990).
Ryman, Rebecca, *Shalimar* (New York: St Martin's Press, 1999).
Saadi, Suhayl, 'Storm in the valley of death', review of *Shalimar the Clown* in *The Independent* Online Edition, 09.09.05, accessed 05.08.06, last updated 09.09.05 http://arts.independent.co.uk/books/reviews/article311190.ece.
Said, Edward, *Culture and Imperialism* (London: Vintage, 1993).
—, *Orientalism* (London: Penguin, 2003, 1978).
—, *Reflections on Exile and other Literary and Cultural Essays* (London: Granta, 2001).
—, 'Travelling Theory Reconsidered', in Nigel C. Gibson, ed., *Rethinking Fanon: the Continuing Dialogue* (Amherst: Prometheus Books, 1999), pp. 197–214.
Samadi, Alyssa, 'Neither Prophets Jesus nor Moses (peace be upon them) ate pork', (last updated 14.08.04), accessed 17.08.06 via http://www.muslimworld.co.uk/porkeater.htm.
Sardar, Ziauddin, 'Extremely wrong about British Muslims', review of *From Rushdie to 7/7*, by Anthony McRoy, 28 April 2006, in the Independent Online, Last updated 28.04.06, accessed 10.07.06 via http://enjoyment.independent.co.uk/books/reviews/article360562.ece.
Sardar, Ziauddin and Merryl Wyn Davies, *Distorted Imagination – Lessons from the Rushdie Affair* (London: Greyseal, 1990).
Sarup, Madan, *An Introductory Guide to Post-structuralism and Postmodernism*, second edition (New York: Harvester Wheatsheaf, 1993).
Schivelbusch, Wolfgang, *Tastes of Paradise – A Social History of Spices, Stimulants and Intoxicants*, translated by David Jacobson (New York: Vintage, 1993).
Schuon, Frithjof, *Understanding Islam* (London: Unwin, 1986, 1963).
Scott Jr, Nathan A. and Ronald A. Sharp, *Reading George Steiner* (Baltimore: Johns Hopkins University Press, 1994).
Selvadurai, Shyam, ed., *Story-Wallah – Short Fiction from South Asian Writers* (New York: Houghton Mifflin, 2005).
Sengupta, Shuddhabrata, 'Jaipur Literature Festival – Requiescat in Pacem', *Kafila*, http://kafila.org/2012/01/21/jaipur-literature-festival-requiescat-in-pacem/#more-11294, 21 January 2012 (accessed 25.09.2012).
Serres, Michel, *Angels – A Modern Myth*, translated by Francis Cowper (Paris: Flammarion, 1993).
Shakespeare, William, *Romeo and Juliet*, edited by T. J. B. Spencer (Harmondsworth: Penguin, 1967).

Sharma, Shailja, 'Salman Rushdie: The ambivalence of migrancy' in *Twentieth Century Literature*, Hempstead, 47(4), (Winter 2001), 596618.
Sharp, Emma, 'Art Restoration: a Chemical Perspective' (London, King's College: 2001) last updated 04.11.01, accessed 11.03.06, via http://www.chemsoc.org/ExemplarChem/entries/2001/esharp/default.htm.
Shohat, Ella and Robert Stam. 'Narrativizing Visual Culture: Towards a Polycentric Aesthetics', in Nicholas Mirzoeff, ed., *The Visual Culture Reader* (London: Routledge, 1998), pp. 27–49.
Simon, Roger, *Gramsci's Political Thought: An Introduction* (London: Lawrence and Wishart, 1982).
Smaller, Margaret, 'Intertextuality: An Interview with Julia Kristeva', in Patrick O'Donnell and Robert Con Davis, eds, *Intertextuality and Contemporary American Fiction* (Baltimore: The Johns Hopkins University Press, 1989).
Smith, Anna, *Julia Kristeva – Readings of Exile and Estrangement* (London: Macmillan, 1996).
Smith, Anne-Marie, *Julia Kristeva – Speaking the Unspeakable* (London: Pluto, 1998).
Solomon, Robert C. and Kathleen M. Higgins, eds, *Reading Nietzsche* (Oxford: Oxford University Press, 1988)
Sontag, Susan, *Illness as Metaphor* (London: Penguin, 1991).
Soueif, Ahdaf, *Sandpiper* (London: Bloomsbury, 1997).
Soyinka, Wole, *The Man Died* (London: Arrow, 1985 [1972]).
Spang, Rebecca L., *The Invention of the Restaurant* (London: Harvard University Press, 2000).
Spirano, Paolo, *Antonio Gramsci and the Party*, translated by John Fraser (London: Lawrence and Wishart, 1979).
Spivak, Gayatri Chakravorty, *A Critique of Postcolonial Reason: Toward a History of the Vanishing Present* (London: Harvard University Press, 1999).
—, *Death of a Discipline* (New York: Columbia University Press, 2003).
—, 'Reading *The Satanic Verses*', in Maurice Birotti and Nicola Miller, eds, *What Is an Author?* (Manchester: Manchester University Press, 1993).
—, 'Subaltern Studies – Deconstructing Historiograhy', in Donna Landry and Gerald Maclean, eds, *The Spivak Reader* (London: Routledge, 1996).
Stein, Burton, *A History of India* (Oxford: Blackwell, 1998).
Steiner, George, *After Babel*, second edition (Oxford: Oxford University Press, 1992).
—, *Language and Silence* (Middlesex: Penguin, 1969).
Stevens, Wallace, *The Necessary Angel – Essays on Reality and Imagination* (London: Faber, 1960).
Stewart, Susan, *On Longing – Narratives of the Miniature, the Gigantic, the Souvenir, the Collection* (London: Duke University Press, 1993).
Strong, Roy, *Feast: A Cultural History of Grand Eating* (London: Jonathan Cape, 2002).
Su, Jung,' Saleem's Quest for Origin: Authenticity and Nation in Midnight's Children'. *Proc. Natl. Sci, Counc. ROC(C)* 10(1), (2000), 6078.

Suleri, Sara, *The Rhetoric of English India* (London: The University of Chicago Press, 1992).

Talbot, Ian, *India and Pakistan* (London: Arnold, 2000).

Teverson, Andrew, *Salman Rushdie* (Manchester: Manchester University Press, 2007).

Thomas, Linda and Shân Wareing, eds, *Language, Society and Power* (London: Routledge, 1999).

Trivedi, Harish, 'Translating Culture vs. Cultural Translation'. *91st Meridian* 4(1) (2005), available via: http://iwp.uiowa.edu/91st/vol4_n1/trivedi/trivedi.html (accessed 15/12/08).

Tymoczko, Maria, 'Post-colonial Writing and Literary Translation', in Bassnett, Susan and Trivedi, Harish, eds, *Post-colonial Translation: Theory and Practice* (London: Routledge, 1999).

Valassopoulos, Anastasia, 'Fictionalising Post-colonial Theory: The Creative Native Informant?' *Critical Survey* 162 (2004), 28–44.

Venuti, Lawrence, ed., *Rethinking Translation: Discourse, Subjectivity, Ideology* (London: Routledge, 1992).

Venuti, Lawrence, *The Translator's Invisibility* (London: Routledge, 1995).

Vergès, Françoise, 'Creole Skin, Black Mask: Fanon and Disavowal'. *Critical Inquiry* 23(3), (Spring 1997), 578–95.

Voltaire, *Candide*, translated by John Butt (Middlesex: Penguin, 1947).

Wadensjö, Cecilia, *Interpreting as Interaction* (London: Longman, 1998).

Warner, Marina, *From the Beast to the Blonde – On Fairy Tales and their Tellers* (London: Chatto & Windus, 1994).

Watson, J. R., *The English Hymn – A Critical and Historical Study* (Oxford: Clarendon Press, 1999).

Watt, W. M., *Islamic Political Thought* (Edinburgh: Edinburgh University Press, 1980, 1968).

Webster, Richard, *A Brief History of Blasphemy: Liberation, Censorship, and 'The Satanic Verses'* (Southwold: Orwell Press, 1990).

Wessing, Robert, 'Sri and Sedana and Sita and Rama: Myths of Fertility and Generation'. *Asian Folklore Studies* 49(2), (1990), 235257.

Westmoreland, Mark, 'Cinematic Dreaming: On Phantom Poetics and the Longing for a Lebanese National Cinema'. *Text, Practice, Performance* IV (2002): 33–50.

White, Hayden, 'The Historical Text as Literary Artifact', in Brian Fay, Philip Pomper and Richard T. Vann eds, *History and Theory – Contemporary Readings* (Oxford: Blackwell, 1998).

Wilson, Peter Lamborn, *Angels* (London: Thames & Hudson, 1980).

Wolfreys, Julian, *Being English – Narratives, Idioms and Performances of National Identity from Coleridge to Trollope* (Albany: State University of New York Press, 1994).

—, *The Derrida Reader* (Edinburgh: Edinburgh University Press, 1998).

—, ed., *Literary Theories - A Reader & Guide* (Edinburgh: Edinburgh University Press, 1999).

—, *Writing London - The Trace of the Urban Text from Blake to Dickens* (London: Macmillan, 1998).

Yamani, Mai, *Feminism and Islam - Legal & Literary Perspectives* (New York: New York University Press, 1996).

Young, Robert J. C., *Colonial Desire: Hybridity in Theory, Culture and Race* (London: Routledge, 1995).

Zipes, Jack, ed., *The Arabian Nights* (London: Penguin, 1997).

Zucker, David J., 'Midrash and Modern Jewish American Literature'. *Studies in American Jewish Literature*, ser.2:11:1 (Spring 1992), 721.

Index